T0323429

New Developments in Evolutionary Innovation

New Developments in Evolutionary Innovation

Novelty Creation in a Serendipitous Economy

Edited by
Gino Cattani and
Mariano Mastrogiorgio

UNIVERSITY PRESS

Great Clarendon Street, Oxford, OX2 6DP,
United Kingdom

Oxford University Press is a department of the University of Oxford.
It furthers the University's objective of excellence in research, scholarship,
and education by publishing worldwide. Oxford is a registered trade mark of
Oxford University Press in the UK and in certain other countries

© the several contributors 2021

The moral rights of the authors have been asserted

First Edition published in 2021

Impression: 2

All rights reserved. No part of this publication may be reproduced, stored in
a retrieval system, or transmitted, in any form or by any means, without the
prior permission in writing of Oxford University Press, or as expressly permitted
by law, by licence or under terms agreed with the appropriate reprographics
rights organization. Enquiries concerning reproduction outside the scope of the
above should be sent to the Rights Department, Oxford University Press, at the
address above

You must not circulate this work in any other form
and you must impose this same condition on any acquirer

Published in the United States of America by Oxford University Press
198 Madison Avenue, New York, NY 10016, United States of America

British Library Cataloguing in Publication Data
Data available

Library of Congress Control Number: 2020951193

ISBN 978–0–19–883709–1

DOI: 10.1093/oso/9780198837091.001.0001

Printed and bound by
CPI Group (UK) Ltd, Croydon, CR0 4YY

Links to third party websites are provided by Oxford in good faith and
for information only. Oxford disclaims any responsibility for the materials
contained in any third party website referenced in this work.

Foreword from Richard Nelson

Economics and the other social sciences grew up in an era when physics was the model of what a strong science should be like, but in recent years more and more social scientists have turned to biology, particularly evolutionary biology, as a model. Today there are significant bodies of research and writing taking an evolutionary perspective on how firms, technologies, industries, broader economic structures, institutions, and various aspect of human culture change over time. The evolutionary conceptions used in these fields of study differ in important ways from those in analysis of biological evolution, but all of this work draws heavily on post-Darwinian evolutionary theory.

This book is concerned with recent developments in evolutionary biology, and how they might be adapted for use in evolutionary social science, particular in study of the evolution of technologies and the artefacts they spawn. The focus is on the concepts of punctuated equilibrium, speciation, and exaptation, with most of the writing concerned with the latter. The book is rich in discussion both of the biology involved, and of how these conceptions can enrich studies of how technologies and their artefacts evolve. While the chapters of this book have a range of authors, the various pieces add up to a coherent whole. A very interesting read.

Richard Nelson

Professor Emeritus of International and Public Affairs, Business, and Law
The Center on Capitalism and Society
Columbia University, New York, United States

Foreword from Franco Malerba

This is a timely and must-read book edited by Gino Cattani and Mariano Mastrogiorgio, two leading scholars in management and innovation quite active in the area of evolutionary economics and strategy. In a sharp and coherent way, the book presents and discusses the impact that recent developments in evolutionary biology have had on innovation studies, management, and economics. Cattani and Mastrogiorgio successfully link new key concepts in evolutionary biology to the understanding of the economy as a continuously evolving system, in which the emergence of novelty plays a major role and in which major unpredictable changes alternate with periods of relative stability.

The book enriches evolutionary thinking in economics, innovation, and management, pioneered by the seminal book *An evolutionary theory of economic change* by Richard Nelson and Sidney Winter in 1982, and expanded over the years by the work of Stan Metcalfe, Giovanni Dosi, Joel Mokyr, Dan Levinthal, Kurth Dopfer, Howard Aldrich, Paolo Saviotti, Luigi Orsenigo, and many other scholars. As it has developed, the evolutionary paradigm has been centred on innovation as a key driver of economic growth and industrial transformation, on adaptation and change as major features of the evolution of technology, industry, and the economy and on three basic mechanisms of evolution (variation, selection, and retention). Needless to say, these developments in evolutionary theory have had a tremendous impact on innovation studies, strategy, and management.

Among the many topics addressed by this book—from evolution, speciation, and unprestateability, to evolutionary theory and simulations, technological evolution and complexity, cognition and innovation, cultural evolution, and social innovation—two stand prominently as pillars for a better understanding of technological change and evolutionary strategies: punctuated equilibrium and exaptation. Up to now, many evolutionary contributions in examining technological change have focused on adaptation and the incremental nature of innovation. The perspective of punctuated equilibrium discussed in the book identifies a pattern of change in technologies and industries in which adaptation and incremental change are interrupted by sudden bursts of disruption and introduction of novelty. This has significant implications for the study of industrial transformation as a process in which periods of gradual change are followed by periods of radical innovations and discontinuities, as shown by the history of industrialized economies over the last centuries, or by the case of the evolution of electronics with the discovery of the transistor, the introduction of the microprocessor, the emergence of the internet, and the rise of mobile phones.

The second pillar is represented by exaptation: a character used for a specific function or application may be suddenly co-opted for a novel and unanticipated function. Thus, a technology or an artefact may have inherent and unpredictable potentials for totally new applications. This is quite common in technological and industrial evolution, as clearly illustrated in the book by the cases of fibre optics by Corning and of the metal monoplane and the airframes revolution by Fokker. But while the notion of exaptation has been a major step forward in evolutionary biology, it has received much less attention in the study of innovation and strategy. This comes as a surprise because exaptation adds a mechanism leading to unexpected and sudden functional shifts in existing technologies, which differs from existing theories of speciation as a process of adaptation of a technology to a new domain of application. Furthermore, the implications of exaptation for strategy are significant. Because of the pervasive presence of uncertainty and serendipity in technological change, it is impossible to identify *ex ante* all of the possible uses and applications of existing technologies. Therefore, evolutionary search strategies and appropriate organizational designs are called for. In the book, Cattani and Mastrogiorgio propose a shadow option approach in order to recognize the potential new applications or the new uses embodied but hidden in the current technologies and artefacts.

Other general considerations on technological and economic evolution may also be drawn from this book. Concepts and theories presented in the book characterize evolution and speciation as a process of horizontal transfer of existing functional modules that generates major innovations. This differs from the well-known evolutionary process of vertical transmission and the gradual accumulation of novelty over time. This characterization has major implications for the understanding of the economy as an evolving, complex system and of technological evolution as a dynamic network with a reticular structure of complementary relationships. Furthermore, this characterization opens a new link between evolutionary biology and biological evolution on one side and the analysis of technological and cultural evolution on the other.

In sum, I am convinced that this book will be of great interest to a large variety of scholars of innovation, strategy, and economics by showing how evolutionary theory is advancing and how fertile it is for a wide range of research questions. Cattani, Mastrogiorgio, and the other authors—Carignani, Felin, Kauffman, Petracca, Palumbo, Unrau, and Gabora—introduce new concepts from evolutionary biology and show why they are significant for our understanding of innovation and strategy. The chapters in the book present a clear and persuasive argument, using various methodologies, from theory, to case studies, to modelling. These methodologies complement each other quite effectively and provide a multidimensional analysis of the progress occurring in evolutionary theory. From this book, the interested reader will acquire a broad view of new perspectives in evolutionary theory, and new ideas of how to develop our understanding of the complexity of technological, industrial, and economic evolution.

Franco Malerba

Professor of Applied Economics
Department of Management and Technology and ICRIOS
Bocconi University, Milan, Italy

Contents

List of Figures

List of Contributors

Giuseppe Carignani is a researcher, engineer, and professor in the Department of Economics and Statistics, University of Udine.

Gino Cattani is Professor of Strategy and Organization Theory at the Stern School of Business, Department of Management and Organizations, New York University.

Teppo Felin is a professor of strategy and the Academic Director of the Diploma in Strategy and Innovation at Saïd Business School, University of Oxford.

Liane Gabora is an interdisciplinary psychology professor at the University of British Columbia.

Stuart Kauffman is an emeritus professor of biochemistry at the University of Pennsylvania and an affiliate faculty member at the Institute for Systems Biology.

Antonio Mastrogiorgio is a researcher at the Laboratory for the Analysis of Complex Economic Systems and at the Neuroscience Lab, IMT School for Advanced Studies Lucca.

Mariano Mastrogiorgio is Assistant Professor of Management at IE Business School, Department of Strategy, where he teaches Introduction to Management and Strategic Management in the undergraduate programmes.

Riccardo Palumbo is Professor of Business and Behavioural Economics and co-ordinator of the Unit of Behavioural Economics and Neuroeconomics in the Department of Neurosciences, Imaging and Clinical Sciences, University of Chieti-Pescara.

Enrico Petracca is a research associate at the School of Economics, Management, and Statistics, University of Bologna.

Mike Unrau is currently an adjunct faculty member at Mount Royal University, Canada, and a PhD student of Interdisciplinary Graduate Studies at the University of British Columbia, Canada.

1

New Developments in Evolutionary Innovation

An Introduction

Gino Cattani and Mariano Mastrogiorgio

The publication of 'An Evolutionary Theory of Economic Change' by Nelson and Winter (1982) has had a major impact on economics and on related fields such as innovation and strategy. All of these fields have received a further impulse owing to recent re-examinations and extensions of evolutionary theory (Nelson et al., 2018; Malerba et al., 2016). At its core, evolutionary theory sees the economy as a system that is continually in motion because of continual changes in technology that are endogenous to the economy and, more importantly, intrinsically evolutionary. A paradigm that underlies several studies in this tradition is the concept of neo-Darwinian evolution, as indicated by Nelson et al. (2018): 'the term "evolutionary economics" obviously carries the connotation that this orientation to economic analysis has something in common with the perspective of Darwinian evolutionary biology' (p. 25). Neo-Darwinian evolution is, in essence, the idea that the unit of the evolutionary process (e.g. a technological artefact) is subject to a dynamic of variation, selection, and retention leading to adaptation to a predefined function.

It is worth noting how Darwin himself recognized the subtleties of adaptive dynamics, particularly the fact that the function of a biological trait may shift during evolutionary history (Darwin, 1859). From the 1970s, these initial observations have received a more systematic treatment in new theories that have profoundly changed the field of evolutionary biology. In this book, we refer to the frameworks of punctuated equilibrium, speciation, and exaptation (Gould, 2007). Despite their significant influence in evolutionary biology, these advancements have been reflected partially in evolutionary approaches to economics, innovation, and strategy. Of course, the field is

Gino Cattani and Mariano Mastrogiorgio, *New Developments in Evolutionary Innovation: An Introduction* In: *New Developments in Evolutionary Innovation: Novelty Creation in a Serendipitous Economy.* Edited by: Gino Cattani and Mariano Mastrogiorgio, Oxford University Press (2021). © Gino Cattani and Mariano Mastrogiorgio. DOI: 10.1093/oso/9780198837091.003.0001 vast, and the exceptions are numerous (e.g. Cattani, 2006; Levinthal, 1998; Tushman and Anderson, 1986). However, to our surprise, a systematic recognition of these topics is still mostly scattered or missing. The aim of this book is to fill this gap, review these advancements, and contextualize them in the current evolutionary debate in economics, innovation, and strategy.

These new advancements can shed new light on some of the key assumptions of evolutionary theory, such as the idea of the economy as a complex system that is continually in motion and is far from equilibrium (if this equilibrium even exists). The concept of 'exaptation' (Andriani and Cattani, 2016; Gould and Vrba, 1982), for instance, refers to technologies, artefacts, and resources that evolved for other uses and functions (or no function at all) and were later co-opted for new functions, very often serendipitously. An example is the drug Marsilid, which was originally designed for tuberculosis, but was discovered to make tuberculotic patients particularly euphoric, thus becoming the first antidepressant drug (Andriani et al., 2017). These developments are pervasive in the history of technology and are highly impactful: they can lead to new dominant designs that shake existing industries, as shown by the turbojet revolution (Carignani et al., 2019), or even to the radical emergence of new industries, as shown by the pharmaceutical and chemical industry, whose birth can be traced back to multiple exaptations starting from coal tar (Andriani and Carignani, 2014). Moreover, owing to their intrinsic nature, these developments are highly unpredictable and fundamentally 'unprestateable'—that is, the phase space of economic evolution is also inherently unstable, a-causal and, perhaps, lawless in a classical sense (Kauffman, 2016; Koppl et al., 2015).

To appreciate these ideas fully, it is useful to recall the concept of 'affordances', which refer to the multiple latent uses and functions embodied in technologies, artefacts, and resources. For example, a kettle can be used to pour boiling water into a tea cup, crack nuts with its bottom surface, and so on (Gibson, 1979). The affordances of an object are potentially infinite, and their emergence—via exaptation and related processes—is highly contextual and mediated by the heterogeneity of actor-specific perception (Felin et al., 2016). Therefore, it is simply impossible to pre-state all the possible affordances, uses, and functions of an object. Assuming that the value of something is, in essence, a reflection of the best use among *all* possible uses, then there is no value for a market price to converge to—in a classical equilibrium-like sense. Moreover, as implied by the causation debate in biology (Okasha, 2009) and as shown by exaptation, existing biological and technological traits and functions are not necessarily the result of natural selection because they could have been originally selected for different functions or have no original function at all. In other words, biological and technological traits may not be *caused* by selection, as implied by neo-Darwinian theory (Okasha, 2009). If by 'cause' we mean some sort of 'differential impact entailed by law' (Koppl et al., 2015: p. 12), the existence of laws that govern evolution becomes problematic, at least in a classical equilibrium-like sense.

The rest of the book explores some of these issues and is organized as follows. Chapter 2 (Cattani and Mastrogiorgio) reviews the developments of evolutionary biology, with a particular emphasis on punctuated equilibrium, speciation, exaptation, and the Woesian model, and their applications to the technological case. This chapter discusses some broad implications, such as the role of serendipity and unprestateability in technological change and, consequently, the importance of innovating through an option-based logic. Chapter 3 (Carignani) digs deeper into exaptation by analysing a case study of the 'airframe revolution'. The chapter reconstructs the microhistorical events that, starting from a modular exaptation in the wing system, led to the emergence of a new dominant design that shook the entire aircraft industry. By building on the concepts, models, and theories introduced in Chapters 2 and 3, Chapter 4 (Cattani and Mastrogiorgio) aims to link the new developments in evolutionary theory to the debate on unprestateability and disequilibrium in economic systems. Owing to the complexity of the debate, this chapter sketches a very general map that builds on the intuitions of others (Mirowski, 1989; Beinhocker, 2007; Kauffman, 2000; Koppl et al., 2015), to which we refer the interested reader for further details. Moving from theory to applications, Chapter 5 (Cattani and Mastrogiorgio) proposes some computational approaches to model the evolutionary phenomena (punctuated equilibrium, speciation, and exaptation) of interest in this volume. A standard approach is the so-called NK modelling approach; however, its application needs to be significantly reconsidered to capture those phenomena properly. Chapter 6 (Cattani and Mastrogiorgio) proposes the possible approaches to empirical analysis that are often used in evolutionary research, with a particular emphasis on patent data. To this end and consistent with some recent developments in evolutionary literature (e.g. 'connectivity analysis'), this chapter stresses the importance of adopting a network approach to patent data. Chapters 7 and 8 delve into some of the key implications of the new evolutionary framework. One of the main implications of punctuated equilibrium, speciation, and exaptation is that the emergence of new technologies, resources, and artefacts is highly contextual, that is, influenced by *environments* at the meso and macro level. The idea of environments as spaces of search for novelty is also central to other streams of evolutionary theory. By building on recent advancements in cognitive and perception science, Chapter 7 (Felin and Kauffman) challenges the classical idea of environments and, in particular, the assumption that environments can be fully represented, exhausted, or accounted for. Accordingly, search becomes a 'hard problem', and a new mechanism of novelty generation is proposed on the basis of question-answer probing and theory-laden inquiries. Chapter 8 (Mastrogiorgio, Petracca, and Palumbo) takes a slightly different stance on environments. By building on recent advancements in extended cognition, this chapter reframes the whole innovation process as being constitutively embodied in the contingent interaction between actors and artefacts in the environment, thus emphasizing the role of practicality and procedural knowledge in the generation of novelty. Closing the circle, Chapter 9 (Cattani and Mastrogiorgio) examines some of the implications that have been anticipated at the beginning, particularly the importance of innovating using an option-based logic. By building on 'redeployability' theory, this chapter not only explains option-based logic but also discusses its limitations by focusing on the notion of 'shadow options', i.e. new uses or applications that are embodied in technologies, resources, and artefacts but are still awaiting recognition, and their importance for strategy and competitive advantage. Chapter 10 (Unrau and Gabora) links together many of the previous topics by discussing another important topic: the cultural evolution of creative ideas that leads to social innovation.

This book is aimed towards academic scholars of innovation and strategy who feel in tune with evolutionary theory and are willing to advance in the field. This book defines a general map of the evolutionary ideas proposed and discussed in previous research (Andriani and Cattani, 2016; Beinhocker, 2007; Cattani, 2006; Kauffman, 2000; Koppl et al., 2015; Mirowski, 1989). Owing to the vastness of the evolutionary field, we may have omitted some ideas and names. Therefore, any omissions and errors are our own responsibility. Last but not least, we benefited from the works and efforts of other authors in completing this book. This book has also benefited from the many insights received from colleagues and friends at various conferences and seminars over the years. A particular source of inspiration was the first and second 'International Workshop on Exaptation' held in 2009 and 2018 in Gargnano del Garda, Italy. Our final thanks go to Adam Swallow and Jenny King of Oxford University Press for their kind help, assistance, and patience during the writing process. The authors would like to thank Enago (www.enago.com) for the English language review.

Research reported in this book was partially funded by the State Research Agency (AEI)-10.13039/501100011033 Grant No. PID2019-104568GB-100.

References

Andriani, P. and Carignani, G. 2014. Modular exaptation: a missing link in the synthesis of artificial form. *Research Policy*, 43(9): 1608–20.

Andriani, P. and Cattani, G. 2016. Exaptation as a source of creativity, innovation, and diversity in evolutionary sciences: introduction to the special section. *Industrial and Corporate Change*, 25(1): 115–31.

Andriani, P., Ali, A., and Mastrogiorgio, M. 2017. Measuring exaptation and its impact on innovation, search and problem-solving. *Organization Science*, 28(2): 320–38.

Beinhocker, E.D. 2007. *The origins of wealth: evolution, complexity, and the radical remaking of economics*. Harvard Business Review Press.

Carignani, G., Cattani, G., and Zaina, G. 2019. Evolutionary chimeras: a Woesian perspective of radical innovation. *Industrial and Corporate Change*, 28(3): 511–28.

Cattani, G. 2006. Technological preadaptation, speciation and emergence of new technologies: how Corning invented and developed fiber optics. *Industrial and Corporate Change*, 15(2): 285–318.

Darwin, C. 1859. *On the origin of species*. John Murray Eds.

Felin, T., Kauffman, S., Mastrogiorgio, A., and Mastrogiorgio, M. 2016. Factor markets, actors and affordances. *Industrial and Corporate Change*, 25(1): 133–47.

Gibson, J.J. (1979). *The ecological approach to visual perception*. Erlbaum.

Gould, S.J. and Vrba, E.S. 1982. Exaptation—a missing term in the science of form. *Paleobiology*, 8(1): 4–15.

Gould, S.J. 2007. *Punctuated equilibrium*. Belknap Press.

Kauffman, S.A. 2000. *Investigations*. Oxford University Press.

Kauffman, S. 2016. *Humanity in a creative universe*. Oxford University Press.

Koppl, R., Kauffman, S., Felin, T., and Longo, G. 2015. Economics for a creative world. *Journal of Institutional Economics*, 11(1): 1–31.

Levinthal, D.A. 1998. The slow pace of rapid technological change: gradualism and punctuation in technological change. *Industrial and Corporate Change*, 7(2): 217–47.

Malerba, F., Nelson, R.R., Orsenigo, L., and Winter, S.G. 2016. *Innovation and the evolution of industries: history friendly models*. Cambridge University Press.

Mirowski, P. 1989. *More heat than light. Economics as social physics: physics as nature's economics*. Cambridge University Press.

Nelson, R.R. and Winter, S.G. 1982. *An evolutionary theory of economic change*. Harvard University Press.

Nelson, R.R., Dosi, G., Helfat, C.E., Pyka, A., Saviotti, P., Lee, K., Dopfer, K., Malerba, F., and Winter, S.G. 2018. *Modern evolutionary economics*. Cambridge University Press.

Okasha, S. 2009. Causation in biology. In Beebee, H., Hitchcock, C., and Menzies, P. (eds.). *The Oxford handbook of causation*. Oxford University Press.

Tushman, M.L. and Anderson, P. 1986. Technological discontinuities and organizational environments. *Administrative Science Quarterly*, 31(3): 439–65.

2

New Frontiers

Punctuated Equilibrium, Speciation, and Exaptation in Innovation

Gino Cattani and Mariano Mastrogiorgio

Evolutionary theory in economics, strategy, and innovation

Since the publication of 'An Evolutionary Theory of Economic Change' (Nelson and Winter, 1982), evolutionary thinking has grown significantly and has had a profound impact on various fields such as economics, strategy, and technological innovation (Aldrich and Ruef, 1999; Dopfer, 2005; Dosi, 2000; Helfat et al., 2007; Malerba et al., 2016; Metcalfe, 1998; Mokyr, 1990; Saviotti, 1996). Evolutionary thinking is centred on the idea that economic systems are constantly evolving and, contrary to neoclassical theory, are not in equilibrium owing to endogenous factors, such as technological innovation, which is also intrinsically evolutionary. This basic idea is not new. Marshall (1890) once argued that 'The Mecca of the economist lies in economic biology' (p. xxv). Despite being one of the founders of neoclassical economics, he emphasized the inherent evolutionary nature of an economic system. The other roots of the idea can be found in Veblen (1898) and later on in Schumpeter's (1942) concept of 'creative destruction' and in his recognition that 'in dealing with capitalism we are dealing with an evolutionary process' (p. 83). For a recent review of evolutionary thinking, we refer the reader to Nelson et al. (2018) and Murmann et al. (2003).

Despite being originally conceived as a contribution to growth economics, it is interesting to note that the book of Nelson and Winter (1982) has been highly influential in the strategy and technological innovation fields. In terms of strategy, the concept of routines and capabilities, which are central to evolutionary economic theory (e.g. Nelson and Winter, 1982), have strongly influenced the resource-based view of the firm and the debate on

Gino Cattani and Mariano Mastrogiorgio, *New Frontiers: Punctuated Equilibrium, Speciation, and Exaptation in Innovation* In: *New Developments in Evolutionary Innovation: Novelty Creation in a Serendipitous Economy.* Edited by: Gino Cattani and Mariano Mastrogiorgio, Oxford University Press (2021). © Gino Cattani and Mariano Mastrogiorgio. DOI: 10.1093/oso/9780198837091.003.0002 the sources of competitive advantage in highly dynamic contexts (Teece et al., 1997). In the context of technological innovation, evolutionary models have been even more impactful and are now well-established. As early as 1863, Butler (1863) noted that there is a Darwin among the machines because these objects undergo continuous evolution. In the 1930s, Gilfillan (1935) argued that innovation is like evolution and very much 'resembles a biologic process' (p. 275). Subsequently, Basalla (1988) presented a systematic theory of technological evolution that is based on historical sources. More recent evolutionary models of innovation can be found in Arthur (2009) and Ziman (2000) among others.

An overview of the current paradigm: neo-Darwinian evolution

An important paradigm that underlies the evolutionary theory of innovation is neo-Darwinian evolution. As stated by Nelson et al. (2018), 'the term "evolutionary economics" obviously carries the connotation that this orientation to economic analysis has something in common with the perspective of Darwinian evolutionary biology' (p. 25). Today, neo-Darwinian evolution is also known as 'modern synthesis', and this originated from the fusion of Darwin's original formulation and Mendel's genetic inheritance theory (Huxley, 1942; Mayr, 1942). Therefore, neo-Darwinian evolution was preceded by Darwin's original formulation and the theory of evolution of Lamarck, who can be considered the precursor of the evolutionary sciences because he was among the first to recognize evolution as the transformation of living things over time. According to Lamarck, living things actively change and learn to meet environmental challenges, and these somatic changes are passed on to subsequent generations. For example, a giraffe stretches its neck to reach a tall tree, and a longer neck is passed on to subsequent generations. In Darwin's original formulation, the transformation of living beings over time is not the result of transmittable modification and learning but of natural selection acting on phenotypes together with more sophisticated transmission mechanisms (that were not yet understood at the time) than those assumed by Lamarck. Owing to the development of Mendelian genetics, neo-Darwinian evolution began to shed light on these mechanisms.

According to neo-Darwinism, the evolution of living beings is gradualist and based on the mechanisms of variation, selection, and retention; in other words, genotypes are subject to variation via recombination and mutation, and the resulting phenotypes are subject to selection, which determines a new pool of genotypes that will be again subjected to variation, selection, and retention (Nelson, 1995). Recombination and mutation act on genes and occur during the cellular processes of meiosis and mitosis. Therefore, evolution is predominantly gene centred (Dawkins, 1976), and macroevolution arises from microevolution; this is consistent with a structuralist view (Gould, 2007). A related concept is that of adaptation, namely, the gradual change—via variation, selection, and retention—of a given trait of a living being towards a function. These processes 'shape a characteristic for its current use' (Dew et al., 2004: p. 72). An important meaning of adaptation refers to the process through which a given trait of the living being is *designed* for a specific function or the process by which we can 'attribute the origin and perfection of this design to a long period of selection for its effectiveness in this particular role' (Williams, 1966: p. 6).

In the innovation context, the evolutionary unit becomes a technological artefact rather than a biological organism. A genotype can be likened to a set—or string—of underlying modules arranged in an architecture that defines the interdependencies between them, whereas the phenotype is a set of observable characteristics, such as the form, behaviour, and functions of the technology. In this setting, variation via recombination or mutation consists of changes in the architecture—planned or unexpected—via several types of modular operators (Baldwin and Clark, 2000). On the other hand, selection is driven by the users and the market. Therefore, adaptation can be seen as the process through which a technology 'gets transformed on the basis of users' selection', and then 'into a market-driven function' (Andriani and Carignani, 2014: p. 1609). Technological adaptation has been studied using fitness landscape models (Wright, 1932), such as Kauffman's (1993) NK model in evolutionary biology, which was introduced by Levinthal (1997) in the innovation and strategy fields (see Baumann et al., 2019).

The NK model is a genotype-phenotype mapping that involves the assigning of a fitness value to each technological configuration among all possible configurations. Fitness values are the numerical values of how much a function/use of the technology is being improved via variation consisting of local or distant movements from one configuration to another. An interesting feature of the NK model is that the shape of the fitness curve is a function of the number of technological components and of the interaction among them (i.e. N and K, respectively). For instance, a higher K corresponds to a more rugged landscape, that is, technological adaptation towards a function becomes complex with a high risk of remaining trapped on a suboptimal peak. A key assumption at the basis of NK modelling and of neo-Darwinian technological adaptation is that there is a unique, pre-given and fixed function of the technology that enables the process of technological adaptation. Therefore, a technology is fit for the current function only through a process of adaptation, design, and fine-tuning oriented towards the function itself. As we will see, new developments in evolutionary theory challenge this assumption.

Towards a new paradigm: punctuated equilibrium, speciation, and exaptation

New theoretical advancements in evolutionary biology have recognized the central role of punctuated equilibrium, speciation, and exaptation in evolution. Introduced in Eldredge and Gould (1972) and Gould (2007), and partly inspired by the notion of allopatric speciation of Mayr (1954), the model of *punctuated equilibrium* contrasts with the model of phyletic gradualism, which is at the core of neo-Darwinian evolution. The model views evolution as a process that is characterized by stasis on a geological scale and is interrupted by short periods of *speciation*. In biology, speciation describes the process through which a new species emerges by divergent selection from a population that gradually adapts to new ecological conditions. A theory of speciation is essentially a theory about how reproductive isolation between two or more previously interbreeding populations arises (Mayr, 1942). Models of speciation tend to emphasize how the development of reproductive isolation may occur between populations that are geographically separated (allopatric speciation). Because of the presence of extrinsic barriers (rivers, mountains, etc.), the evolution of intrinsic barriers to gene flow (e.g. preferences for different mating habitats or genetic incompatibilities) promotes speciation. Geographically isolated populations can in fact diverge freely or, if they are small, be subject to random variation in gene frequency or genetic drift (Via, 2001).

Although allopatric speciation has been the dominant model of speciation, new theoretical work and empirical evidence (see Turelli et al., 2001) have recently pointed to other mechanisms favouring speciation when no extrinsic barriers impede the homogenizing effect of gene flow. The emphasis on geography in limiting gene flow contrasts with the role that *ecology* and especially natural selection plays in fostering speciation (Via, 2001: p. 381). The role of ecology in evolutionary divergence and species formation is now integral to models of *ecological* speciation (Schluter, 1996, 2001). According to the ecological hypothesis of speciation, the barriers to gene flow between populations evolve as a result of ecologically based divergent selection (i.e. contrasting selection forces characterizing distinct resource environments). Under ecological speciation, reproduction isolation 'evolves ultimately as a consequence of divergent (including disruptive) selection on traits between environments' (Schluter, 2001: p. 372). Populations facing different environments or exploiting different resources experience contrasting natural selection pressures on traits that directly or indirectly cause the evolution of reproductive isolation. In this sense, ecological speciation by divergent selection is consistent with the classic model of allopatric speciation (Mayr, 1942). The degree of correlation between divergent selection and the rate at which reproductive isolation evolves affects the speed of the overall process. Rapid evolution in natural populations can be observed in a relatively short time span (e.g. Reznick et al., 1997). The rate and patterns of change determined by natural selection might account for patterns observed in fossil records (i.e. long periods of little or no change [stasis] punctuated by brief periods of rapid change). Therefore, in natural populations, sustained directional selection may explain the rapid change leading to new species formation without invoking other evolutionary forces (e.g. a macro mutation) (see Cattani, 2019).

Overall, while neo-Darwinian evolution places emphasis on mutation, punctuated equilibrium places more emphasis on the macro and ecological context as the driver of novelty leading to new species. Therefore, punctuated equilibrium implies a non-structuralist view because it considers evolution as less gene-centred, less driven by microevolution, and influenced by alternative mechanisms of variation. In this regard, if one looks at historical changes in the evolution of an adaptation, it is possible that an organ served the same function at every stage (the evolution of the eye is a good example because in all stages it probably performed visual functions), or could possibly have performed different functions in the earlier stages. The classical Darwinian term for the second possibility is *preadaptation*, whereby the earlier stage is described as a preadaptation for the later stage. According to Bock (1959), 'the pre-adapted level is a threshold at which there is a functional shift, not a morphological shift. Because this shift has great functional and evolutionary significance, it may appear that it also involves a large morphological change; however, this "morphological change" is more apparent than real' (p. 209). For instance, feathers were most likely selected for thermal insulation, bones originated as excess calcium repositories, and so on.

The idea that the function of a trait might shift during its evolutionary history originated with Darwin (1859: Chapter 6), who gave functional *change* and *improvement* equal emphasis in his discussion of the origin of complex adaptations, as most major evolutionary biologists have done since then. The idea that current traits or structures have adaptive origins has been challenged by Gould and Vrba (1982), who suggested that the concept of *exaptation* should be used to describe the case wherein a trait or structure is a nonadaptation. Exaptation refers to the process whereby 'characters, evolved for other usages (or for no function at all)' are 'later "coopted" for their current role' (Gould and Vrba, 1982: p. 6). In particular, they argue (see Table 1 on p. 5 in their paper) that an exaptation is observed when (1) a character that was previously shaped by natural selection for a particular function (an adaptation) is co-opted for a new use and when (2) a character whose origin cannot be ascribed to the direct action of natural selection (a nonadaptation) is co-opted for a current use. While adaptation refers to the process through which a given trait is optimized for a function, exaptation refers to the process through which a given trait optimized for a function (or for no function at all) is later on co-opted for a new one. A classic example of exaptation in biology are wings, which hypothetically evolved for ancestral functions such as capturing prey or climbing trees and were later on co-opted for flight (Gatesy and Baier, 2005).

Despite being established in the evolutionary sciences, punctuated equilibrium, speciation, and exaptation have received less attention in innovation studies compared to neo-Darwinian theory. There are of course exceptions because the new evolutionary paradigm is becoming increasingly common. For instance, punctuated equilibrium has been proposed as a framework to reconcile different perspectives on technological change, particularly perspectives that view technological change as either gradual or discontinuous (Gersick, 1991; Mokyr, 1990b; Romanelli and Tushman, 1994; Tushman and Anderson, 1986). In contrast to the punctuated perspective, the model of technological speciation sheds light on the inherently gradual nature of technological change (Adner and Levinthal, 2002; Cattani, 2006; Levinthal, 1998). For example, Levinthal (1998) noted how punctuated equilibrium rests on speciation, which is defined as 'the application of existing technological know-how to a new domain of application', rather than mutation events (p. 218). His model of speciation is based on niche pressures (both in the old and new domains) and can be applied to the evolution of wireless communication technology. Cattani (2006) (see Figure 1, p. 307) examines the key technological antecedents (i.e. technologies developed for other, more or less related, technological fields or applications) that contributed to Corning's development of fibre optics. Most of this prior accumulated (technological) knowledge was actually adaptation for the particular (but different) uses for which it was originally created. However, this knowledge also proved valuable with respect to the new (though unanticipated) application, that is, fibre optics for long-distance telecommunications.

More recently, exaptation has also entered the scene, where the concept has been used to illustrate further the mechanics of speciation. As indicated by Andriani and Cattani (2016), there is indeed a clear linkage between speciation and exaptation. However, while the extant theory of speciation focuses on the adaptation trajectory of a technology *once* it is redeployed to a new domain of application, exaptation focuses on the functional shift itself and on what caused this shift. As stated by Andriani and Cattani (2016), 'an evolutionary theory on the emergence of novelty must explicitly account for what causes the "functional shift" of an existing technological artefact, i.e. the functional discontinuity that is central to the notion of exaptation' (p. 4). Therefore, a literature on exaptation is slowly emerging (La Porta et al., 2020) and focuses on different aspects of the phenomenon. For a recent and systematic review of this literature, we refer to the ICC special issue (Andriani and Cattani, 2016). We also refer the reader to Dew et al. (2004) for a definition of the phenomenon, of its economic significance, and for several anecdotal examples. We then refer to Cattani (2006) for an in-depth historical case study on the exaptation of capabilities from glass manufacturing to fibre optics. Finally, we refer to Andriani and Carignani (2014) and Mastrogiorgio and Gilsing (2016) for a discussion of the microdrivers of exaptation, such as modularity. An illustrative case of exaptation via modularity is the first microwave oven, namely, the Radarange, which resulted from the serendipitous discovery of a novel functionality of a module of the radar called the 'magnetron'; this happened when Mr Spencer, who was a military engineer working in the US army, was sitting close to a radar and discovered that the magnetron caused a candy bar in his pocket to melt (Andriani and Carignani, 2014).

Recent developments of exaptation research have shed light on other aspects such as the uncertain and unprestateable nature of exaptation and on the implications for search (Andriani et al., 2017), market efficiency, and economic opportunity (Felin et al., 2014, 2016). Unprestateability refers to multiple latent—and thus inherently unpredictable—functions and uses of technological artefacts (Felin et al., 2016). As we will see, unprestateability has important implications for evolutionary thinking in economics, strategy, and innovation, particularly for the idea of change, evolution, and disequilibrium, of which unprestateability is a source. Before delving into the previous questions, the next section discusses an often-overlooked issue: is evolutionary thinking fit for technological innovation?

In other words, is there a true parallel between biological evolution and technological evolution?

A short digression: is there a true link between biology and technology?

Before discussing the parallelism between biological and technological evolution, we must introduce an important concept: the phylogenetic tree, which is also known as the 'tree of life' (Darwin, 1859). The phylogenetic tree is a visual representation of the relationships between different species. It consists of a set of lineages that progressively branch out from a common ancestor. Each lineage represents a different species because it evolves through a gradual process of novelty accumulation via variation, selection, and retention. This is the visual representation of the phyletic gradualism assumed by neo-Darwinism in the modern synthesis (see Figure 2.1a), which contrasts with the visual representation of punctuated equilibrium that assumes that stasis is interrupted by sudden bursts of change (see Figure 2.1b).

According to Tëmkin and Eldredge (2007), technology and culture certainly evolve, but 'to what degree the processes of cultural change mirror biological evolution remains an unsettled question' (p. 146). According to them, there is a fundamental difference between biological and technological evolution: biological evolution unfolds through the vertical transmission of genetic information from parents to offspring on the basis of the mechanisms described before (Nelson, 1995). However, cultural and technological evolution unfolds through the transmission of 'memes' and technological components/modules, whereby the memes are the gene-correspondent units of cultural information (Cavalli-Sforza and Feldman, 1981; Dawkins, 1976). A fundamental difference is that memes and components can be transmitted via long vertical jumps along lineages or horizontally via lateral jumps across different lineages (Kelly, 2010; Tëmkin and Eldredge, 2007). Long vertical jumps mean that adaptive trajectories are faster, more abrupt, and less incremental than in biology and, more importantly, able to bring back to life old components and designs. As Kelly (2010) argued, 'the greatest difference between the evolution of the born and the evolution of the made is that species of technology, unlike species in biology, almost never go extinct' (p. 51). Several examples can be found in North American Amish communities (Kelly, 2010) or in the evolution of cornets, which is also characterized by horizontal jumps (Tëmkin and Eldredge, 2007). Overall, as shown in Figure 2.1c, long vertical jumps go from points I to II,

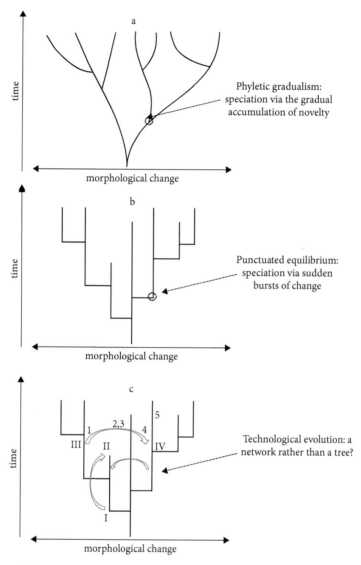

Figure 2.1 Phylogenetic trees: phyletic gradualism, punctuated equilibrium, and technological evolution

whereas lateral jumps go from III to IV. Therefore, in technological evolution, the graph looks like a reticulate structure, and what we see is a network rather than the trees of Figures 2.1a and 2.1b. This reticulate structure is indeed evident in patent data when represented in a network form, in which patents/technologies are nodes and in which patent citations are the links between nodes in the network (Solé et al., 2013).

Does the presence of a reticulate structure signal an irreconcilable difference between biological and technological evolution? There are several reasons to suggest the opposite. As argued by Mokyr (2000), technology 'contains an irreducible component of utilizing nature's regularities' (p. 4). First, biological and technological evolution can be both seen as an autopoietic self-organized process out of complex networks, that is, technology also falls within the category of the living (Kauffman, 1993). Second, unlike technological evolution, biological evolution is not Lamarckian because phenotypic/somatic features are not transmitted to subsequent generations, with the genotype being the only material to be transmitted (Ziman, 2000). However, this difference becomes less clear when considering 'epigenetic inheritance systems' or transgenerational epigenetic inheritance in biology, that is, the transmission of information from one generation to the next without altering the genetic material (Jablonka and Ziman, 2000). In this regard, the etymological root of 'epigenesis' is illuminating: the Greek prefix 'epi' stands for 'beyond'. Therefore, epigenesis stands for 'beyond genes'. A third reason has to do with 'horizontal genetic transfer', which consists of the transmission of genetic material among cells without vertical reproduction. Woese (2002, 2004) was the first to advance a model of evolution that explicitly incorporates horizontal gene transfer—in addition to vertical inheritance—as a key mechanism of evolution, thus leading to the speculation that 'a natural [tree-like] hierarchy may not extend into the bacterial world' (Carignani et al., 2019: p. 513). In other words, a phylogenetic network—rather than a tree—is the right structure, similar to that in technology. Carignani et al. (2019) have recently shown how this model can generate novel insights for studying technological evolution because it enables the reconciliation of different perspectives on technological evolution (gradualism versus discontinuity) by placing speciation and exaptation at the centre via artefact modularity.

Woesian models of technological evolution

On the premise that technological artefacts can be conceptualized as consisting of distinct functional modules (e.g. Ulrich, 1995), Carignani et al. (2019) recently proposed a novel perspective on technological change that is based on the Woesian model (Woese, 2002, 2004) of cell evolution to study technological change and, in particular, the origins of radical innovation. The model identifies horizontal gene transfer (HGT) as a critical force that drives evolution and complements the Darwinian theory of vertical inheritance. By building on the Woesian model of cell evolution (Woese, 2002, 2004), they highlight the central role of the horizontal transfer of existing functional modules in prompting radical innovation. In two influential articles, Woese (2002, 2004) advanced a new model of cell evolution that is still rooted within the modern synthesis, in which HGT complements vertical transfer (VT) as the main force that creates variation and prompts evolution. According to his model, bacterial cells—the only living organisms at the very beginning of life—freely exchanged parts of their replicators within a common pool via HGT. The result was the assemblage of modules with different origins in the same organism—that is, an evolutionary chimera (Woese, 2002). The ensuing variation did not originate from simple mutations but from a sort of genetic information reshuffling via the horizontal transfer of parts of modules (Ganfornina and Sanchez, 1999). Given that these modules impart new and consequential functions, they are called functional modules (Wolf and Arkin, 2003).

By building on this model, Carignani et al. (2019) examined the key role of the horizontal transfer of functional modules in generating (radical) innovation and strengthening the analogy between biological and technological evolution. In particular, they proposed a five-stage evolutionary model that mirrors key phases and events that characterize bacterial evolution: acquisition (1), retention (2), selection (3), fixation (4), and amelioration (5) (see Figure 2.1c). These follow the functional module starting from when it is transferred from a lineage into a new assembly (1); to when the new assembly gains selective advantage (2, 3), which creates a new lineage (4); and to when the adaptation of the new assembly happens vertically along the new lineage (5) (Carignani et al., 2019: p. 518). Phase 1 can be exaptive when the functional module is shifted to new functions after having been previously selected for other functions and can lead to speciation via phase 4.

In elaborating their Woesian model of technological change, Carignani et al. (2019) used the turbojet revolution to illustrate the main features of the model and to elucidate the conditions under which horizontal transfer is a crucial evolutionary force that leads to (radical) innovation. In their study, one of the main findings is that the first developments in aviation consisted of the horizontal transfer of exapted functional modules, such as compressors and turbines; these developments then became the basis of successive phases, including lineage generation. An important implication of this study is to place modularity at the centre of evolution theory, both biological and technological (Callebaut and Rasskin-Gutman, 2005). As Carignani et al. (2019) argued and demonstrated, modules are indeed central in artefact-based theories of technological evolution that are inspired by the new paradigm (see Andriani and Carignani, 2014; Mastrogiorgio and Gilsing, 2016). An important implication of adopting a Woesian model of evolution is that it is possible to propose a more general framework in which gradualist and discontinuous perspectives of change in technological evolution can be fruitfully reconciled (Carignani et al., 2019).

Serendipity, unprestateability, and disequilibrium: a new paradigm

The new paradigm views technological evolution as a fundamentally uncertain process and endogenous generator of economic disequilibrium, which is a potential source of value and profits. A concept that illustrates uncertainty is serendipity. Despite having its roots in sociology, the concept of serendipity is closely related to new evolutionary theories, particularly exaptation, which can be seen as the underlying mechanism of serendipity (Andriani and Cattani, 2016; Cattani, 2006, 2008; Dew et al., 2004). The word 'serendipity' comes from Walpole's story of the princes of Serendip (Sri Lanka), who made accidental discoveries thanks to their sagacity. Serendipity, which is defined as 'finding something of value while seeking something entirely different' (Merton and Barber, 2004: p. 14), is pervasive in innovation, where it has shaped the birth of single technologies, such as the abovementioned microwave oven (Andriani and Carignani, 2014), or entire industries, such as the pharmaceutical industry (Meyers, 2007). Serendipity via exaptation is very common in the pharmaceutical industry, where drugs that were originally approved for a specific disease often end up being prescribed for very different diseases via the off-label route (Andriani et al., 2017). This also happens in unpredictable ways. Merton and Barber (2004) traced the theoretical roots of serendipity and its saliency in science. Academic research on the role of serendipity is slowly emerging. For instance, Yaqub (2018) argued that serendipity comes in different forms and proposes a taxonomy that is based on four different types. On the other hand, Cunha et al. (2010) discussed the organizational conditions that make serendipity more likely, whereas Dew et al. (2004) discussed the value implications of serendipity. In this regard, an interesting direction is to link serendipity to profits via fundamental uncertainty (Dew et al., 2004): the impossibility of pre-stating all possible functions, uses, and markets that emerge via serendipity/exaptation is a form of fundamental uncertainty. According to Knight (1921), this situation is a source of value and profits. More recently, Felin et al. (2016) argued that the continual emergence of new functions and uses poses a challenge for the efficiency of markets, thus constituting a source of value and profits.

A recent concept that further develops the link between evolution, fundamental uncertainty, and disequilibrium is that of 'unprestateability'. The concept of unprestateability refers to the idea that organisms and technological artefacts 'embody myriad functionalities and uses that cannot be prestated' *ex ante* (Felin et al., 2014: p. 9). It can be seen as a 'modern' version of Knightian uncertainty because the impossibility of pre-stating all possible functions and uses means that a space of events does not exist, thus invalidating any type of probability statement. A classic example is the screwdriver, which can be used to screw in a screw, open a door, kill a predator, or for other multiple and undefinable function and uses (Longo et al., 2012). The concept of unprestateability has been recently placed at the centre of disequilibrium-based theories of economic opportunity (Felin et al., 2016; Koppl et al., 2015). These theories claim that economic environments are blossoming in terms of diversity because of the continual emergence of new technological artefacts, products, and assets. This catalyses the continual emergence of novel functions and uses of other (existing) artefacts. For example, following the invention of the can, the screwdriver eventually 'acquired' a new function as a can opener. The core intuition here is that given the diversity of technologies, products, and assets, the number of possible interactions giving rise to novel functions and uses is unprestateable.

This has deep economic implications. Two key economic aggregates are prices and quantities, as illustrated in textbook models where supply and demand intersect at a point of equilibrium, towards which prices and quantities converge hypothetically. As Koppl et al. (2015) noted, equilibrium becomes problematic when we remove the Arrowian assumption of 'contingent claims' (Arrow and Debreu, 1954), according to which 'all future artefacts or states can be mapped and calculated' (p. 7). This implies that the unprestateability of functions and uses via serendipity and exaptation is a source of disequilibrium (Kauffman, 2000). Similar claims have been also made by Denrell et al. (2003), who claimed that equilibrium (and efficiency) holds only when we assume that all possible functions and uses can be listed (i.e. 'exhaustive entrepreneurship'). In this regard, it is useful to think about the ontological meaning of the 'price' of a technology, product, or asset as the *value of the best use we can make of it among all possible ones*. However, if the set of all possible uses changes owing to unprestateability, the value of the best use and the price will also change, thus implying disequilibrium. This intuition is important because it links back to the core evolutionary debate on the limitations of the equilibrium concept in neoclassical economics.

As Georgescu-Roegen (1971), Mirowski (1989), and Beinhocker (2007) noticed, neoclassical equilibrium is nothing more than a consequence of borrowing physical concepts, particularly the first law of thermodynamics, which assumes energy conservation in a *closed* system. However, real economies are open systems—that is, increasing diversity and consequent functional expansion continually drives economies out of stasis and into a state of constant, inherent disequilibrium.

Innovating without planning: an option-based logic

As discussed until now, most of the current evolutionary theories in economics, strategy, and innovation are grounded on the paradigm of neo-Darwinian evolution. By contrast, new evolutionary theory is progressively adopting a new paradigm that challenges old assumptions and aims to offer a view of technological evolution as a complex and out-of-equilibrium process in which serendipity, fundamental uncertainty, and unprestateability play a central role. What are the main practical implications of the new theory for understanding technological innovation? We propose three broad implications that adopt an option-based perspective.

First, we should note the emphasis of current evolutionary theory on the idea of 'innovation systems' (Nelson, 1993). With the risk of oversimplifying a much broader debate, the idea of innovation systems somehow originates from the core assumptions of evolutionary theory. In particular, owing to disequilibrium and the perfectible nature of markets, other nonmarket institutions are seen as necessary to complement the functioning of markets: in fact, national innovation systems refer to public support to innovation (through increasing spending, tax deductions, and so forth) in the form of R&D conducted at universities, laboratories, and public research centres. From this perspective, the government matters, as suggested by defence spending during the internet revolution in the United States (Mazzucato, 2013). Indeed, innovation systems are presumed to have a positive impact on economic outcomes despite significant cross-industry variations (Nelson et al., 2018). However, some industries also reveal the fallacies of innovation systems, particularly fallacies that are implicit in a 'planning approach' to innovation, according to which R&D unfolds in a linear fashion towards prespecified targets and goals. An example of these fallacies is the lost war on cancer by the National Cancer Institutes (Leaf, 2013), whereby massive research investments have resulted in low productivity levels, owing to a 'throw money at it' and target-oriented approach to drug development (Scannell et al., 2012). Andriani et al. (2017) noted that 'randomness, luck, serendipity, and chance play a fundamental role even in science-driven sectors', with 'ample evidence about the role of unintended events [rather than goal-driven strategies] in innovation' (p. 335). By acknowledging the importance of new processes such as horizontal transfer and exaptation, the evolutionary theory we propose is better equipped to conceptualize on the role of the unexpected, thus affording a new perspective on technological innovation that enriches (and perhaps goes beyond) current approaches.

This brings us to a second point: how can we stimulate the unexpected in organizational contexts? This issue has been discussed, directly or indirectly, in multiple contributions. For instance, Merton and Barber (2004) offered general recommendations on how science, research, and innovation should be managed to increase the chances of unexpected discoveries. According to them, R&D managers should avoid *ex ante* planning and should define very general (and flexible) goals and targets that grant individual scientists and inventors freedom to experiment. Cunha et al. (2010) discussed more specific recommendations centred around the role of destructured—rather than ordered, controlled, and predictable—organizational processes such as deadline removal, boundary spanning, teamwork, bottom-up rather than hierarchical power, and the opportunity to play with ideas. In the context of exaptation, Andriani et al. (2017) emphasized distributed processes in which users play a key role owing to their ability to bring ideas from different domains freely, without being subject to hierarchical authority. Multiple examples of these policies abound in start-up settings and in technology firms such as Pixar, 3M, Corning, Google, and so on. For instance, William McKnight, former chairman of 3M and the person responsible for fostering the company's entrepreneurial culture, introduced the policy known as the '15 percent rule' to encourage 'managers to allow employees time to work on projects of their own personal interest' (Gundling, 2000: p. 58). By allowing 3M engineers to spend up to 15 per cent of their work time pursuing whatever project they like, the rule is still today essential to the corporate culture of 3M. Since its introduction, 'the 15 percent rule has been credited for the invention of many radical technologies, some of which—like 3M's Post-it notepad—were eventually used for different applications than those for which they were originally intended' (Cattani, 2019: p. 403). By the same token, Google's '70–20–10' per cent rule allows employees to dedicate 20 or 10 per cent of their time to the pursuit of novel (and often risky) projects (Schmidt et al., 2014). The aim of this policy is to incentivize individuals to explore beyond the firm's core business within an organizational culture in which failure is actively promoted rather than being punished. This policy has generated multiple innovations that are often very unexpected and novel, such as Google's Sky Map, Street View, and Gmail (Schmidt et al., 2014).

Overall, these examples point to the importance of free experimentation within a model of technological innovation that is governed by inherent serendipity, unprestateability, and fundamental uncertainty.

This brings us to the very last point: the need to adopt an option-based philosophy. As the previous discussion implies, a technological artefact has multiple latent functions that emerge serendipitously. These multiple functions can be seen as multiple options embedded in the technological artefact. This suggests a possible point of contact between the new evolutionary paradigm and the theory of 'real options'. Option theory originated in finance (Black and Scholes, 1973) and was later on expanded in other fields (Myers, 1977), including innovation and R&D (Oriani and Sobrero, 2008). In the innovation field, a real option refers to the fact that a technology embeds the right (but not the obligation) to expand further the initial investment when a new function of an existing technology is discovered. This is the case when a new treatment is discovered using a drug originally developed for other reasons, but the exercise of this new option requires further investments in new clinical trials. A new research stream of real options theory, which is still underexplored from the evolutionary angle, looks at 'resource redeployability' (Sakhartov and Folta, 2014). Redeployability specifically refers to the redeployment of resources (and technologies) into different domains, which is seen as a source of corporate diversification (Helfat and Eisenhardt, 2004). However, for the purposes of this discussion, what is important to stress is that technological functions are *latent*, which means that the real options embedded in technologies are *shadow*, that is, they cannot be known *ex ante* (Bowman and Hurry, 1993). As Andriani and Cattani (2016) emphasized, 'a shadow option refers to the case in which an existing bundle of resources provide options (or investment opportunities) awaiting recognition' (p. 12). This raises several important questions: how does the process of recognition (i.e. transforming a shadow option into a real one) unfold? Which approach should be adopted to determine the value of a shadow option? Given the unprestateability of latent functions, is the classical financial approach (such as real options) the right approach? Should we rather rely on a historical, case-based approach? We do not have a clear answer to these questions; thus, we leave them to future research. A possible insight is that the recognition of shadow options (i.e. new functions, uses, and possibilities) is a fine-grained, path-dependent, idiosyncratic, not-yet-understood process that may unfold in different ways in different organizations via the gradual sense making, reactivation, and synthetization of old knowledge preserved for old uses (Cattani, 2005, 2006; Garud and Nayyar, 1994; Leiblein et al., 2017).

References

Adner, R. and Levinthal, D.A. 2002. The emergence of emerging technologies. *California Management Review*, 45(1): 50–66.

Aldrich, H.E. and Ruef, M. 1999. *Organizations evolving*. SAGE.

Andriani, P. and Carignani, G. 2014. Modular exaptation: a missing link in the synthesis of artificial form. *Research Policy*, 43(9): 1608–20.

Andriani, P. and Cattani, G. 2016. Exaptation as a source of creativity, innovation, and diversity in evolutionary sciences: introduction to the special section. *Industrial and Corporate Change*, 25(1): 115–31.

Andriani, P., Ali, A., and Mastrogiorgio, M. 2017. Measuring exaptation and its impact on innovation, search and problem-solving. *Organization Science*, 28(2): 320–38.

Arrow, K.J. and Debreu, G. 1954. Existence of an equilibrium for a competitive economy. *Econometrica*, 22(3): 265–90.

Arthur, W.B. 2009. *The nature of technology*. Free Press.

Baldwin, C.Y. and Clark, K.B. 2000. *Design rules: the power of modularity*. MIT Press.

Basalla, G. 1988. *The evolution of technology*. Cambridge University Press.

Baumann, O., Schmidt, J., and Stieglitz, N. 2019. Effective search in rugged performance landscapes: a review and outlook. *Journal of Management*, 45(1): 285–318.

Beinhocker, E.D. 2007. *The origins of wealth: evolution, complexity, and the radical remaking of economics*. Harvard Business Review Press.

Black, F. and Scholes, M. 1973. The pricing of options and corporate liabilities. *Journal of Political Economy*, 81(3): 637–54.

Bock, W.J. 1959. Pre-adaptation and multiple evolutionary pathways. *Evolution*, 21(2): 194–211.

Bowman, E.H. and Hurry, D. 1993. Strategy through the option lens: an integrated view of resource investments and the incremental-choice process. *Academy of Management Review*, 18(4): 760–82.

Butler, S. 1863. *Darwin among the machines*. Published in The Press Newspaper.

Callebaut, W. and Rasskin-Gutman, D. 2005. *Modularity: understanding the development and evolution of natural complex systems*. MIT Press.

Carignani, G., Cattani, G., and Zaina, G. 2019. Evolutionary chimeras: A Woesian perspective of radical innovation. *Industrial and Corporate Change*, 28(3): 511–28.

Cattani, G. 2005. Pre-adaptation, firm heterogeneity and technological performance: a study on the evolution of fiber optics, 1970–1995. *Organization Science*, 16(6): 563–80.

Cattani, G. 2006. Technological preadaptation, speciation and emergence of new technologies: how Corning invented and developed fiber optics. *Industrial and Corporate Change*, 15(2): 285–318.

Cattani, G. 2008. Reply to Dew's (2007) commentary: pre-adaptation, exaptation and technology speciation: a comment on Cattani (2006). *Industrial and Corporate Change*, 17(3): 585–96.

Cattani, G. 2019. The origins and recognition of radical innovation: a multi-disciplinary perspective. In *Stato e Mercato* (Il Mulino, English version), 117(3): 377–410.

Cavalli-Sforza, L.L. and Feldman, M. 1981. *Cultural transmission and evolution: a quantitative approach*. Princeton University Press.

Cunha, M.P., Clegg, S.R., and Mendonça, S. 2010. On serendipity and organizing. *European Management Journal*, 28(5): 319–30.

Darwin, C. 1859. *On the origin of species*. John Murray Eds.

Dawkins, R. 1976. *The selfish gene*. Oxford University Press.

Denrell, J., Fang, C., and Winter, S.G. 2003. The economics of strategic opportunity. *Strategic Management Journal*, 24(10): 977–90.

Dew, N., Sarasvathy, S.D., and Venkataraman, S. 2004. The economic implications of exaptation. *Journal of Evolutionary Economics*, 14(1): 69–84.

Dopfer, K. 2005. *Evolutionary foundations of economics*. Cambridge University Press.

Dosi, G. 2000. *Innovation, organization and economic dynamics: selected essays*. Edward Elgar.

Eldredge, N. and Gould, S.J. 1972. Punctuated equilibria: an alternative to phyletic gradualism. In Schopf, T.J.M. (ed.). *Models in paleobiology*. Freeman Cooper.

Felin, T., Kauffman, S., Koppl, R., and Longo, G. 2014. Economic opportunity and evolution: beyond landscapes and bounded rationality. *Strategic Entrepreneurship Journal*, 8(4): 269–82.

Felin, T., Kauffman, S., Mastrogiorgio, A., and Mastrogiorgio, M. 2016. Factor markets, actors and affordances. *Industrial and Corporate Change*, 25(1): 133–47.

Ganfornina, M.D. and Sánchez, D. 1999. Generation of evolutionary novelty by functional shift. *BioEssays: News and Reviews in Molecular, Cellular and Developmental Biology*, 21(5): 432–9.

Garud, R. and Nayyar, P.R. 1994. Transformative capacity: continual structuring by intertemporal technology transfer. *Strategic Management Journal*, 15(5): 365–85.

Gatesy, S.M. and Baier, D.B. 2005. The origin of the avian flight stroke: a kinematic and kinetic perspective. *Paleobiology*, 31(3): 382–99.

Georgescu-Roegen, N. 1971. *The entropy law and the economic process*. Harvard University Press.

Gersick, C.J.G. 1991. Revolutionary change theories: a multilevel exploration of the punctuated equilibrium approach. *Academy of Management Review*, 16(1): 10–36.

Gilfillan, S. 1935. *Inventing the ship*. Follett Publishing.

Gould, S.J. 2007. *Punctuated equilibrium*. Belknap Press.

Gould, S.J. and Vrba, E.S. 1982. Exaptation—a missing term in the science of form. *Paleobiology*, 8(1): 4–15.

Gundling, E. 2000. *The 3M way to innovation. Balancing people and profit.* Kodansha International.

Helfat, C.E. and Eisenhardt, K.M. 2004. Inter-temporal economies of scope, organizational modularity, and the dynamics of diversification. *Strategic Management Journal*, 25(13): 1217–32.

Helfat, C.E., Finkelstein, S., Mitchell, W., Peteraf, M.A., Singh, H., Teece, D.J., and Winter, S.G. 2007. *Dynamic capabilities: understanding strategic change in organizations.* Blackwell Publishing.

Huxley, J. 1942. *Evolution: the modern synthesis.* Allen & Unwin.

Jablonka, E. and Ziman, J. 2000. Biological evolution: processes and phenomena. In Ziman, J. (ed.). *Technological innovation as an evolutionary process.* Cambridge University Press.

Kauffman, S. 1993. *The origins of order.* Oxford University Press.

Kauffman, S.A. 2000. *Investigations.* Oxford University Press.

Kelly, K. 2010. *What technology wants.* Viking Press.

Knight, F.H. 1921. *Risk, uncertainty, and profit* (8th edn). Kelley and Millman.

Koppl, R., Kauffman, S., Felin, T., and Longo, G. 2015. Economics for a creative world. *Journal of Institutional Economics*, 11(1): 1–31.

La Porta, C., Zapperi, S., and Pilotti, L. 2020. *Understanding innovation through exaptation.* Springer.

Leaf, C. 2013. *The truth in small doses: why we're losing the war on cancer—and how to win it.* Simon & Schuster paperbacks.

Leiblein, M.J., Chen, J.S., and Posen, H.E. 2017. Resource allocation in strategic factor markets; a realistic real options approach to generating competitive advantage. *Journal of Management*, 43(8): 2588–608.

Levinthal, D.A. 1997. Adaptation on rugged landscapes. *Management Science*, 43(7): 934–50.

Levinthal, D.A. 1998. The slow pace of rapid technological change: gradualism and punctuation in technological change. *Industrial and Corporate Change*, 7(2): 217–47.

Longo, G., Montevil, M., and Kauffman, S. 2012. No entailing laws, but enablement in the evolution of the biosphere. In Proceedings of the genetic and evolutionary computation conference.

Malerba, F., Nelson, R.R., Orsenigo, L., and Winter, S.G. 2016. *Innovation and the evolution of industries: history-friendly models.* Cambridge University Press.

Marshall, A. 1890. *Principles of economics.* MacMillan.

Mastrogiorgio, M. and Gilsing, V. 2016. Innovation through exaptation and its determinants: the role of technological complexity, analogy making and patent scope. *Research Policy*, 45(7): 1419–35.

Mayr, E. 1942. *Systematics and the origin of species from the viewpoint of a zoologist.* Columbia University Press.

Mayr, E. 1954. Geographic speciation in tropical echinoids. *Evolution*, 8(1): 1–18.

Mazzucato, M. 2013. *The entrepreneurial state: debunking the public vs. private myth in risk and innovation*. Anthem Press.

Merton, R.K. and Barber, E. 2004. *The travels and adventures of serendipity*. Princeton University Press.

Metcalfe, J.S. 1998. *Evolutionary economics and creative destruction*. Routledge.

Meyers, M.A. 2007. *Happy accidents: serendipity in major medical breakthroughs in the twentieth century*. Arcade Publishing.

Mirowski, P. 1989. *More heat than light. Economics as social physics: physics as nature's economics*. Cambridge University Press.

Mokyr, J. 1990. *The lever of the riches: technological creativity and economic progress*. Oxford University Press.

Mokyr, J. 1990b. Punctuated equilibria and technological progress. *American Economic Review*, 80(2): 350–4.

Mokyr, J. 2000. Natural history and economic history: is technological change and evolutionary process? Unpublished manuscript.

Murmann, J.P., Aldrich, H.E., Levinthal, D., and Winter, S.G. 2003. Evolutionary thought in management and organization theory at the beginning of the new millennium: a symposium on the state of the art and opportunities for future research. *Journal of Management Inquiry*, 12(1): 22–40.

Myers, S.C. 1977. Determinants of corporate borrowing. *Journal of Financial Economics*, 5(2): 147–75.

Nelson, R.R. 1993. *National innovation systems: a comparative analysis*. Oxford University Press.

Nelson, R.R. 1995. Recent evolutionary theorizing about economic change. *Journal of Economic Literature*, 33(1): 48–90.

Nelson, R.R., Dosi, G., Helfat, C.E., Pyka, A., Saviotti, P., Lee, K., Dopfer, K., Malerba, F., and Winter, S.G. 2018. *Modern evolutionary economics*. Cambridge University Press.

Nelson, R.R. and Winter, S.G. 1982. *An evolutionary theory of economic change*. Harvard University Press.

Oriani, R. and Sobrero, M. 2008. Uncertainty and the market valuation of R&D within a real options logic. *Strategic Management Journal*, 29(4): 343–61.

Reznick, D.N., Shaw, F.H., Rodd, F.H., and Shaw, R.G. 1997. Evaluation of the rate of evolution in natural populations of guppies (*Poecilia reticulate*). *Science*, 275(5308): 1934–7.

Romanelli, E. and Tushman, M.L. 1994. Organizational transformation as punctuated equilibrium: an empirical test. *Academy of Management Journal*, 37(5): 1141–66.

Sakhartov, A.V. and Folta, T.B. 2014. Resource relatedness, redeployability, and firm value. *Strategic Management Journal*, 35(12): 1781–97.

Saviotti, P.P. 1996. *Technological evolution, variety and the economy*. Edward Elgar.

Scannell, J.W., Blanckley, A., Boldon, H., and Warrington, B. 2012. Diagnosing the decline in pharmaceutical R&D efficiency. *Nature Reviews Drug Discovery*, 11(3): 191–200.

Schluter, D. 1996. Ecological speciation in post-glacial fishes. *Philosophical Transactions of the Royal Society of London. Series B: Biological Sciences*, 351(1341): 807–14.

Schluter, D. 2001. Ecology and the origin of species. *Trends in Ecology and Evolution*, 16(7): 372–80.

Schmidt, E., Rosenberg, J., and Eagle, A. 2014. *How Google works*. Grand Central Publishing.

Schumpeter, J.A. 1942. *Capitalism, socialism and democracy*. Harper.

Solé, R.V., Valverde, S., Rosas-Casals, M., Kauffman, S.A., Farmer, D., and Eldredge, N. 2013. The evolutionary ecology of technological innovations. *Complexity*, 18(4): 15–27.

Teece, D.J., Pisano, G., and Shuen, A. 1997. Dynamic capabilities and strategic management. *Strategic Management Journal*, 18(7): 509–33.

Tëmkin, I. and Eldredge, N. 2007. Phylogenetics and material cultural evolution. *Current Anthropology*, 48(1): 146–54.

Turelli, M., Barton, N.H., and Coyne, J.A. 2001. Theory and speciation. *Trends in Ecology and Evolution*, 16(7): 330–43.

Tushman, M.L. and Anderson, P. 1986. Technological discontinuities and organizational environments. *Administrative Science Quarterly*, 31(3): 439–65.

Ulrich, K. 1995. The role of product architecture in the manufacturing firm. *Research Policy*, 24(3): 419–40.

Veblen, T. 1898. Why is economics not an evolutionary science? *Quarterly Journal of Economics*, 12(4): 373–97.

Via, S. 2001. Sympatric speciation in animals: the ugly duckling grows up. *Trends in Ecology and Evolution*, 16(7): 381–90.

Williams, G.C. 1966. *Adaptation and natural selection*. Princeton University Press.

Woese, C.R. 2002. On the evolution of cells. *Proceedings of the National Academy of Sciences of the United States of America*, 99(13): 8742–7.

Woese, C.R. 2004. A new biology for a new century. *Microbiology and Molecular Biology Reviews*, 68(2): 173–86.

Wolf, D.M. and Arkin, A.P. 2003. Motifs, modules and games in bacteria. *Current Opinion in Microbiology*, 6(2): 125–34.

Wright, S. 1932. The roles of mutations, inbreeding, crossbreeding and selection in evolution. Proceedings of the 11th international congress of genetics.

Yaqub, O. 2018. Serendipity: towards a taxonomy and a theory. *Research Policy*, 47(1): 169–79.

Ziman, J. 2000. *Technological innovation as an evolutionary process*. Cambridge University Press.

3

On The Origins of The Airframe Revolution

Managing Exaptive Radical Innovation

Giuseppe Carignani

Introduction

The *airframe revolution* (*c.*1926–39) was the greatest development in aviation history after the Wright brothers. It transformed the aviation industry from wood-and-doped-fabric truss airframes (the dominant design in military planes at the end of WWI) to internally braced all-metal aircraft, whose distinctive elements were cantilever wings and monocoque fuselages. The airframe revolution marked the advent of the new *dominant design in aero-structures*, an architecture that is still largely in existence in modern general aviation. Although the importance of the airframe revolution can hardly be denied, its origin remains poorly understood. The common opinion is that the development of new materials and theoretical advancements in aero-dynamics and construction science were the drivers of the transition.

However, the historical record tells a different story. By using a narrative method, this chapter reconstructs the microhistorical events that led to the airframe revolution and clarifies their meaning via an evolutionary framework. This demonstrates that a punctual event of *modular internal exaptation* triggered the inception of the revolution several years before its manifestation. After this technological discontinuity, which went almost unnoticed even within the aviation industry, a cascade of synergistic developments (i.e. advances in material performance, thanks to new aluminium alloys, and theoretical progress in construction science and in aerodynamics) gradually perfected the revolution and led to the emergence of the novel dominant design.

This chapter proposes a new definition of *gradual revolution* to indicate an innovation pattern of *slow radical innovation*. This novel pattern reconciles

Giuseppe Carignani, *On The Origins of The Airframe Revolution: Managing Exaptive Radical Innovation* In: *New Developments in Evolutionary Innovation: Novelty Creation in a Serendipitous Economy*. Edited by: Gino Cattani and Mariano Mastrogiorgio, Oxford University Press (2021). © Giuseppe Carignani. DOI: 10.1093/oso/9780198837091.003.0003 the gradualistic Darwinian vision with the discontinuous character of radical innovation. Gradual revolutions analogous to the airframe revolution are by no means rare in the history of technology. Accordingly, this chapter proposes a stylized general model elucidating the critical subprocesses. To this end, the analysis of the Fokker case shows how identifying exaptive phenomena is possible and can provide firms with sustained competitive advantages on the basis of the engineering of VRIN (valuable, rare, inimitable, and non-substitutable) resources[1] that they already possess. The final paragraph of this chapter discusses the managerial implications from the case analysis by proposing a novel approach to managing radical exaptive innovation. Adopting this approach requires a novel attitude towards technology: opening the black box of creative engineering—a VRIN resource that many firms own—could move Knightian true uncertainty into the realm of manageable risk.

The airframe revolution

The silent inception of the airframe revolution in Fokker's memoir

In 1919, during the troubled and chaotic period that followed the defeat of the German Empire in WWI, an unusually long freight train crossed the German-Dutch border to export goods to the Netherlands. To make the inspection more difficult, the train was deliberately made longer than the forty trucks that the sidings at the frontier could accommodate. Nonetheless, it was inspected at Saltsbergen by German and Allied frontier patrols and at Hengelo by the Dutch. However, nothing wrong was found with its cargo of wood and steel tubing. The successful border crossing was also helped by 'greased' tracks. The customs officers were bribed with money or gifts consisting of sewing machines and bicycles, which were coveted items in impoverished post-war Europe, as well as Fokker model planes. Anthony Fokker himself, the famous Dutch inventor and entrepreneur, was the man behind the daring smuggling scheme. After the first train got safely across, five other trains followed. When the 'Great Smuggling Plot' (Fokker, 1938: p. 196) was completed, Fokker had shipped an impressive stock of aviation *materièl* (military material), which had been previously hidden in barns and rural buildings

---

[1] Valuable, rare, imperfectly imitable, and nonsubstitutable resources are, according to Barney (1991), the sources of sustained competitive advantage for a firm.

Figure 3.1 Fokker D.VIII 'parasol' monoplane

Anthony Fokker (standing, on the right, in a necktie) emphasizes the strength of the novel plywood-sheathed stressed-skin wing. The structural function has already been transferred to the 'thick wing'. (Smithsonian Institution)

near his factory in Schwerin, tricking the Allied inspectors who had previously visited Fokker's facilities.

According to his memoirs, Fokker (1938) was able to smuggle a total of 400 aviation engines, 120 D.VII planes, and 'a score' of D.VIII new fighters. Both types were remarkable aircraft. The Fokker D.VII, as Fokker proudly emphasized in his memoirs, was the only warplane that the armistice explicitly required be turned over to the Allies. The D.VIII was the latest development of Fokker designs, the innovative wing of which could deliver exceptional performance (Figure 3.1). This wing adopted a subtle yet critical design concept—it was much thicker than the theory and best practices required (almost three times as thick). The understanding of the advantages of this new counterintuitive design provided Fokker with a sustained advantage that was enough to support his firm's development from near bankruptcy at the end of WWI to a prominent and profitable role within the European and American aviation industry. The D.VIII wing design was 'used on Fokker aircrafts for many years' (Loftin Jr, 1985: p. 40). In particular, the Fokker Trimotor of 1926, which heralded modern civil aviation in the United States, still used the all-wood 'thick wing' pioneered in 1918. Unbeknown to both aviation experts and most aviation firms, including Fokker's competitors, in 1918, with the D.VIII wing, the airframe revolution had silently begun.

The airframe revolution: contradictory background

Over a century, aviation historians have defined only two radical innovations as revolutions: the turbojet revolution, for which 'the ultimate accolade of successful technological revolution' was 'to be acclaimed by pundits as age' (Constant, 1980: p. 1), and the less-known airframe revolution, which is also called 'the revolution in aerostructures' (Constant, 1980: p. 129) or the 'design revolution' (Loftin, 1985). Although less conspicuous to the layman, the airframe revolution was as important as the jet revolution: without the former, the latter would never have occurred. As Constant (1980) put it: 'During the 1930s, piston engine and propeller design co-evolved with revolutionary developments in aircraft structures. That revolution in aero-structures…was essential to the coming of the turbojet' (p. 129). Rather than a *discontinuous breakthrough*, the airframe revolution consisted of a complex process of *gradual modular evolution* from 'strut-and-wires' aero-structures (the dominant design in military planes at the end of WWI) to internally braced, all-metal architectures whose distinctive elements were cantilever wings and monocoque fuselages, which became the new domin-ant design in aerostructures. This design was established in the 1920s and 1930s, and is still in existence in modern general aviation.

Despite its impact, the airframe revolution remains poorly understood. According to some scholars (e.g. Geels, 2006), the airframe revolution can be described as an accumulation of design changes (all-metal, mono-wing planes using stressed-skin structures, retractable landing gear, Fowler air flaps, and leading-edge slats). However, the word 'accumulation' hardly cap-tures the causal chain leading to the revolution. The common view of the origins of the revolution posits that advances in material technology, which led to the adoption of new aluminium alloys, and theoretical progress in construction science played a critical role. Constant (1980) embraces this view by emphasizing how 'the really critical revolution in airframes was the development of monocoque, stressed-skin structures in which the aluminium itself was made to carry a significant portion of the structural load' (p. 131). Hence, the traditional assumption is that materials were the critical factor underlying the structural revolution in aeronautics.

This explanation is not supported by historical records. As aviation histor-ian Peter Jakab (1999) shows, 'the prevalent assumption regarding the transition...that the building material acted as the primary driver of structural design change is clearly at odds with the historical record. Indeed, several successful aircrafts featuring the major structural innovations characterizing the design revolution were built well before the availability of the novel materials. They were prototyped during WWI and were all-wood and doped-fabric aircraft' (p. 914). Innovative aircrafts that anticipated the coming revolution 'were developed largely independent of the material' (Jakab, 1999: p. 914). The all-wood D.VIII fighters designed (and smuggled) by Fokker (Figure 3.1) are the obscure yet iconic demonstration that metal was not the primary driver of fundamental change. As a result, the airframe revolution constitutes a quintessential case of radical innovation that marked the demise of an existing dominant design and the advent of a new one, thus unravelling the entire aviation industry and opening new important markets, most notably civil aviation. However, the general explanation that most innovation historians have accepted is proven false by historical records.

The exaptive origins of the airframe revolution

This chapter proposes an interpretative description of the microhistorical events that initiated the airframe revolution. It takes the form of a narrative that aims to make sense of the puzzling events occurring in 1918, the effects of which were to trigger an avalanche of radical innovations shaping the entire aviation industry. The *narrative method* complements the theoretical framework of *modular exaptation* and unveils the unexpected and counterintuitive decision-making by 'identifying a series of key events and capturing the perspective of the actors involved' (Beltagui et al., 2020: p. 6).

Exaptation. Exaptation can be defined as the co-opting of a technology or biological trait or module for a function for which it was not designed or selected. Poetically described as 'The wonderful metamorphoses in function' by Darwin himself (in *On the Origin of Species*, 1859, Chapter 6), the concept was later reconsidered and defined as 'preadaptation' by the French naturalist Lucien Cuènot (1914). Gould and Vrba (1982) in their seminal paper reframed the concept and introduced the term 'exaptation' to describe the process of functional shift in biological evolution. Gould and Vrba (1982) contrasted exaptation (i.e. the discovery of a new function for an existing trait) with adaptation, which is defined as the improvement of a trait via natural selection. Although exaptation originated in biology, it has also been recognized as a powerful force of technological change. The analogy between biological and technological exaptation is well-founded (Andriani and

Carignani 2018), particularly when considering bacteria rather than eukarya as the evolving entities in the base domain (Carignani et al., 2019).

Modular exaptation. A powerful extension of the concept of exaptation is derived by considering it within the framework of *modular systems*. Modularity as a general property of complex systems was first theorized by Simon (1962), who proposed modularity as a systemic concept for describing how a complex system can be decoupled into subsystems (modules) that perform nearly independently of each other. He called this property near-decomposability. Near-decomposability applies to various levels of a complex system as it 'is composed of interrelated subsystems, each of the latter being, in turn, hierarchic in structure' (Simon, 1962: p. 468). Near-decomposability is common in complex systems, particularly in biological and technological systems. According to Baldwin and Clark (2004), technological systems are modular when the 'elements of their design are split up and assigned to *modules* according to a formal *architecture*' (p. 175).[2] All aircraft, including WWI fighters, are *modular artefacts*.

The concepts of modularity and exaptation are tightly linked in biology and technology. This connection has been recognized in the concept of *modular exaptation* (Andriani and Carignani, 2014), defined as 'the process in which a functional module previously designed and manufactured for a certain function is later selected (i.e. replicated) for a different function' (Andriani and Carignani, 2018: p. 495).[3] Modular exaptation can be classified along two dimensions that distinguish between cases in which functional shifts affect an internal module of the artefact while preserving the existing function of the whole artefact and cases in which a whole artefact changes its function. By framing it this way, four different types of exaptation can be identified (Figure 3.2). Of particular interest for this chapter is the top right quadrant, which is labelled *internal exaptation*. The term describes the exaptation of an internal module of an artefact (here the aircraft) but without changing the function of this artefact.

---

[2] For example, the propulsion function is provided by one or more engines (a functional module), whereas the function of providing lift is attributed to the wings. This could seem trivial and obvious, but it is not. For example, in flying organisms, the 'wings' provide both the propulsion and lift function, a completely different modular architecture unsuccessfully adopted by unusual aircraft called ornithopters.

[3] In contrast with Baldwin and Clark (2000), I implicitly adopt in this chapter the etiological concept of function, that is, the consensus concept used in biology (aka *'proper function'*). Following this definition, the 'function' of an artefact is not what the artefact (or module) is *designed* for but what it is *selected* for: i.e. 'the proper function of an item is to do whatever it was selected for' (Neander, 1991: p. 171). A detailed discussion of the issue and other epistemological and methodological critical points can be found in Andriani and Carignani (2018).

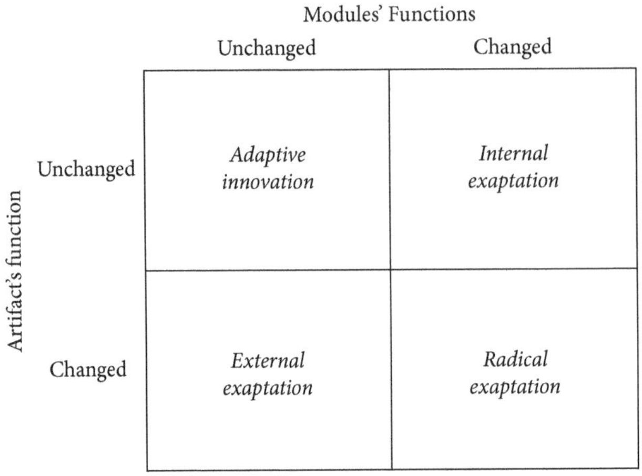

Modules' Functions

Figure 3.2 Modular exaptation: dimensions and taxonomy

Modular operators. Modular systems can evolve as their modular architecture can change over time. These changes, including internal exaptations, can be effectively described by the concept of 'modular operator' (Baldwin and Clark, 2004: p. 199), namely, a deliberate design action that, applied to a modular system, modifies its modular architecture. Several modular operators have been discussed in the literature, and six of them are discussed in Baldwin and Clark (2000): 'splitting' (a module), 'substituting' (a newer module design for an older one), 'excluding' (a module from the modular system), 'augmenting' (the system by adding a module that was not there before), 'inverting' (collecting and connecting several modules and reorganizing them at a different hierarchic level), and 'porting' (creating a shell around a module to make it transferable to another system). Subsequent empirical research has identified other modular operators, such as 'linking' (two pre-existing modules), 'recombining' (two previously separated modules, the opposite of splitting), and 'extending' (a pre-existing module).

Modular operators are powerful descriptors of engineering and managerial choices. However, the concept falls short of providing clear prescriptions to managers because the feasibility of modular operations falls outside the field of management and into that of engineering. For example, the successful design of the revolutionary 'thick wing' can be certainly described as the *recombination* of two previously different modules (thus the application of one of Baldwin and Clark's modular operators) because it recombined in the cantilever wing the structural module previously external to it (the truss-and-wire bi- and tri-plane structure). Figure 3.3, at the top, shows the modular process. However, the recombination required the recognition of the

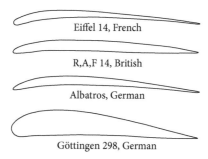

Figure 3.3 Morphological change in WWI airfoils

The transition is clearly detectable between the Albatros and the Gottingen 298 airfoils. (figure from Loftin, 1985)

technological opportunity and the right timing to implement it, as epitomized by Anthony Fokker's airframe revolution.

On the true origins of the airframe revolution: a microhistorical account

The story of Anthony Fokker paralleled the evolutionary trajectory that led to the airframe revolution. More than any other of the actors involved in the early phases of the revolution, Fokker embodies the role of the entrepreneur because his career sheds light on the shrewd, daring, and timely decision processes that are the trademark of successful entrepreneurial action. Fokker's innovations—including the one initiating the airframe revolution— were often modular, and showed deceptively minor changes that had major effects on the performances of his aircraft. This pattern is apparent in the first successful fighter plane built by Fokker, namely, the E.1 Eindecker (Monoplane). Although it was a mediocre aircraft because the controls were 'archaic even by 1914 standards' (Loftin, 1985: p. 11) and was very uncomfortable to fly (Tallman, 1973), the E.1 Eindecker represented a revolutionary modular innovation: the synchronized forward-firing machine gun.

Entering service in 1915, the E.1 introduced a new revolutionary concept to air combat by 'aiming' the whole plane (instead of a swivelling machine gun) at the enemy aircraft. The new fighter plane gave the German air force complete air superiority and inaugurated a period called 'Fokker Scourge', during which unfortunate Allied aircraft meeting E.1 fighters became simply 'Fokker Fodder'. The idea was 'suggested' to Fokker by the Germans (a Dutch national, Fokker was at the time providing aircraft to the German Army).

Fokker himself admits that he was shown a captured French fighter with a very crude version of the forward-firing machine gun (Fokker, 1938). Shortly thereafter, Fokker designed and prototyped a better but rather simple engineering solution: a synchronizing mechanism connecting the engine and the machine gun that prevented the bullets from hitting and smashing the propeller blades. From the very beginning, Fokker demonstrated his attitude towards picking up and expeditiously exploiting good ideas.

In 1918, after having designed and produced several successful fighters, including the famous DR.1 triplane and the D.VII already mentioned, Fokker prototyped the D.VIII monoplane fighter. The D.VIII was a strange 'chimera' (Carignani et al., 2019) because it was composed of modules from different aircraft: a traditional and rather conservative Fokker fuselage, an archaic rotary engine, and an innovative 'parasol' wing (Figure 3.1). The wing was covered with sheets of plywood, which had a structural function. In short, it introduced a novel structural concept that was later defined as 'monocoque', in which the stressed skin (plywood in Fokker's military and later commercial planes and metal in successive developments) contributed to resisting the bending, shearing, and torsional loads. The monoplane 'parasol' architecture of the Fokker D.VIII, though unusual, was not an absolute novelty. The wing was the truly revolutionary component: it was extraordinarily strong (Figure 3.1) and gave an otherwise very ordinary aircraft an outstanding 'climb rate',[4] the very best among WWI fighters, thus allowing it to surpass all its competitors (Loftin, 1985: p. 480) (Table1). This sharp increase in performance was the result of the wing geometry alone.

In the following years, on the basis of a series of adventurous entrepreneurial feats, including the 'Great Smuggling Plot' narrated in the introduction, Fokker 'evolved the design (of the D.VIII wing) into a series of very successful single- and multiengine transport aircraft that played a significant role in the burgeoning air passenger industry during the 20s' (Jakab, 1999: p. 915). The successful Lockheed designs of the early 1930s (including Amelia Earhart's Vega and Charles Lindberg's modified Sirius) 'were fitted with plywood-covered, stressed-skin, cantilevered wings virtually identical to those of the Fokker transports' (Jakab, 1999: p. 916). Even the famous all-metal Ford Triplane replicated—with a different material—the earlier all-wood Fokker Triplane. A few years later, the Boeing 247, which, together with the Douglas DC-3, was the aircraft that made air transport profitable, adopted a structure that was 'essentially the same as the cantilevered monoplane wing developed

---

[4] The climb rate, i.e. the ascensional speed, was the primary performance metric for WWI fighter planes.

by Fokker during WWI, except that is was constructed of metal' (Jakab, 1999: p. 917).

Exaptive radical innovation: who invented the thick wing?

The successful 'Great Smuggling Plot' of aircraft material into the Netherlands helped Fokker resume his entrepreneurial activity after the war, first in Europe and then in the United States. However, more than the material per se, Fokker's key to success and the origins of the airframe revolution is deeply rooted in his understanding of the advantages of the D.VIII 'thick wing' in 1918. The origin of the revolution can be traced to the design of the obscure Fokker D.VIII fighter plane. Therefore, its story needs a more detailed micro-historical narrative analysis to unveil the reasons and meaning of the technical and entrepreneurial decision-making.

During most of WWI, the cross-section of aircraft wings was extremely thin: 4 per cent to 6 per cent 'airfoil ratios', which is the thickness of the wing divided by the 'wing chord',[5] were the norm. Indeed, the consensus among aircraft designers was that 'thick wings' would have produced unsustainable drag forces (Loftin, 1985: p. 11). The best structural solution allowed by this very limited thickness was the 'truss (strut-and-wire) design', in which the wing, spars, and wires bear axial forces but no (or very small) bending moments (e.g. the Sopwith Triplane shown in Figure 3.4, top left). The design and adoption of thin airfoil were supported by early experimental results from the Wright brothers. Unfortunately, the experimental base was characterized by low 'Reynolds numbers',[6] thus pointing early aeroplane designers 'in the wrong general direction' because they had 'no way to know what they were missing' (Anderson, 1997: p. 308). What they were missing emerged in Germany in the following war years (1914–18) as a result of an intertwined chain of events. Although contrasting versions appear in the literature, the following account seeks to reconcile them.

While pioneering the design of all-metal aeroplanes during WWI, Hugo Junkers, who was a professor at a technical college in Aachen, a brilliant inventor and an aircraft designer, was the first to recognize and prove the aerodynamic advantages of thick airfoils. In 1914 and 1915, in wind tunnels at Aachen as well as at his company in Dessau, Junkers conducted a series of

---

[5] The wing chord is the dimension of the wing measured in the direction of the slipstream.

[6] Reynolds' number is a non-dimensional quantity expressing the ratio of inertia to viscous forces seen in fluids, tightly related to the speed of the flow. Thick airfoils became efficient at higher Reynolds' numbers. The transition became possible as more powerful engines became available.

tests on thin and thick airfoils. After the war, in 1923, he presented the surprising results of his tests at the Royal Aeronautical Society: '...my most extravagant expectations were surpassed. The thick airfoils proved not only equivalent to the thin ones of some series but even superior, within certain limits.' Of course, Junkers had a specific reason for conducting these wind tunnel tests: for structural reasons, he had to use a thick airfoil on his all-metal aeroplane, the Junkers J1. Without considering other potential outcomes for his 'serendipitous' discovery,[7] Junkers went on to design his all-metal aeroplanes with thick airfoil sections (Anderson, 2003: p. 145). Thereafter, in 1916, the German Army forced a merger between the firms of Hugo Junkers and Anthony Fokker. Richard Byers (2008) accurately described the reasons behind this unhappy merger and the subsequent troubles between the two great pioneers of aviation.

According to Byers, in April 1917, Fokker informed Junkers that he wanted to use Junkers' patented wing designs, whose characteristics far exceeded any known characteristics by Fokker and his designers. Fokker appropriated the thick airfoil concept from Junkers and used it in his V.4 and DR.1 triplanes (1917). According to Weil (1965), the actual shape of the thick airfoil of the DR.1 was drawn 'by eye' by Fokker's designer, Reinhold Platz. This was an extraordinary achievement because designing 'the Dr.1 airfoil by eye, without any benefit of testing and subsequent fine-tuning, and to have that airfoil shape perform as well as it did on the DR.1 and the D.VII, seems fortuitous beyond belief' (Anderson, 2003: p. 146). Meanwhile, in 1917, Ludwing Prandtl, the scientist who founded modern aerodynamics, initiated a series of detailed measurements of the performance of several different airfoil shapes in the new Gottingen wind tunnel. Each shape was labelled with a number that indicated its sequence in the tests, starting with the Gottingen 1. The tests continued through 1919, with Gottingen airfoils numbered up to the Gottingen 460. There was no logical technical progression in the airfoil shape from one number to another. Many of the airfoil shapes were taken from existing aeroplanes. For example, the Gottingen 298 airfoil, which was subjected to tunnel tests in 1918, was taken from that designed for the Fokker DR.1, as documented in an early NACA report (NACA, 1921: p. 437).

---

[7] The term is often used in its generic meaning of 'unexpected' discovery. However, in this case, it is used in the more specific meaning of 'always making discoveries of things which they were not in quest of', like the Princes of Serendip, accurately describing the historical events (Merton and Barber, 2011). Indeed, Hugo Junkers was deliberately pursuing the design of all-metal aircraft (when metals were heavy and underperforming for aviation purposes), when he discovered the unexpected good aerodynamic performances of the thick airfoil. Although serendipity is often associated with exaptation, this is the only truly serendipitous event in the causal chain that eventually initiated the airframe revolution.

The thick airfoil gave the Fokker DR.1 not only several valuable combat advantages, such as a high maximum lift coefficient, a high climb rate, and excellent manoeuvrability, but also other benefits that eventually culminated in the airframe revolution. The key point is that 'there was sufficient room for the wing structure to be made completely internal.[8] That is, the wings of the DR.1 involved a cantilever design, which obviated the need for the conventional bracing used in other aircraft. In turn, this eliminated the high drag associated with such wires. For that reason, the DR.1 had a zero-lift drag coefficient of 0.032, among the lowest for WWI airplanes' (Anderson, 1997: p. 310). These words, by aviation historian Anderson (1997, 2014), seem to confirm that the origin of the airframe revolution was this morphological change in the geometry of the wing and, more specifically, the radical increase of the wing thickness (Figure 3.3).

The mechanism is consistent with the notion of *modular exaptation* (Andriani and Carignani, 2014). Therefore, it can be viewed as a case of *internal exaptation*. This exaptive mechanism could just as well be described using Darwin's words from *On the Origin of Species*. His description of the functional shift from the swim bladder to the lung essentially describes the transition from truss to internally braced wings: 'The swimbladder is homologous, or ideally similar, in position and structure with the lungs of the higher vertebrate animals: hence there seems to me to be no great difficulty in believing that natural selection has actually converted a swimbladder into a lung, an organ used exclusively for respiration' (Darwin, 1859: p. 190). Indeed, 'there was sufficient room for the wing structure to be made completely internal' (Anderson, 1997: p. 310), which suggests how the thick airfoil was ideal 'in position and structure' for becoming a cantilever internally braced wing, by using existing technologies and made entirely with wood.

The emergence of a new market: evolving the modern airliner

The pattern of internal exaptation is coherent with Darwin's gradualist evolutionary theory because it implies *architectural continuity*. Indeed, the exaptive process is *internal* to an existing artefact (in this case the aircraft), and it improves its performance while maintaining the function desired by the user

---

[8] Given that flexural resistance is proportional to the thickness squared, tripling the thickness multiplies the wing strength by nine, thus giving an advantage to the cantilever wing over the strut-and-wire design, *which is independent of the material.*

(its fitness to the existing environment/market) by slowly changing the functional architecture with far-reaching consequences, including the extension of the existing market and the opening of new markets at different modular levels. In the long run, the airframe revolution evolved from early warplanes to modern airliners. The uncomfortable, unprofitable, and rather dangerous Fokker (and Ford) tri-motors of the mid-1920s paved the way to new profitable civil airliners (e.g. the Boeing 247 and DC-3, some of which are still flying today).

The evolutionary interpretation of the airframe revolution seems robust: the thicker wing became preadapted for internal exaptation because its morphology was suitable in 'position and structure' (in Darwin's words) to absorb internally the whole structural function. Although advancements in aerodynamics played a critical role in the origin of the airframe revolution, it was not scientific knowledge that directly launched it. The origin can instead be traced to the morphological change. In originating the airframe revolution, Junkers' intuition and experimental work, Prandtl's scientific analysis, and Fokker's entrepreneurial acumen—not to mention Platz's gifted drawing hand—initiated the innovation cascade that inevitably, in hindsight, led to the modern all-metal aircraft more than a decade later.

The preadaptation of several aircraft components (e.g. the monocoque construction and the retractable undercarriage) and aviation engines (e.g. turbosuperchargers and heat-resistant alloys) were also fundamental in fostering the following turbojet revolution (1939–46) (Constant, 1980; Carignani et al., 2019). Thus, we can recognize the distinctive elements of any evolutionary process: variation, selection, and retention. The wealth of experimental aircraft built by manufacturers during WWI—an era in which designing, building, and testing a new plane in combat took just a few weeks—provided the diversity necessary for a Darwinian selection process. Unexpectedly, but inevitably, owing to the increase of Reynolds' numbers following the availability of more powerful engines, the thick airfoil wing was designed, selected, and retained, thus triggering the revolution.

The dynamics of gradual revolution: a stylized model

The novel construct of gradual revolution reconciles the gradualistic Darwinian vision with the discontinuous character of radical innovation. The discontinuity due to modular exaptation triggered the onset of the revolution, but its complete development took years and was marked with incremental innovations, particularly at lower modular levels.[9] A stylized process describing in abstract terms the airframe revolution (and possibly a general process of gradualist revolution) could be described as follows (and exemplified in Figure 3.4). It could provide a consistent pattern of gradual revolution and clarify the inception of architectural innovation (Henderson and Clark, 1990) by unveiling its early mechanisms.

- *Dominant design.* The initial state is characterized by the modular architecture of an artefact and is usually recognized as the 'dominant' design: in the case of the airframe revolution, the wood-and-doped-fabric, strut-and-wires aircraft (often a biplane, sometimes a triplane) exemplified in Figure 3.4 by the Sopwith Triplane of 1917 (top left).
- *Modular preadaptation.* Through 'normal technology'[10] (Vincenti, 2000; Constant, 1980), some of the modules could over time become preadapted for different functions for which they were not originally designed: in Figure 3.4 (top right), the transfer of the structural function of the cantilever 'thick wing' of the Fokker DR.1 is made evident by the lack of diagonal wires. The morphological change marking the transition between phases 1 and 2 (modular preadaptation, i.e. the increase of the airfoil thickness, a morphological change that suggested the possibility of transferring the whole structural function to the 'thick wing') is evident in Figure 3.3 (evolution of the airfoils, where the discontinuity is evident).
- *Internal exaptation.* The event of modular exaptation is brought about by an inventor (or a team) who understands the potential of the novelty and exploits it. In the case of the airframe revolution, the Fokker D.VIII (Figure 3.4, top middle) successfully introduced the stressed skin. This radical change in wing structural engineering was independent of materials because the stressed skin was made with plywood.[11]
- *Selection.* The exaptive event improves the fitness of the artefact in the existing environment (often a market), thus resulting in the selection of the artefact. The Fokker D.VIII was the overall winner in a competition

[9] An important example among many is the adoption of the retractable undercarriage, which also followed a modular evolutionary path (Vincenti, 2000). Preadaptation was a critical issue because the thickness of the wing made it easier to find the necessary room for retracting the undercarriage.

[10] Normal technology is what firms and engineers usually do, that is the improvement of the accepted technological tradition or its application under new conditions (Constant 1980: p. 10).

[11] The fact that the wooden 'skin' was rather thick made easier the new design because it was immune from structural instability in compression, a phenomenon relatively unknown at that time. Structural instability makes designing a thinner metal skin much more difficult.

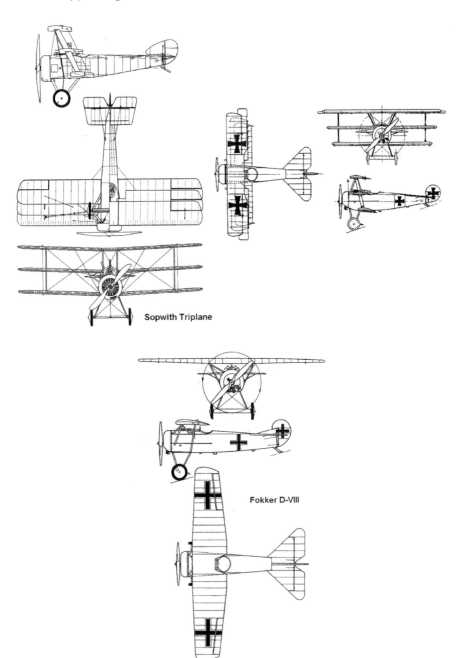

Sopwith Triplane

Fokker D-VIII

Figure 3.4　Thick wings. Stylized process of gradual revolution (graphical representation)
1. Old dominant design (Sopwith Triplane, 1917); 2. Preadaptation (Fokker DR.1, 1917); 3. Exaptation (Fokker D.VIII, 1918); 4. Scaling up (Fokker Trimotor, 1926); 5. Co-evolution: new materials (Ford Trimotor, 1928); 6. Novel dominant design (Douglas DC 3, 1935).

The Sopwith Triplane (1917) conforms to the truss (struts-and-wire) dominant design in aerostructures preceding the airframe revolution (notice the diagonal wires) even though it is

(*cont.*)

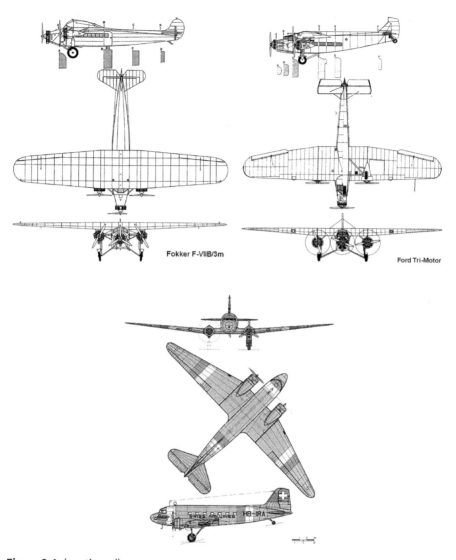

Figure 3.4 (continued)

characterized by the unusual triplane architecture. The Fokker DR.1 Triplane (1917) is deceptively similar but already adopts the *thick wing*. The wing plan (rectangular) and the wood-and-doped-fabric construction are still dominant designs. However, there are no wires nor the struts are necessary (the struts are only a vibration-reducing device). In the Fokker D.VIII (1918), the cantilever wing is characterized by the new plywood 'stressed skin'. Appears the new tapered wing plan, suggested by both structural and aerodynamic reasons. The scaled-up wing is the same one adopted in the Fokker Trimotor (1926). Almost identical in morphology, the Ford Trimotor (1928) adopts an all-metal construction. After the 'synergistic' modular evolution, the new all-metal, stressed-skin, cantilever-wing dominant design emerges (iconic example, the Douglas DC3).

sponsored by the German Air Force in June 1918, in which twelve firms presented twenty-five prototypes. An order to produce 400 fighters was placed with Fokker, and a more severe selection process took soon place in combat.

- *Modular evolution.* A subsequent and often co-evolutionary process further improves the artefact and redefines the other elements of the artefact's architectures (e.g. the retractable landing gear), thus showing features of architectural and modular innovation at the lower modular level. The overall effect of this continuous and complex process of modular evolution is slow and gradual, but its overall result is 'revolutionary' (i.e. discontinuous).
- *New dominant design.* Eventually, a novel dominant design could emerge (e.g. the Fokker Trimotor, Ford Triplane) and initiate a technological trajectory that eventually led to the Boeing 247 and DC 3 airliners, and the beginning of civil aviation (Figure 3.4, bottom).

The hidden riches of engineering: how normal technology can foster radical innovation

Exaptation-driven gradual revolutions are by no means rare in history. For example, six cases are cited in Andriani and Carignani (2014). Even when limiting a preliminary inquiry to cases in which only structural functions are involved, one can find some significant cases, and these cases are briefly discussed below.

The transfer of the structural function into an already existing module, coherent with the stylized model of the airframe revolution, occurred in the car industry (Andriani and Carignani, 2014) and agricultural tractor industry (Dew et al., 2004). In both cases, it was a gradual revolution triggered by the preadaptation of functional modules due to technological advances. Existing modules (the body of the car and the engine block in the tractor case) became preadapted to the structural function. The successful exploitation was initiated by the first entrepreneurs who were able to recognize the opportunity given by the preadapted module: Vincenzo Lancia introduced the Lancia Lambda in 1922, and Henry Ford introduced the Fordson tractor in 1917.

Outside the transportation industry but still connected with structural issues, another famous case of radical innovation whose origins can be also recognized as a modular preadaptation is the origin of Gillette's safety razor.

This case is also related to the functional shift of structural functions. King Camp Gillette applied for his first razor patent in 1899. He was granted his first two US patents in 1901 and 1904, and his British patent in 1903. At first sight, Gillette's razor resembles a 'hoe-type' safety razor, one of the architectures that were dominant in the industry at the time. The first US patent (# 775134) listed thirty-one claims, among them 'a detachable razor-blade of such thinness and flexibility as to require external support to give rigidity to its cutting edge'. Gillette's claims about the transfer of the structural function to a different module (external support) were essential in assuring the 'detachability' of the razor blade. The concept became feasible when William Nickerson, who was an associate of Gillette, perfected the tools and machines required to manufacture the thin blade. Before this technological preadaptation (providing the opportunity of manufacturing low-cost thin blades), the functional shift (modular exaptation via a 'splitting' modular operator) could hardly have been possible.

Finally, several internal exaptations triggered by modular preadaptation and implemented via modular operators show up in contemporary modular evolution in several industries, thus suggesting that the pattern is pervasive, particularly when considering low-level modules. Examples such as spark plugs used as sensors, earplug wires as aerials, transfer of keyboards from hardware to touch screens in mobile phones, and e-readers seems to demonstrate that internal exaptation is still an evolutionary force that is able to explain contemporary technological innovation.

Discussion

The airframe revolution: summarizing the case

The airframe revolution was initiated in 1917 by a single event—the *morphological change* of a *functional module*, namely, the *thick airfoil*, which was pioneered by Hugo Junkers and was successfully introduced in operational aircraft by Antony Fokker. The evolutionary consequence was the transfer of a function from a functional module to another. This occurred when Fokker transferred the structural function of the truss structure characterizing the biplane architecture to the internally bracing of the cantilever wing, first in his triplane fighters (Fokker V.4 and Fokker DR.1) of 1917 and then in the Fokker D.VIII monoplane in 1918 (see Figure 3.4). On the basis of a narrative whose microhistorical events and decision-making were interpreted via the theoretical framework of *modular exaptation* (Andriani and Carignani, 2014), this account provides a robust explanation of the causal chain that triggered the airframe revolution as a case of *internal exaptation* (Figure 3.2, top right quadrant). The cascade of connected innovations or 'synergistic developments' (Loftin, 1985), i.e. advances in material performance (new aluminium alloys), in construction science, and aerodynamics, were not the actual drivers of the airframe revolution; rather, they were the consequences of the initial exaptive event. The history of technology is replete with instances of innovation processes that are similar to the airframe revolution in that they are often cases of exaptive innovation triggering a slow process of modular innovation that eventually results in the emergence of a novel dominant design.

This novel pattern of *gradual revolution* helps reconcile the gradualist Darwinian vision with the discontinuous character of radical innovation. The discontinuity marked by modular functional shift is evident in the very beginning of the revolution, but its complete development required years and was characterized by incremental innovations, particularly at lower modular levels. Wartime technological innovation is usually much faster than its peaceful counterpart: during WWI, experimentation in aviation was inexpensive and was not constrained by budget issues. Daring creative engineers could design and prototype hundreds of experimental aircraft that collectively produced unprecedented performance improvements. However, the extreme contextual circumstances in which the revolution took place began to reveal—instead of concealing—its evolutionary character. The microhistorical narrative approach adopted in this chapter has shown several puzzling, contradictory, and counterintuitive decisions marking the inception of the gradual revolution. Focusing on the engineering meaning of these decisions bears the promise of deriving interesting implications for managing radical innovation.

Is exaptation really unpredictable? Rethinking an ideological tenet

Exaptation is intrinsically characterized by serendipity, unpredictability, and unprestateability (e.g. Gabora et al., 2013). This theoretical tenet is deeply rooted in the theory of modular complex systems. The unpredictability of exaptation (and other properties and processes of evolving complex systems) is considered ontological: it is associated with the huge number of potential configurations of complex systems that makes impossible any type of information processing. Moreover, bifurcations between trajectories leading to different configurations may be triggered by noise or minimal events, thus making predictability inherently impracticable (Andriani and Carignani, 2018). However, the airframe revolution narrative tells a different story.

Anthony Fokker was able to recognize *ex ante* the exaptive opportunity that led to the airframe revolution: he *designed and prototyped the critical module* in 1918, several years before historians agreed on the *inception* of the revolution (Loftin, 1985). What Fokker did was not to *invent* the thick airfoil: he appropriated it from Junkers by taking advantage of the forced merger of their firms in 1917 after Junkers had demonstrated the unexpectedly good characteristics of the counterintuitive design feature. Fokker *recognized* a technology-driven strategic opportunity. After having ascertained the advantages of Junkers' airfoils, he transferred the structural function into the new 'thick wing'[12] and designed plywood stressed skin, which gave the wing great strength and stiffness. Although revolutionary in hindsight, all these design actions were completely within the bounds of engineering theory and practice at the time. This entrepreneurial action, which occurred in the desperate war years of 1917–18, gave Fokker's firms a sustained advantage lasting a decade. Indeed, the Fokker Aircraft Corporation of America became the leading firm in airliners in the United States when the famous Fokker Triplane transport took the lead in early civil aviation, 'inspiring' Ford to create his famed all-metal triplane.[13]

The tale of the Fokker Aircraft Corporation can be interpreted through several managerial theories. However, as we shall see, all of them fall short of founding an effective managerial action. It is apparent that Fokker's firms demonstrably possessed what management scholars call *dynamic capabilities*: key immaterial resources of the innovative firm aimed at '*doing the right things, at the right time, based on new product (and process) development*' (Teece, 2014: p. 22). However, neither the material nor its usage were technological novelties: *timing* in seizing and exploiting the right ideas was the watermark of Fokker's success, as seen in another case, namely, the Eindecker synchronized machine gun. The concept of 'kairos' (opportune moment) proposed by Garud et al. (2016) seems to apply perfectly to Fokker's entrepreneurial

---

[12] He also modified the wing plan. Notice the tapered wing, which is a feature characterizing all following developments (Figure 3.4). This geometry of the wing has aerodynamic advantages but also reduces the bending moments of the wing, thus making the cantilever solution feasible.

[13] Notice the identical geometry of the aircraft in Figure 3.4. The narrative of a naïve event of industrial espionage appears rather believable.

action: 'these "kairotic moments" represent a capacity to understand the strategic importance of unexpected anomalies encountered in the interstices of time' (Garud et al., 2016: p. 159). Anthony Fokker was surely a master in seizing *kairotic moments*. All the same, the concept describes his entrepreneurial action but hardly explains its secrets. Finally, it is apparent that Fokker recognized and exercised a *shadow option* (Cattani, 2006), but his decision-making was based on technological reasoning and not financial reasoning.

All these managerial constructs (*dynamic capabilities, kairotic moments,* and *shadow options*) are apt to capture some aspects of Fokker's entrepreneurial attitude and managerial action. However, it seems clear that the real basis of a method for managing technological exaptation belongs to the technological realm and should be based on engineering understanding. The case shows that at a technological micro level the opportunity of exapting new functions from existing modules is perfectly understandable to technically minded creative people. Engineers are often considered just executives that are implementing what higher-level managers have wisely decided. On the contrary, they are the ones that can understand *ex ante* exaptive opportunities in existing technological modules and could be able to detect promising radical innovations at their very beginning.

Predictable exaptations: towards a methodology for managing radical innovation

Why are certain entrepreneurs able to recognize with perfect kairotic timing the shadow option of exaptive innovation when it first arises, whereas many experts, firms, and institutions are left in the dark? Does it require an extraordinarily gifted inventor or is it amenable to theoretical inquiry and managerial methodology? To address this dilemma, it is important to emphasize that engineers and experts usually know the promise of recombining the functional modules they design or use.[14] Unfortunately, they also often suffer from a sort of *inattentional blindness,*[15] which is possibly associated with their deep knowledge of the limited performances of

---

[14] For example, dozens of innovation projects recombining compressors, burners, propellers, fans, and turbines were designed and prototyped in the early phases of the turbojet revolution, but the different modular architectures were just a handful (Carignani et al., 2019; Constant, 1980).

[15] Inattentional blindness is the failure to notice a fully visible, but unexpected object, because attention is engaged on another task, event, or object.

state-of-the-art modules at their disposal. Therefore, they tend to discard certain solutions early on.[16] This could explain why the Allies' aviation designers did not understand the 'thick wing' innovation, which was easily detectable with the naked eye (see Figure 3.4). However, it also suggests that the difficulties in developing a prescriptive theory on radical innovation lie more in managerial inattention in supporting the right creative technological attitude than in the lack of technological knowledge per se. Such a theory could be developed on the basis of the evolutionary steps characterizing radical innovation:

1. Variation: considering potential recombinations in a specific industry. The ontological unpredictability of complex system evolution 'is associated to the huge number of potential configurations of complex systems that will eschew any type of information processability' (Andriani and Carignani, 2018: p. 485). However, similar to a good chess or bridge player who does not consider all possible moves and their astronomically huge number of consequences but only the configurations that make sense to his or her trained eye, a good creative engineer would not consider any naive recombination and would only consider those who make engineering sense—albeit not yet practicable.[17]

2. Timing of selection: recognizing the kairotic moment, i.e. when impracticable recombinations come within reach, owing to technological advances often from different industries. The concept of pre-adaptation is central here (Cattani, 2006). Engineering theory makes a predictable—albeit often risky—task to prototype a novel artefact when recombinations have been hypothesized because the performance requirements can be computed within engineering practice. By focusing on some kairotic moments in aviation history—each of which initiated a revolution—we can accurately pinpoint the moment in which the inventor was able to translate risky modular recombinations into an engineering question:

    i. Which *power/weight* ratio is necessary for a heavier-than-air flying machine?

---

[16] For example, Alan Griffith, who was a leading expert in gas turbines, rejected more than once the turbojet proposal, the recombination which eventually brought about the turbojet revolution (Carignani et al., 2019).

[17] Garud et al. (2016) propose several activities (or serendipity arrangements) that can propitiate the conceiving of unusual recombinations.

   ii. How *thick* should a wing be to host the entire structure inside?

   iii. What *compression ratio* is needed for a turbojet compressor?

The answer to these technical questions revolutionized the aviation industry. It is historically documented that Wilbur Wright, Anthony Fokker, and Frank Whittle knew the required modular *performance* well *before* they were able to prototype their successful inventions.[18] Here are their answers:

   i. '...an engine of 6 horsepower, weighing 100 pounds, would answer the purpose. Such an engine is entirely practicable. Indeed, working motors of one-half this weight per horsepower (9 pounds per horsepower) have been constructed by several different builders' (Wilbur Wright, lecture to the Western Society of Engineers, 1901, quoted by Hobbs, 1971).

   ii. 'The thick airfoils proved not only equivalent to the thin ones of some series, but even superior, within certain limits' (Junkers, *circa* 1914, quoted by Anderson, 2003: p. 145).

   iii. Whittle's proposal required a compressor with a 4:1 pressure ratio and at least 75 per cent efficiency.

After deriving from engineering principles the *specifications* of critical modules, these engineers were able to *recognize the incipient preadaptation* of the available components. Historical records show how all were met with industry experts' scepticism or outright hostility, and finding the resources for designing and prototyping their revolutionary recombinations proved rather difficult. Eventually, history showed they had been right.

Conclusions

Anthony Fokker, Vincenzo Lancia, Henry Ford, and King Camp Gillette were able to seize their kairotic moment: they recognized and exercised the shadow options that eventually resulted in radical innovations that enabled their firms to achieve enduring success. They were visionary people who had the necessary engineering knowledge at both the modular and the architectural levels and the resources to bear the risk of developing a

---

[18] Frank Whittle is the recognized British inventor of the turbojet.

novel architecture. Given that the conceptual design of novel recombinations has already been hypothesized, a straightforward engineering procedure was able to confidently derive the *specifications* of the missing modules. There is recurring historical evidence that good engineers (such as the Wright Brothers or Frank Whittle, as exemplified in the previous paragraph) are generally able to calculate the correct specifications of the key components necessary for their invention. When the requirements are known, radical uncertainty can be translated into manageable risk. It is up to innovation managers to search for preadapted modules, considering that they can emerge in different industries and require not only local search but also jumps to different spots of the technological landscape. However, the task is within the realm of management theory and practice. For example, Raghu et al. (2016) suggest 'arrangements' that can be embraced by a firm to *contextualize scientific discovery*: similar arrangements could also be practised to keep track of modular preadaptation in distant industries. Many manufacturing firms possess engineering modular and architectural knowledge, which is a VRIN resource that is often ignored by innovation managers. Exploiting these resources requires a novel managerial attitude towards technology by opening the black box of creative engineering. However, it bears the promise of recasting Knightian true uncertainty into manageable risk.

Acknowledgments

I would like to gratefully acknowledge Peter Jakab and John Anderson (at the Smithsonian Institution in Washington DC, USA), for enabling me to ascertain the microhistorical details that triggered the airframe revolution, and my colleague Mauro Darida (Istituto Malignani, Udine, Italy) for his revision. I could not have written this chapter without their help.

GLOSSARY

Airfoil (or airfoil) ratio The term 'airfoil' (or airfoil) refers to the shape of the cross-section of a wing. The 'airfoil ratio' is the ratio between the wing thickness and the 'wing chord', i.e. the dimension of the wing measured in the direction of slipstream. Figure 3.3

Airframe (or aerostructure) The structure of an aircraft, usually composed by its fuselage, wings, an empennage, and an undercarriage, and excluding the engine.

Climb rate Ascensional speed.

Internally braced cantilever wing A wing whose structure is completely enclosed in its aerodynamic shape, without any external brace. Figures 3.4(3), (4), (5), (6)

Monocoque (fuselage) A structural concept whose distinctive feature is the 'stressed' skin (made of wood or aluminium alloys), which gets the entire structural function, or (in the semi-monocoque version) part of it.

Parasol (wing, architecture) A monoplane architecture in which the wing is supported above the fuselage by an arrangement of struts. Figure 3.1

Reynolds' number A non-dimensional quantity expressing the ratio of inertia to viscous forces in the fluid show, tightly related to the speed of the flow.

Truss (or strut-and-wire) wing A wing system based on the truss structural scheme, which is a triangulated system of straight interconnected structural elements, and is usually composed of two or even three wings (biplane or triplane architecture) connected by struts and wires. Figure 3.4(1)

Wood and doped fabric The dominant design of a WWI airframe, made of wood and fabric doped with glue to stretch it tight and provide waterproofing.

References

Anderson, J.D. 1997. *A history of aerodynamics.* Cambridge University Press.

Anderson, J.D. 2003. *The airplane: a history of its technology.* American Institute of Aeronautics and Astronautics.

Andriani, P. and Carignani, G. 2014. Modular exaptation: a missing link in the synthesis of artificial form. *Research Policy,* 43(9): 1608–20.

Andriani, P. and Carignani, G. 2018. Complex analogy and modular exaptation: some definitional clarifications. In Mitleton-Kelly, E., Paraskevas, A., and Day, C. (eds.). *Handbook of research methods in complexity science theory and applications.* Edward Elgar.

Baldwin, C.Y. and Clark, K.B. 2000. *Design rules: the power of modularity Volume 1.* Cambridge University Press.

Baldwin, C.Y. and Clark, K.B. 2004. Modularity in the design of complex engineering systems. *Complex Engineered Systems Understanding Complex Systems,* January: 175–205.

Barney, J. 1991. Firm resources and sustained competitive advantage. *Journal of Management,* 17: 99–120.

Beltagui, A., Rosli, A., and Candi, M. 2020. Exaptation in a digital innovation ecosystem: the disruptive impacts of 3D printing. *Research Policy,* 49(1): 103833.

Byers, R. 2008. An unhappy marriage: the Junkers-Fokker merger. *Journal of Historical Biography,* 3(Spring): 1–30.

Carignani, G., Cattani, G., and Zaina, G. 2019. Evolutionary chimeras: a Woesian perspective of radical innovation. *Industrial and Corporate Change*, 28: 511–28.

Cattani, G. 2006. Technological pre-adaptation, speciation, and emergence of new technologies: how Corning invented and developed fiber optics. *Industrial and Corporate Change*, 15(2): 285–318.

Constant, E. 1980. *The origins of the turbojet revolution*. Johns Hopkins studies in the history of technology.

Cuènot, L. 1914. Thèorie de la prèadaptation. *Scientia*, 16: 60–73.

Darwin, C. 1859. *On the origin of species*. New York D Appleton (Vol. 5).

Dew, N., Sarasvathy, S.D., and Venkataraman, S. 2004. The economic implications of exaptation. *Journal of Evolutionary Economics*, 14: 69–84.

Fokker, A. 1938. *Flying Dutchman, the life of Antony Fokker*. Penguin.

Gabora, L., Scott, E., and Kaufman, S. 2013. A quantum model of exaptation: incorporating potentiality into evolutionary theory. *Progress in Biophysics and Molecular Biology*, 113(1): 108–16.

Garud, R., Gehlman, J., and Giuliani, A.P. 2016. Technological exaptation: a narrative approach. *Industrial and Corporate Change*, 25(1): 149–66.

Geels, F.W. 2006. Co-evolutionary and multi-level dynamics in transitions: the transformation of aviation systems and the shift from propeller to turbojet (1930–1970). *Technovation*, 26: 999–1016.

Gould, S. and Vrba, E. 1982. Exaptation—a missing term in the science of form. *Paleobiology*, 8: 4–15.

Henderson, R.M. and Clark, K.B. 1990. Architectural innovation: the reconfiguration of existing product technologies and the failure of established firms. *Administrative Science Quarterly*, 35: 9–30.

Hobbs, L.S. 1971. *Wright brothers' engines and their design*. Smithsonian Institution Scholarly Press.

Jakab, P.L. 1999. Wood to metal: the structural origins of the modern airplane. *Journal of Aircraft*, 36(6): 914–18.

Loftin Jr, L.K. 1985. Quest for performance: the evolution of modern aircraft. *NASA History Office*, 1–410. https://ntrs.nasa.gov/citations/19850023776.

Merton, R.K. and Barber, E. 2011. *The travels and adventures of serendipity: a study in sociological semantics and the sociology of science*. Princeton University Press.

NACA. 1921. Aerodynamic Characteristics of Airfoils—II (Report No.124).

Neander, K. 1991. Function as selected effects: the conceptual analyst's defense. *Philosphy of Science*, 58: 168–84.

Simon, H. 1962. The architecture of complexity. *Proceeding of the American Philosophical Society*, 106: 467–82.

Tallman, F. 1973. *Flying the old planes*. Doubleday.

Teece, D. A 2014. A dynamic capabilities-based entrepreneurial theory of the multi-national enterprise. *Journal of International Business Studies,* 45: 8–37.

Vincenti, W.G. 2000. Real-world variation-selection it the evolution of technological form: historical examples. In *Technological innovation as an evolutionary process* (pp. 174–89). Cambridge University Press.

Weyl, A.R. 1965. *Fokker: the creative years.* Putnam.

4

A Non-Predictive View

Evolution, Unprestateability, Disequilibrium

Gino Cattani and Mariano Mastrogiorgio

Evolution, unprestateability, and disequilibrium

One of the central tenets of evolutionary economics is that economic systems are continually evolving out of equilibrium owing to endogenous factors such as technological innovation, which is also intrinsically evolutionary. This view contrasts with that of neoclassical economists, who assume the existence of economic equilibria between quantities and prices that result from efforts by consumers and firms to maximize their respective utility and profit functions. These equilibria correspond to the points where demand and supply functions intersect with each other (Nelson et al., 2018). Given the rise of 'neoclassical theory at the end of the nineteenth century, mainstream economics has regarded the determination of equilibrium conditions as the Holy Grail of theoretical discovery' (Hodgson, 2009: p. xx). As we will see, the neoclassical view, with its emphasis on equilibrium, traces its historical roots to classical physics. In the beginning, an important source of inspiration was the first law of thermodynamics, which implies balance assuming that energy is preserved in a closed system (Mirowski, 1989). However, economic systems are open, interconnected, and exposed to growing diversity in terms of technologies, products, and processes, which generates new uses for existing things and leads to disequilibrium. Therefore, disequilibrium is an intrinsic feature of these systems.

These ideas and the related debate on the physical roots of economics have taken different forms in different 'schools' of economic thought that have also embraced disequilibrium. For our purposes, we will review some insights of the Austrian school (Hayek, 1937), nonequilibrium economics (Berger, 2009; Fisher, 1983), Georgescu-Rogen's view (Georgescu-Rogen, 1971), and recent developments in complexity economics (Beinhocker, 2007).

Gino Cattani and Mariano Mastrogiorgio, *A Non-Predictive View: Evolution, Unprestateability, Disequilibrium* In: *New Developments in Evolutionary Innovation: Novelty Creation in a Serendipitous Economy.* Edited by: Gino Cattani and Mariano Mastrogiorgio, Oxford University Press (2021). © Gino Cattani and Mariano Mastrogiorgio.
DOI: 10.1093/oso/9780198837091.003.0004

These ideas have also received systematic attention in the field of evolutionary economics (Nelson et al., 2018), where the latest developments are particularly insightful (Dosi and Stiglitz, 2020).[1] In this regard, the debate on exaptation and unprestateability is of particular interest (Longo et al., 2012). Technologies, organisms, and, generally speaking, *evolution* 'embody myriad functionalities and uses that cannot be prestated' (Felin et al., 2014: p. 9) and this is a source of disequilibrium. As we will argue, this is the foundation of a view of economic systems wherein such systems are inherently non-predictive and, under certain conditions, better described as evolving entities with an irreducible history rather than in terms of classical trajectories that unfold in predefined phase spaces.

An excursus on equilibrium in the economic debate

The idea of disequilibrium is central to some versions of the Austrian school of economics, even though this school is deemed to have contributed significantly to mainstream economics (e.g. via early formulations of marginalism). This is particularly evident in the work of the Austrian economist Hayek (1937), who remarked how equilibrium rests on restrictive theoretical assumptions (e.g. economic agents have perfect knowledge). In reality, the differences in the amount of information and knowledge that agents have or control are a source of disequilibrium. To better understand this intuition, it is useful to start from standard microeconomic theory, which considers equilibrium as the point at which the demand function and the supply function intersect each other (i.e. a point identified by a quantity and a price on the x and y axes, respectively). The demand function results from the demand aggregation of consumers who seek to maximize their utility function under budget constraints, whereas the supply function results from the aggregation of the production function of producers who seek to maximize their profit. A price (or quantity) is an equilibrium price (or quantity) when it is stable, that is, the point of arrival of a process of oscillation or 'tatonnement', which originated from a hypothetical situation of excess demand or oversupply. If there is excess demand, the price increases; thereafter, new production is

---

[1] We would like to stress that this chapter is just a very broad overview of a vast debate in economic thinking that spans decades and could occupy entire books (see Roncaglia, 2017). Some of the ideas contained in this chapter have already been discussed by others, to whom we refer the reader for further details (see Mirowski, 1989; Koppl et al., 2015; and Beinhocker, 2007). Moreover, as the reader will notice, a lot of emphasis is given to the demand side and to concepts such as 'utility' because they are at the core of the 'marginalist' revolution in economics and subsequent neoclassical syntheses based on the equilibrium paradigm (Roncaglia, 2017). Any omissions or errors are our own responsibility.

added up to a point where this translates into an oversupply, which decreases the price. If there is an oversupply, prices go down; thereafter, new consumption is added until that translates into excess demand, which increases the price. This tatonnement stops when the price reaches equilibrium.

It is interesting to note that equilibrium builds on strategic assumptions (see Farmer and Geanakoplos, 2009) that, in turn, rest on underlying behavioural assumptions (Thomsen, 1992). The strategic assumptions can be illustrated by a simple Bertrand setting (Watson, 2002): in a competitive situation, the equilibrium price is equal to the marginal cost and brings zero profits to the firms. In a game-theoretic sense, this happens because firms converge on the strategy of selling at the equilibrium price instead of cooperating among each other on setting a price that is higher than the equilibrium price and would then bring them positive profits. In a nutshell, the equilibrium is a Nash configuration in prices, which is similar to a classical prisoners' dilemma, in which players avoid cooperation even if this would bring them higher payoffs. The equilibrium also rests on underlying behavioural assumptions. This has been stressed by economists such as Stiglitz (1987), who noted that 'the equality of demand and supply should not be taken as a definition of equilibrium, but rather as a consequence following from more primitive behavioural postulates' (Thomsen, 1992: p. 28). These behavioural assumptions include *rationality*, which indicates that firms do not vary the equilibrium price because they know that no other profit opportunities are available. A given product, in other words, has no other *uses* and *functions*. Firms are assumed to know all possible uses and functions. Several Austrian economists have called this assumption into questions by pointing out that firms—and, in general, economic agents—have only limited knowledge and foresight because they are endowed with different knowledge stocks. Therefore, they cannot anticipate all available profit opportunities, as well as alternative uses and functions for their products. As Hayek (1937) stated, 'we have come to a point where we all realise that the concept of equilibrium itself can be made definite and clear only in terms of assumptions concerning *foresight*, although we may not yet all agree what exactly these essential assumptions are' (p. 34, emphasis added). Overall, it is because of these different stocks of knowledge and the ability of some companies to discover new possibilities that prices (and quantities) tend to deviate from their equilibrium level. This keeps the economy in a state of motion that is characterized by the continual emergence and disappearance of profit opportunities, consistent with a Schumpeterian creative destruction process.

These intuitions have received a systematic attention in evolutionary economics (Nelson and Winter, 1982), complexity economics (Beinhocker, 2007) and nonequilibrium economics (Berger, 2009). Veblen (1898), who is regarded as the first evolutionary economist, argued that economics must go beyond equilibrium and embrace disequilibrium and, in so doing, draw inspiration from Darwinian evolution. Of particular interest are his early intuitions about the role played by the changing nature of human behaviour as a driver of disequilibrium. In his words, 'The physical properties of the materials accessible to man are constants: it is the human agent that changes, his insight and his appreciation of *what these things can be used for*' (Veblen, 1898: p. 387, emphasis added).

A second important contribution to evolutionary economics is the work of Schumpeter (1934). Although he opposed biological analogies and sympathized with some formal approaches of neoclassical economics, particularly the approach of Walras (Hart, 2013), Schumpeter strongly opposed the idea of equilibrium. For instance, in reference to Walrasian equilibrium, he wrote the following: 'I felt very strongly that this was wrong, and that there was a source of energy within the economic system which would of itself disrupt any equilibrium that might be attained' (Schumpeter, 1934: p. 166). Schumpeter turned his efforts to building a theory of disequilibrium where the role of the entrepreneur and innovation is the engine of economic change.

However, the beginning of modern evolutionary economics coincides with the fundamental work of Nelson and Winter (1982), which is based on Nelson's first criticism of traditional growth theory and on Winter's criticism of maximization hypotheses (Hart, 2013). Evolutionary economics integrates Schumpeter's emphasis on the role of innovation, Veblen's emphasis on evolution, and Simon's notion of bounded rationality. Similar to the first contributions, the critique of equilibrium is central. Subsequent versions of evolutionary economics took these original perspectives to a new level by modelling disequilibrium by using simulations of heterogeneous agents and complexity theory (Delli Gatti et al., 2018). This is where evolutionary economics meets complexity and nonequilibrium economics (Beinhocker, 2007; Berger, 2009). Agent-based economics aims to replicate empirical patterns (e.g. the business cycle) by modelling the economy as a complex adaptive system of interacting elements that gives rise to emergent properties such as power-law distributions, sudden bursts of change, and disequilibrium (Delli Gatti et al., 2018).[2]

---

[2] An extensive treatment of complexity economics can be found in Beinhocker (2007), whereas Berger (2006) reviews the debate on disequilibrium.

Originating at the Santa Fé Institute in the late 1980s, complexity economics encompasses a set of research programmes whose main objective was to study the economy as an out-of-equilibrium system. After 'two centuries of studying equilibria—patterns of consistency that call for no further behavioral adjustments—economists are beginning to study the unfolding of patterns in the economy' (Arthur, 2010: p. 149). An important topic on this agenda is that of 'increasing returns' (Arthur, 1989). Increasing returns refer to the case in which the more a technology that competes against other technologies is adopted, the more it becomes dominant. This means that multiple equilibria exist (rather than a single equilibrium), and the type of equilibrium that is eventually selected is a path-dependent and history-driven process.[3]

The physical roots of equilibrium

An often-neglected fact is that economic equilibrium has roots in classical physics. The most comprehensive discussion of this linkage can be found in Mirowski (1989) and, in a more accessible way, Beinhocker (2007). Given that our goal here is to offer a summary treatment of these topics, we refer the interested reader to them for further details. Classical physics refers to the premodern theories of physics, such as Newtonian motion, which precede the developments of relativity theory and quantum mechanics. As Mirowski (1989) indicated, the influence of classical physics on economic equilibrium was mainly due to historical reasons: early neoclassical economists were influenced by the (progressively mathematized) developments in science during those years. A significant example is that of Irvin Fisher, who made key contributions to utility theory and whose PhD thesis advisor was Josiah Willard Gibbs, the famed thermodynamicist. As we will see, early neoclassical economists were particularly influenced by 'energetics' and the first law of thermodynamics, which assumes the conservation of energy within a closed system and, by implication, equilibrium (Mirowski, 1989). The closed system assumption is particularly problematic because economies are open systems that are in a state of imbalance when information and resources flow 'to and from' the surrounding environment. What is truly substantial is how these assumptions are at the centre of the neoclassical apparatus of supply and demand. More importantly, despite major

---

[3] Another key implication of increasing returns is that they subvert the conditions leading to an equilibrium of supply and demand (Hodgson, 2009).

developments in the physical and biological sciences, their impact on the theoretical development of economics has been limited, with the exception of what lies outside the mainstream. This is paradoxical because 'an irresistible field of force' (the economy) is forced to meet 'an immovable object' (the theory of equilibrium) (Mirowski, 1989: p. 193).

How has economics appropriated the notion of equilibrium from physics? The history is complex, and the origins can be traced to Adam Smith. According to Smith, wealth comes from the division of labour, which involves trade in goods between skilled workers, in which trade was viewed as governed by personal interest and occurred in competitive markets via a (not yet understood) balancing mechanism of supply and demand. The work of Turgot and Gossen further elucidated this balancing mechanism. On the supply side, Turgot hypothesized the diminishing returns of production as a balancing mechanism. On the demand side, Gossen hypothesized diminishing returns on 'utility' (a concept introduced by Bentham, which refers to the pleasure of consuming a basket of goods). More specifically, decreasing utility returns mean that marginal utility (increased utility from increased consumption of the good) is decreasing. The consumer will require more of the good provided that the marginal utility is higher than the marginal cost of purchasing an additional unit of that good. Therefore, as the price of the goods increases, the consumer will ask for less. Likewise, diminishing returns on production mean that the marginal return on production is decreasing: the producer will then supply more of a good if the price of this good increases. The decreasing returns on utility and production imply a balancing mechanism that occurs through supply and demand and is mediated by price, which is the 'key information shared by producers and consumers' (Beinhocker, 2007: p. 29).

These ideas received further development in Walras' work, which drew inspiration from physics (albeit indirectly) in approaching the balancing mechanism as a process that ultimately leads to equilibrium. The key contribution of Walras (who mainly focused on the demand side) was to conceive a market as an exchange process supervised by an auctioneer, i.e. the so-called Walrasian auctioneer. The idea is that there is a set of individuals who each has a random endowment of goods with corresponding utilities (Walras, 1874). Owing to discrepancies between utilities and good endowments (due to random initialization), individuals begin to exchange their goods between them through a process that is supervised by the auctioneer and in which an excess of supply or demand translates into a price increase or decrease until an equilibrium is reached. The physical analogy became even more explicit in the work of Jevons (1871), who conceptualized utility as a form of energy, symbolized by the willingness of individuals to trade (given their random endowment). In his view, 'utility only exists when there is on the one side the person wanting and on the other the thing wanted... Just as the gravitating force of a material body depends not alone on the mass of that body, but upon the masses and relative positions and distances of the surrounding material bodies, so utility is an attraction between a wanting being and what is wanted' (Jevons, cited in Beinhocker, 2007: p. 29). More importantly, Jevons started to think about equilibrium in explicit physical terms. He did so by borrowing the system of the lever. A lever is in balance when the ratio between two masses m_1 and m_2 on the lever is equal to the ratio between the distances d_1 and d_2 of these masses from the fulcrum below the lever. Similar to a lever, Jevons conjectured that a condition of economic equilibrium is when the ratio between the marginal utilities of consumption of two goods (the so-called 'marginal rate of substitution') is equal to the ratio between their market prices.

Overall, these examples show how physical analogies were central in the work of leading 'marginalists', such as Walras and Jevons, who established the theoretical foundations of neoclassical economics (Beinhocker, 2007; Mirowski, 1989). Later on, this influence continued with Arrow and Debreu (1954) proving the existence of a general equilibrium in the case of multiple markets and, in different forms, in the market efficiency tradition of financial studies (Fama, 1970). It is worth mentioning that even Alfred Marshall advocated the use of physical analogies. Evolutionary economists often refer to Marshall's famous quote: 'the Mecca of the economist lies in economic biology...' (Marshall, 1890: p. xxv). However, as Mirowski (1989) emphasized, very few pay attention to the following sentence in Marshall's textbook: '[...] but biological conceptions are more complex than those of mechanics; a volume on Foundations must therefore give a relatively large place to mechanical analogies' (Marshall, 1890: p. xxv).

The energetics analogy according to Mirowski

Despite the significant contribution of the marginalists, mechanical analogies became most evident in the work of Fisher, who was the first to explore these mechanical analogies in great detail (Mirowski, 1989). The influence of Gibbs, who was a thermodynamicist and Fisher's thesis advisor, was critical. The key contribution of Fisher was the further development of the energetics analogy by viewing consumer's utility as a form of energy. Let's consider a ball that moves from point a to point b in a bi-dimensional physical space

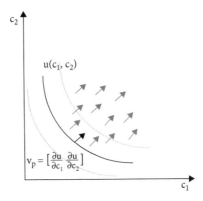

Figure 4.1   Indifference curves of utility

defined by the axes x and y (representing positions). As the ball moves, it generates a total amount of work (or change in kinetic energy) equal to the integral, on the interval a–b, of the forces multiplied by the incremental displacements: $\int_a^b F_x \partial x + F_y \partial y$, where ∂x and ∂y are the incremental displacement values with respect to x and y, respectively, and F_x and F_y are the forces with respect to x and y, respectively. According to Newton's laws, force is equal to mass times acceleration, where acceleration is the change in velocity. In the analogy of Fisher, the particle became a consumer who moves into a bidimensional commodity space defined by the axes c_1 and c_2 (representing the consumption levels of goods 1 and 2), whereas work/energy became the utility, which is now equal to the integral of the marginal utilities times the incremental consumptions: $\int_a^b \frac{\partial u}{\partial c_1} \partial c_1 + \frac{\partial u}{\partial c_2} \partial c_2$, where ∂c_1 and ∂c_2 are the incremental consumption values of goods 1 and 2, respectively, and $\partial u / \partial c_1$ and $\partial u / \partial c_2$ are the marginal utility values with respect to goods 1 and 2, respectively. Therefore, one of the key ideas in Fisher's work was the explicit interpretation of marginal utilities as forces. This is evident when we think about the well-known 'indifference curves' of utility, which are illustrated in Figure 4.1.

On these curves, the utility is the same; therefore, the consumer is indifferent to different combinations of goods 1 and 2 that give her the same utility. Indifference curves can also be represented in terms of their respective gradients. Considering a point p on a given indifference curve, the gradient in that point is the vector v_p of marginal utilities $\partial u / \partial c_1$ and $\partial u / \partial c_2$, which expresses the direction and magnitude (i.e. the force) of greater utility when additional consumption is possible. Considering that an indifference curve

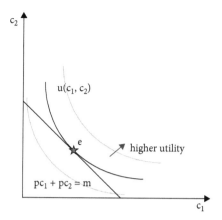

Figure 4.2 Indifference curves of utility and the budget constraint

can be represented as a set of gradients in the different points of the curve, the whole commodity space can be seen as a field of forces (Mirowski, 1989).

It is important to specify that what generates equilibrium is not utility per se, but the imposition of a budget constraint on the maximization of utility. This is the classical consumer problem, in which the utility function $u(c_1, c_2)$ is maximized with respect to c_1 and c_2 under the budget constraint $pc_1 + pc_2 = m$, where m is the available budget that can be spent on consumptions c_1 and c_2 of goods 1 and 2 at, respectively, prices p_1 and p_2. The classical consumer problem is represented graphically in Figure 4.2, where one of the indifference curves of the utility function meets the budget constraint in point e. This point is where the utility is maximized under the budget constraint. Point e is an equilibrium point in terms of quantities c_1 and c_2, which are consumed at prices p_1 and p_2, respectively. It is here that the underlying assumption of a conservation principle (and the first law of thermodynamics) comes into play.

In a nutshell, the first law of thermodynamics establishes that energy is not destroyed (nor created) because it simply changes its form, with reference to a system which—in a relevant way for us—is presumed to be closed, thus achieving equilibrium. Let us consider the example of a bowl (see Beinhocker, 2007). The limited potential energy (e.g. gravity) of a ball that is about to fall into the bowl meets the attrition of the bowl as the ball falls into it and, consequentially, gets transformed into work and heat, thus changing its form. The energy is limited, and the system is closed. Therefore, new energy does not enter the system, and nothing moves the bowl. The ball eventually reaches the equilibrium after some tatonnement around it. Moving to the consumer problem, we

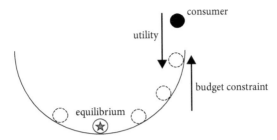

Figure 4.3 The consumer problem seen through Beinhocker's bowl analogy

should think of the ball as the consumer, the potential energy as the utility, and the surface of the ball as the budget constraint (Figure 4.3).

What the conservation principle here means is that the utility, whose energy is a potential, is not destroyed but gets transformed into expenditure. The system is closed, thus indicating that the consumer eventually settles on the equilibrium. If U is the potential energy of a particle (utility) and if T is the total work (expenditure), then 'it is the *total* energy of the particle, T + U, which is conserved through any motion of the particle' (Mirowski, 1984: p. 367). If we assume that the price increases (e.g. let's say p_1), the equilibrium consumption c_1 decreases; by contrast, if the price decreases, the equilibrium consumption increases. This determines the shape of the demand function, which results from the aggregation of multiple consumer choices and expresses the set of equilibrium quantities that consumers are willing to consume for given prices. Therefore, it is the intersection of the demand function with the supply function that identifies the equilibrium quantity and price in the market as a whole. The key analogy is that of market prices as physical forces that determine consumption choices between different goods and keep the system in equilibrium, as in the lever, thanks to the aforementioned equality—in equilibrium—of the marginal rate of substitution to the ratio of prices. In summary, the economic equilibrium rests on underlying physical analogies, particularly the assumption of energy conservation and the first law of thermodynamics in a closed system. As we will further discuss, this assumption is problematic, thereby making the adoption of an evolutionary perspective necessary.

Equilibrium and market efficiency

The theory of equilibrium is closely related to the recent debate in finance on the market efficiency hypothesis (Fama, 1970). According to the market efficiency hypothesis, markets are efficient in the sense that they constitute a better way to organize economic activity with respect to state intervention in the economy. Markets are efficient because of a system of price signals that guide agents in their economic allocation decisions and, more generally, coordinate economic activity. The market is believed to coordinate economic activity efficiently even though economic agents are bounded and have only local knowledge. By contrast, state intervention requires, at least in theory, an exhaustive global knowledge of all the possible transformations in the economy (Denrell et al., 2003; Hayek, 1945). In other words, the market can produce a complex smartphone through the coordination of several suppliers with local knowledge via the price system, whereas state centralization requires some degree of exhaustive planning, engineering, and scheduling knowledge at the top of the hierarchy. Therefore, the difference is subtly epistemological.

Although the idea of market-based coordination is certainly valuable, the idea of market efficiency is more problematic. As Farmer and Geanakoplos (2009) argued, market efficiency is a form—or, better, a consequence—of equilibrium. This means that the empirical detection of market efficiency (or inefficiency) can be seen as a test of equilibrium (disequilibrium). In reality, the link between market efficiency and equilibrium is much more complex. We refer the reader to Farmer and Geanakoplos (2009) for a comprehensive review of this debate. Other useful reviews are those of Mandelbrot and Hudson (2004) and Malkiel (2003). For the purposes of this discussion, we emphasize how market efficiency refers to the trading of financial securities (rather than goods) in a time context (rather than a static one) and is characterized by uncertainty. This brings us to the core hypothesis of market efficiency, according to which stock prices and returns instantly reflect all the information available on the market, thus preventing investors from making abnormal profits. The idea that prices instantly reflect all the available information means that they behave like a random walk: $p_t = p_{t-1} + e_t$, where p is the price of a financial security (e.g. a stock), and e is white noise that reflects public information about future expected events, namely, information about future earnings, changes in the management of a company, imposition of tariffs, and so forth. If the market is not efficient, prices reflect information with a delay rather than instantly, that is, what is reflected in p_t is not only e_t but also past information. In other words, there is a correlative pattern, as well as memory, in the series of prices. This has profit implications: for instance, if someone can anticipate that the slope of the price pattern will be positive, then he or she could borrow 10€ to buy a stock at a price of 10€ at time t, sell the stock at a price of 11€ and return 10€ to the bank at t + 1, thus making a profit of 1€.

There are three types of tests on the market efficiency hypothesis (Malkiel, 2003). The first test consists of directly testing the presence or absence of patterns (or more sophisticated correlations) in the series of prices, which may or may not support the efficiency hypothesis. The second test is based on the series of returns rather than prices and consists of testing whether investors can gain abnormal profits with respect to underlying market indexes; this may or may not support the efficiency hypothesis. The third test consists of looking at whether fundamental information, which is expressed by specific accounting numbers such as earnings, is reflected into returns series with a delay or rather immediately. However, inefficiency and disequilibrium, broadly speaking, also have also other ways to manifest themselves, such as long-term memory patterns, volatility clustering, or skewed distributions of returns (Farmer and Geanakoplos, 2009; Mandelbrot and Hudson, 2004). In this regard, power-law distributions (i.e. the fact that returns have fat tails instead of being normally distributed) are particularly interesting. Power laws are universally recognized as the 'signature' of complex systems (Andriani and McKelvey, 2009) and are often associated with dynamics of thermal *disequilibrium* (Farmer and Geanakoplos, 2009). The bottom line is that there are several approaches to detect economic disequilibrium; however, 'the fact that we have no [...] disequilibrium theory in economics is clearly a serious problem' (Farmer and Geanakoplos, 2009: p. 26). This is striking because markets are rarely efficient. Interestingly, while Fama received the Nobel Prize in economics for his theory of efficiency, Shiller also received it for challenging this theory. Shiller views markets as inherently inefficient and being characterized by what he calls bubbles of 'irrational exuberance' (Shiller, 2000) that may be caused by the introduction of a new technology, news-based amplification mechanisms, and the bounded psychology of investors. From an evolutionary perspective, Shiller's view of technology as a possible trigger of economic bubbles and the whole out-of-equilibrium dynamic of prices and returns is particularly insightful.

Beyond equilibrium: unprestateable evolution

The distinctive aspect of evolutionary thinking is the idea of the economy as a continually evolving system out of equilibrium owing to endogenous factors such as technology, which also evolves (Nelson and Winter, 1982). Similar to equilibrium, disequilibrium can be seen as having physical roots, specifically the second law of thermodynamics. Unlike the first law of thermodynamics, the second law recognizes the role of change, evolution, and disequilibrium.

The contribution of Georgescu-Roegen (1971) to the debate on thermodynamics in the economic process is central here. Trained at Harvard under the supervision of Schumpeter, Georgescu-Roegen started his career as a 'traditional' economist. However, towards the end of his career, he acknowledged the limitations of traditional economics and looked for new answers in the domains of physics and evolution. His main contributions are contained in the magnum opus 'The entropy law and the economic process' (Georgescu-Roegen, 1971). Although the first law of thermodynamics (and the principle of conservation) was already implicit in consumer theory, Georgescu-Roegen recognized the importance of the second law of thermodynamics. According to this law, although energy is transformed into different states, the system is subject to an irreversible process of degradation because it loses structure, order, and information: in other words, the entropy of the system increases. For example, we might think of an assembled puzzle in the trunk of our car while driving on a damaged mountain road. The puzzle progressively becomes a collection of disconnected pieces. The structure, order, and information of the puzzle decrease: therefore, the entropy of the puzzle increases. This is the so-called 'arrow of time', the idea that entropy in the universe augments irreversibly over time. In other words, entropy can be seen as a sort of clock that measures the advancement of time or the pace of evolution itself (Prigogine and Stengers, 1984). However, the fact that entropy increases in the universe does not mean that it increases in all its subsystems. Considering a specific subsystem, the increase of degradation and entropy can be kept under control (or even decreased) by opening up the system and importing energy from the outside. Returning to the example, to preserve the shape of the puzzle, we could open the trunk of the car and bring in a friend who puts his energy and effort into continually reassembling the puzzle during our bumpy journey. In this regard, evolution can be also seen as a struggle against the irreversible increase in entropy (that leads to thermal stasis) via the appropriation of energy, resources, and information from the outside. As a consequence, the system evolves out of balance.

Georgescu-Roegen's intuition was to transfer these ideas into the economic process (particularly from the production side), which he considered intrinsically bound by the second law and consisting of a continual transformation of inputs into outputs in a fight against entropy. In hindsight, a key contribution by Georgescu-Roegen was the conceptualization of the economic system as an open system by recognizing the role of evolution and

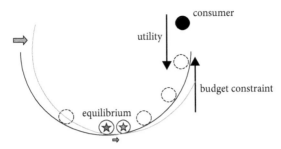

Figure 4.4 The bowl as an open system: second law and disequilibrium

imbalance in the economy. In summary, the first law of thermodynamics states that energy is conserved in a closed system, but it can change form; therefore, the system reaches equilibrium. The second law of thermodynamics states that, in a closed system, energy degrades and entropy increases and the system reaches equilibrium. According to the second law, the opening of the system implies the import of energy, which allows the system to change and thus *evolve* out of balance (Schrödinger, 1944). Returning to the bowl analogy (Beinhocker, 2007), we hypothesize that it is *openness* that continuously *moves* the bowl, as well as the ball inside it, from its static position and thus out of equilibrium (Figure 4.4).

How does disequilibrium in price dynamics develop? This problem is complex; therefore, we do not pretend to offer a comprehensive answer. For the purposes of this discussion, some insights can be found in the recent debate on unprestateable evolution, a key source of which is functional expansion via exaptive innovation (Felin et al., 2014; Longo et al., 2012; Felin et al., 2016; Kauffman, 2008). Before defining unprestateability, we must define the concept of phase space. A phase space is a mathematical space where we represent the trajectory of a Newtonian body. A phase space is typically defined by a horizontal axis $x(t)$, where the position x of the body at time t can be indicated, and by a vertical axis $x'(t)$, where the velocity x' of the body at time t can be indicated. Let us consider a simple oscillating pendulum. For the pendulum, the trajectory on the phase space looks like a spiral that wraps itself into the resting point (0,0) at the intersection of the two axes. Instead of the pendulum, we could also think about a price that is 'tatonning' towards the resting point given by the intersection of demand and supply as the excesses of demand and supply cancel out, respectively. For a classical Newtonian body, a law—in the form of a precise mathematical equation—can be pre-stated and used to make predictions about the position and velocity of the body in the future, given a proper knowledge of the initial conditions. This is the so-called prestateability or 'determinism', which is also known as the 'Laplacian dream' for classical mechanics (Kauffman, 2016). However, the key point of unprestateability is that this type of law cannot be pre-stated or used to make predictions about the future for evolving complex entities such as molecules, organisms, or technologies. To get a better idea, let us consider a complex molecule like a protein that consists of a long string of (for example) 200 amino acids. What do we mean by phase space in this case? We must think of the phase space as a space in which 'trajectory' does not mean that a classical atomistic body moves from one position to another in a three-dimensional context. Instead, it means moving from one possible configuration (string) of the molecule to another. Yet the number of possible configurations of a protein with 200 amino acids is trans-finite and probably higher than the number of particles in the universe; this indicates that the trajectory will never explore the entire phase space but only a small part of it in the expanding environment of past configurations. This is the so-called problem of 'non-ergodicity', a key consequence of which is the impossibility to pre-state a mathematical law for the evolution of a complex entity (Longo et al., 2012). This implies that evolution must be addressed not in terms of mathematical laws, but in terms of history, idio-syncratic contingencies, and path-dependent progress into the 'adjacent pos-sible' (Kauffman, 2000).[4]

Things become even more intricate if we consider entities such as tech-nologies, owing to their greater dimensionality, the greater number of pos-sible combinations made possible by the lack of reproductive closure, and, above all, by their interaction with the functional space: the space of possible functions, uses, and applications of these technologies. It is here that exapta-tion comes into play as a key factor in functional expansion that eventually may drive economic aggregates such as prices and quantities out of equilib-rium. In this regard, it is useful to think of the 'ontological' meaning of price in a broad sense. The price of a product, technology, or resource changes depending on market conditions. However, such changes should ultimately reflect what economic agents consider as the fundamental value of a given good. In turn, the fundamental value reflects the best of all possible func-tions, uses, and applications of the good in question. The fundamental value can therefore be defined as the *value of the best function among all possible functions of the good in question.* Let us consider the classical 'screwdriver', whose best function is to 'screw in a screw' in a 'house context', to which we attach a value of 1€. Let us now consider the very same good but in

---

[4] For a system under investigation, such as a technology, the concept of 'adjacent possible' refers to the possible states of the system that are near the current state and in which the system can evolve (Kauffman, 2000).

a 'savannah context', which is an environment full of predators (and without a shadow of human presence). In this context, the screwdriver is much more valuable (100€) owing to its possible function as 'defence weapon against an approaching lion'. The bottom line is that, contrary to the assumptions of Arrow and Debreu (1954), it is impossible to pre-state all the possible functions afforded by a good, or even define a stable hierarchy of best functions, owing to their dependence on the context of use, which, in a dynamic economy, changes continually. The key implication is that there is no better stable function or a fundamental value, in a classical sense, that acts as an anchor for ever-changing price signals. This evaluation problem is particularly accentuated for complex technologies (or other types of resources) owing to their uniqueness and non-commoditized nature, which is the cause of market incompleteness. As Denrell et al. (2003) emphasized, 'valuation in incomplete markets depends crucially on the knowledge economic agents have about alternative transformations' (p. 983). However, such exhaustive knowledge of possible transformations and functionalities goes beyond the possibilities of human reasoning; therefore, valuation remains problematic. Accordingly, the same idea of equilibrium via market efficiency (Fama, 1970) (i.e. prices that immediately reflect fundamental values) is problematic.

What is the driver of functional expansion, that is, the emergence of new functions, uses, and applications of existing products, technologies, and resources? Koppl et al. (2015) point to the role of 'cambiodiversity', which is similar to biodiversity and refers to the increasing diversity of artefacts in the economy (see also Felin et al., 2016). To get an intuitive idea of how diversity favours functional expansion, it is useful to think of a general-purpose technology (for example, the internet) that has generated a cascade of new features, along with extinctions, for mobile phones (in the form of maps), cars (autonomous driving), or refrigerators (dash buttons). Consequently, our modern economy can be seen as a complex network in which artefacts have links between them (such as the internet and mobile phones), which represent complementary relationships that incorporate new functional activations. The network is certainly not static but increases in size as new products are gradually added. It also changes in terms of topological structure as new links progressively appear while others disappear. Furthermore, beyond certain critical thresholds, the network dynamics are self-catalytic and give rise to power-law statistical regularities for creation and extinction events (Kauffman, 2008; Hanel et al., 2007). More importantly, these complex networks (and their dynamic) constitute a possible engine of disequilibrium in

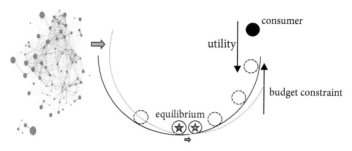

Figure 4.5 Complex networks and disequilibrium

economic aggregates: as diversity goes up, functional expansion increases, thus leading to a continual reshuffling of the hierarchies of best functions, fundamental values, and price signals in *open* markets of buyers and sellers. Therefore, closing the circle on the bowl analogy (Beinhocker, 2007), we can speculate that it is *openness to a diverse and continually evolving network* that continually *moves* the bowl, as well as the ball inside, from its static position and thus out of equilibrium (Figure 4.5).

In summary, the previous debates point to an evolutionary view of the economy as a system in disequilibrium because of the inherent unprestatea-bility of functional expansion in the adjacent possible (Kauffman, 2000). The core implication is that we cannot reduce the economy to the classical laws of equilibrium that still permeate much of the neoclassical tradition (Mirowski, 1989). We should rather see the economy as a system that is con-tinually evolving, innovative, and creative in unpredictable ways (Nelson and Winter, 1982; Kauffman, 2016). This places a premium on a non-predictive evolutionary theory in economics, strategy, and innovation. At this point, we should emphasize that although it is difficult to make predictions about spe-cific events, this does not prevent us from extracting general statistical pat-terns to be used for scientific analysis or policy recommendations. As Kauffman (2008) noted, 'science may fail to predict the concrete details [...], yet capture major statistical features critical for understanding economic growth and evolution' (p. 171). Another key point is that if a new physical analogy is still sought, a starting point is the second law of thermodynamics, under the assumption that systems are open to the exchange of resources, energy, and information (Georgescu-Roegen, 1971). Some versions of post-war economics have progressively embraced the second law via an increas-ing emphasis on information processing and computation (see Mirowski, 2002). Although we are still in the realm of speculation, it is reasonable to expect a further 'tectonic shift' of the debate from physics to biology, and this will perhaps get us closer to Kauffman's (2000) proposal of an additional law of thermodynamics for open systems in an increasingly diverse economy that expands into the adjacent possible.

References

Andriani, P. and McKelvey, B. 2009. From Gaussian to Paretian thinking: causes and implications of power laws in organizations. *Organization Science*, 20(6): 1053–71.

Arrow, K.J. and Debreu, G. 1954. Existence of an equilibrium for a competitive economy. *Econometrica*, 22(3): 265–90.

Arthur, W.B. 1989. Competing technologies, increasing returns, and lock-in by historical events. *The Economic Journal*, 99(394): 116–31.

Arthur, W.B. 2010. Complexity, the Santa Fe approach, and non-equilibrium economics. *History of Economics Ideas*, 18(2): 149–66.

Beinhocker, E.D. 2007. *The origins of wealth: evolution, complexity, and the radical remaking of economics*. Harvard Business Review Press.

Berger, S. 2009. *The foundations of non-equilibrium economics*. Routledge.

Delli Gatti, D., Fagiolo, G., Gallegati, M., Richiardi, M., and Russo, A. 2018. *Agent-based models in economics*. Cambridge University Press.

Denrell, J., Fang, C., and Winter, S.G. 2003. The economics of strategic opportunity. *Strategic Management Journal*, 24(10): 977–90.

Dosi, G. and Stiglitz, J.E. 2020. ICC announcement: annual special issue on macro economics and development. *Industrial and Corporate Change*, 29(3): 577–80.

Fama, E. 1970. Efficient capital markets: a review of theory and empirical work. *Journal of Finance*, 25(2): 383–417.

Farmer, J.D. and Geanakoplos, J. 2009. The virtues and vices of equilibrium and the future of financial economics. *Complexity*, 14(3): 11–38.

Felin, T., Kauffman, S., Koppl, R., and Longo, G. 2014. Economic opportunity and evolution: beyond landscapes and bounded rationality. *Strategic Entrepreneurship Journal*, 8(4): 269–82.

Felin, T., Kauffman, S., Mastrogiorgio, A., and Mastrogiorgio, M. 2016. Factor markets, actors and affordances. *Industrial and Corporate Change*, 25(1): 133–47.

Fisher, F.M. 1983. *Disequilibrium foundations of equilibrium economics*. Econometric Society Monographs in Pure Theory.

Georgescu-Roegen, N. 1971. *The entropy law and the economic process*. Harvard University Press.

Hanel, R., Kauffman, S.A., and Thurner, S. 2007. Towards a physics of evolution: critical diversity dynamics at the edges of collapse and bursts of diversification. *Physical Review E*, 76(3): 036110.

Hart, N. 2013. *Alfred Marshall and modern economics: equilibrium theory and evolutionary economics*. Palgrave Macmillan.

Hayek, F.A. 1937. Economics and knowledge. *Economica*, 4(13): 33–54.

Hayek, F.A. 1945. The use of knowledge in society. *American Economic Review*, 35(4): 519–30.

Hodgson, G.M. 2009. Foreword. In Berger, S. (ed.). *The foundations of non-equilibrium economics*. Routledge.

Jevons, W.S. 1871. *The theory of political economy*. Macmillan.

Kauffman, S.A. 2000. *Investigations*. Oxford University Press.

Kauffman, S. 2008. *Reinventing the sacred: a new view of science, reason, and religion*. Basic Books.

Kauffman, S. 2016. *Humanity in a creative universe*. Oxford University Press.

Koppl, R., Kauffman, S., Felin, T., and Longo, G. 2015. Economics for a creative world. *Journal of Institutional Economics*, 11(1): 1–31.

Longo, G., Montevil, M., and Kauffman, S. 2012. No entailing laws, but enablement in the evolution of the biosphere. In *Proceedings of the Genetic and Evolutionary Computation Conference*.

Malkiel, B.G. 2003. The efficient market hypothesis and its critics. *Journal of Economic Perspectives*, 17(1): 59–82.

Mandelbrot, B.B. and Hudson, R.L. 2004. *The (mis)behavior of markets: a fractal view of risk, ruin and reward*. Profile Books.

Marshall, A. 1890. *Principles of economics*. MacMillan.

Mirowski, P. 1984. Physics and the 'marginalist revolution'. *Cambridge Journal of Economics*, 8(4): 361–79.

Mirowski, P. 1989. *More heat than light. Economics as social physics: physics as nature's economics*. Cambridge University Press.

Mirowski, P. 2002. *Machine dreams: economics becomes a cyborg science*. Cambridge University Press.

Nelson, R.R., Dosi, G., Helfat, C.E., Pyka, A., Saviotti, P., Lee, K., Dopfer, K., Malerba, F., and Winter, S.G. 2018. *Modern evolutionary economics*. Cambridge University Press.

Nelson, R.R. and Winter, S.G. 1982. *An evolutionary theory of economic change*. Harvard University Press.

Prigogine, I. and Stengers, I. 1984. *Order out of chaos: man's new dialogue with nature*. Flamingo.

Roncaglia, A. 2017. *A brief history of economic thought.* Cambridge University Press.

Schrödinger, E. 1944. *What is life? The physical aspect of the living cell.* Cambridge University Press.

Schumpeter, J.A. 1934. *The theory of economic development: an inquiry into profits, capital, credit, interest, and the business cycle.* Harvard University Press.

Shiller, R.J. 2000. *Irrational exuberance.* Princeton University Press.

Thomsen, E.F. 1992. *Prices and knowledge: a market process perspective.* Routledge.

Veblen, T.B. 1898. Why is economics not an evolutionary science? *Quarterly Journal of Economics,* 12(3): 373–97.

Walras, L. 1874. *Éléments d'économie politique pure.* Corbaz & C.

Watson, J. 2002. *Strategy.* Norton & Company.

5

New Evolutionary Theory Via Simulation

NK Landscapes and Beyond

Gino Cattani and Mariano Mastrogiorgio

NK landscapes in evolutionary theory

Computational modelling is common in evolutionary economics, strategy, and innovation. A well-established simulation framework is the NK model of fitness landscapes. Building on the early intuitions of Wright (1932), the NK modelling approach was formally developed by Kauffman (1993) and then further extended by Altenberg (1996) to deal with more general systems (such as technologies with multiple functions). The key idea is to model a process of adaptation, the difficulty or easiness of which is reflected in how a fitness landscape behaves as a function of the number of components and their interdependencies. A fitness landscape becomes increasingly rugged (or multipeaked) as the number of components and interdependencies (N and K, respectively) increases owing to conflicting constraints that make the process of adaptation more difficult.

The NK model was introduced into the strategy and innovation fields by Levinthal (1997). Since then, a vast literature has emerged. From a theoretical point of view, the NK literature rests on Herbert Simon's notions of problem complexity, bounded rationality, and sequential search. Several problems (e.g. the development of a new technology) are complex because they consist of interdependent choices that mutually affect each other (Simon, 1962). Owing to bounded rationality (Simon, 1955), these complex problems are difficult (if not impossible) to solve through global optimization. An alternative approach is to engage in sequential search, which is a form of localized trial-and-error learning process that involves changing slightly the current configuration, observing the resulting performance, and implementing the

Gino Cattani and Mariano Mastrogiorgio, *New Evolutionary Theory Via Simulation: NK Landscapes and Beyond* In: *New Developments in Evolutionary Innovation: Novelty Creation in a Serendipitous Economy.* Edited by: Gino Cattani and Mariano Mastrogiorgio, Oxford University Press (2021). © Gino Cattani and Mariano Mastrogiorgio. DOI: 10.1093/oso/9780198837091.003.0005 change if performance improves (then repeating the steps sequentially). However, a challenge posed by problem complexity is the high variability of performance outcomes, which increases the likelihood that agents may remain trapped on suboptimal solutions (peaks in the performance or fitness landscape) during sequential search. Levinthal (1997) was the first to use the NK modelling approach to examine search and adaptation.

Several scholars have used this approach to explore other questions. A first stream of research has looked at alternative search procedures, particularly different forms of distant search, for example, search via analogy preceded by simplified cognitive representations of the problem structure and solution space (Gavetti and Levinthal, 2000; Gavetti, 2012). A second stream has studied how search can be enhanced via problem decomposition by reducing the dimensionality of the problem or its internal interdependencies through modularization (Ethiraj and Levinthal, 2004). A third stream has examined distributed search, namely, search procedures across firms or across organizational units and actors within firms (Marengo and Pasquali, 2012). A few other scholars have focused on the relationship between problem decomposition and distributed search, optimal problem decomposition, temporal dynamics, and so forth.

Despite all these theoretical insights, there has been limited testing of the main predictions in empirical research (Baumann et al., 2019). Some empirically oriented research has emerged on the basis of large-sample studies, experiments, and case studies. Of particular interest are large-sample studies relying on patent data. Fleming and Sorenson (2001) tested the main predictions of the NK modelling approach by using patent data. Specifically, they considered patents (and the underlying technology) as the unit of analysis. They measured N with the number of a patent's technological subclasses, K with the historical difficulty (empirically observed) of recombining them, and the fitness in terms of the forward citations received by the patent. On the basis of Fleming and Sorenson (2001), other studies have followed a similar approach (see Ganco, 2017). Overall, the available evidence supports the main predictions of the NK model, particularly the link between interdependence and ruggedness, thus implying complex adaptation (Levinthal, 1997). However, evidence is still mixed (Ganco, 2017), and further research is necessary to shed light on the different aspects of the NK modelling approach, which remains an important approach in evolutionary-inspired economics, strategy, and innovation. As we will see, the NK model and its generalization are also suitable for simulating certain aspects of new evolutionary phenomena (though with some caveats). Before illustrating these applications, the next section reviews the classical version of the NK.

The classical NK landscape

We define a technology as a configuration of components expressed by a vector $\overline{X} = \left[x_1, x_2, x_3, \ldots \right]$, where $x_i = \{0,1\}$ for i = 1, 2...N. N is the number of components, and F indicates the fitness of the configuration.[1] Considering this generic case, there are 2^N possible configurations of components and related fitness values. Along with N, another key parameter is the interdependence between components, and this is expressed by K = 0, 1,...N−1. Interdependencies are also known as 'epistatic relations' (Kauffman, 1993). When an epistatic relation exists between a component and other components, changing the state of the component affects the fitness both through the component itself and the other epistatically related components. In the simple case with N = 3, for instance, there are eight possible configurations that each occupy a different position on the landscape L (and represented close to its neighbours, one mutation away). Each configuration has a fitness value, which is expressed by a height on the fitness F axis and is illustrated in Figure 5.1.

The calculation of fitness values depends on the value of K. When K = 0 (no interdependence), the fitness of a configuration is the average fitness

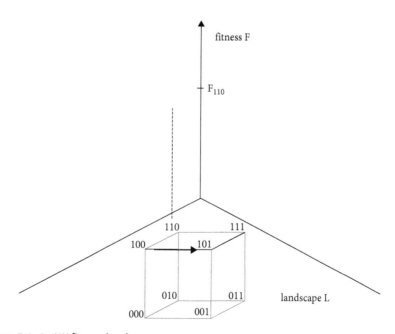

Figure 5.1 An NK fitness landscape

---

[1] For a detailed description of the classical NK model, we refer to Kauffman (1993) and Frenken (2006).

contribution of individual components, where the fitness contribution of an individual component is a random draw from a uniform unit distribution for each possible value (zero or one) of the component; therefore $F(\overline{X}) = \frac{1}{N}\sum_{i=1}^{N} f_{x_i}(\overline{X})$, where f_{x_i} is independent of other i. When K > 0 (interdependence), the fitness of a configuration is the average fitness contribution of individual components, where the fitness contribution of an individual component now also depends on the changes of other components owing to the existence of such epistatic relations; therefore, $F(\overline{X}) = \frac{1}{N}\sum_{i=1}^{N} f_{x_i}(\overline{X})$, where f_{x_i} is not independent of other i. For example, when K = 2, the fitness contribution of an individual component depends not only on the value of the component, whether it changes from zero to one or vice versa, but also on the value of two other components.

On the basis of Kauffman (1993), we assume a process of technological adaptation via local search, which is also known as 'hill climbing'. This means that, starting from a given configuration such as '100', we move to a neighbour configuration such as '101', thus changing one component at a time, and accept the move/change if it implies a fitness improvement and reject it otherwise. If the move/change is accepted, local search continues from the new configuration '101' until a peak is found, i.e. a configuration with higher fitness than the neighbouring peaks. The peak is a global or local optimum depending on whether it is the highest in the landscape. The key insight is that owing to conflicting constraints, increasing K (the level of interdependence) leads to a higher number of local optima; therefore, the distribution of fitness values looks more rugged (and less correlated). As the figures below show, when K = 0 (no interdependence, above), moving from '100' to '101' implies a less abrupt change in fitness compared with the K = 2 case (maximum interdependence, below) (Figure 5.2).

The main effect of increasing K is the higher likelihood of remaining stuck on a suboptimal configuration during hill climbing (unless search starts in the 'basin of attraction' of the global optimum): in general, this implies greater uncertainty in technological adaptation via local search. In reality, more specific implications can be derived formally, or from simulation results. For instance, it has been observed that as K increases, the number of local optima grows exponentially, their average fitness value becomes lower (for very large K), and they are more spread out over the search space. K is a disadvantage only when it is significantly high because systems with low to moderate levels of interdependence have positive characteristics such as a higher average fitness level and wider basins of attractions of local optima. The above conclusions derive from a specific type of search known as hill

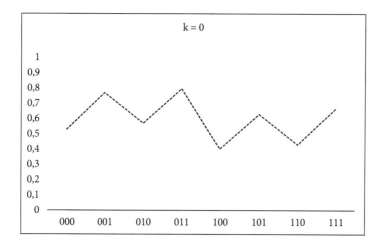

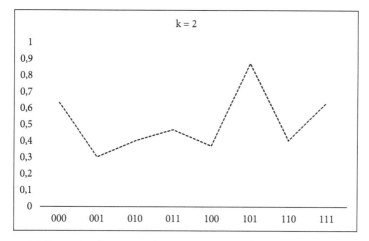

Figure 5.2   NK fitness landscapes with varying degrees of complexity

climbing; therefore, different conclusions can be drawn for different search processes (see Frenken, 2006).

Generalized NK landscapes

The most important feature of the generalized NK model is that a technology can have multiple functions whose number is not necessarily equal to the number of components.[2] This allows multifunctional systems and other key aspects to be simulated (e.g. modularity). Similar to that above, we define a

---

[2] For a more detailed discussion of the generalized NK model, see Frenken (2006) and Altenberg (1996).

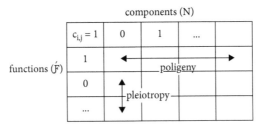

Figure 5.3 Genotype-phenotype mapping in a generalized NK

technology as a configuration of components expressed by a vector $\overline{X} = \left[x_1, x_2, x_{3,} \ldots \right]$, where $x_i = \{0,1\}$ for i=1, 2…N. N is the number of components, F indicates the fitness of the configuration, and $\acute{F}$ is the number of functions. The generalized NK model is based on a map connecting components and functions, which is known as the 'genotype–phenotype' map and is specified in the matrix shown in Figure 5.3, where columns identify the components, rows identify the functions, and a cell (e.g. cell i, j; for i=1,2,…N, j=1,2…$\acute{F}$) is equal to one if component i affects a function j and zero otherwise. We define 'pleiotropy' as the number of functions affected by changes of component i and 'polygeny' as the number of components affecting function j. Pleiotropy is the sum of ones in a particular column (i.e. $pl_i = \sum_{j=1}^{f} c_{i,j}$), whereas polygeny is the sum of ones in a particular row (i.e. $po_j = \sum_{i=1}^{N} c_{i,j}$), where $c_{i,j} = \{0,1\}$.

The genotype-phenotype map is the basis for calculating the fitness values of technological configurations. Let us again consider the N = 3 case with eight possible configurations. Starting from a given configuration (e.g. '100'), when we change a component and move to a neighbouring configuration (e.g. '101'), a new random value (from a uniform unit distribution) is assigned to each function affected by the component, as specified in the pleiotropy vector of the component. Therefore, the calculation of fitness values follows the same logic, similar to the original NK modelling approach, even though the fitness of a configuration is now given by $F(\overline{X}) = \frac{1}{f} \sum_{i=1}^{f} f_i(\overline{X})$. The key difference is that N is not necessarily equal to $\acute{F}$. On the contrary, in the original NK model, N is equal to $\acute{F}$ by definition; this is consistent with the assumption that each component has its own fitness contribution (function) to the overall fitness, which is an average of individual fitness contributions. Another key difference is that complexity is parametrized by the genotype-phenotype map rather than K. Accordingly, the original NK model of Kauffman (1993) can be understood as a special case of the NK model of Altenberg (1996).

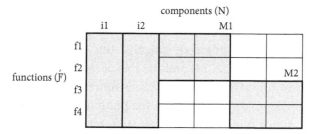

Figure 5.4 Modularity in a generalized NK

An advantage of the generalized NK model is the ease in modelling modularity (Frenken, 2006; Frenken and Mendritzki, 2012). A modular system (e.g. a technology) is composed of subsystems (i.e. the modules) connected to each other through interface standards. A 'modular' system is 'near-decomposable' in the sense that the majority of interdependencies are within modules, with fewer interdependencies connecting them. The reason why the generalized NK model is suitable for studying modularity is the (above-mentioned) presence of components that do not directly contribute to the overall fitness but are available as interface standards. In the original NK model, on the other hand, each component is assumed to contribute to the overall fitness. An example is given in Figure 5.4.

In this example, a modular system with two 2 × 2 modules (shaded squares) is connected via two interface standards (shaded columns, on the left). As we can see, interface standards i1 and i2 are related to functions f1 and f2 affected by module M1, and to functions f3 and f4 affected by module M2, thus mediating the epistatic relations between the components of M1 and those of M2.

Functional expansion

The generalized NK can be used to model some specific aspects of exaptation. At this point, however, a caveat is necessary: the NK apparatus and the concept of landscape (broadly speaking) is problematic for modelling novelty via exaptation owing to the inherently unprestateable nature of new functions and opportunities, whose emergence is continual and highly contextual (Felin et al., 2014, 2016). Despite this inherent limitation, the generalized NK setting is a useful starting point. A first possibility (I) is to model the optimization of technology with multiple functions on an *ex post* basis, that is, *after* new functions have emerged via exaptation (meaning that they are prespecified in the model). Although this does not explain the emergence of new functions and exaptation per se (i.e. where they come from), it can help shed light on the phase of adaptive fine tuning to new functions (Andriani and Carignani, 2014) and the role of modularity in reducing conflicting constraints between old and new functions. Studying conflicting constraints is also important but from the point of view of 'exploiting' exaptation (i.e. *after* new functions have emerged serendipitously). A second possibility (II) is to model a multifunctional technology in a more dynamic setting, in which new components are progressively added to the system and N grows, as in a 'constructional' setting (Altenberg, 1996). This growth can be seen as the proxy of an increasingly large (and diverse) ecological environment to which technology is exposed, in a process that reveals new affordances, uses, and functions.

An important question is how to model functional expansion in a system in which, by definition, the number of functions ($\acute{F}$) is prespecified. One possibility is to model multifunctional optimization (see I) in comparative settings with different (and growing) levels of $\acute{F}$. However, this leaves again the emergence of new functions unexplained. Therefore, a third approach (III) could be based on a weighted fitness function:

$$F(\overline{X}) = \sum_{i=1}^{f} w_i f_i(\overline{X}), \text{where } w_i \geq 0 \text{ and } \sum_{i=1}^{f} w_i = 1.$$

Frenken (2006) proposed a weighted fitness for incorporating user heterogeneity in a generalized NK setting: for a technology with multiple functions, the idea is that there are different user groups where each user group assigns a different set of weights w and thus a different preference ordering to the functions. To model exaptation, a possible variation is to use weights to capture *latent* functions and their emergence via exaptation. For instance, one could assign weights w = 0 to latent functions, as in Figure 5.5, where function f4 is latent (expressed by a weight $w_4 = 0$, which may eventually become positive).

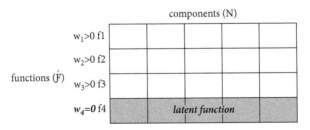

Figure 5.5 Modelling exaptation: latent function emergence in a generalized NK

Exaptation refers to features that 'evolved for other usages (or for no function at all) and were later "coopted" for their current role' (Gould and Vrba, 1982: p. 6). In the context of technology, the emergence of a new function could be addressed by assigning a zero weight to the function (when it is in a latent state), which then becomes positive; on the other hand, the weights of the old functions become zero when the function is activated and the technology is reused for this new function. Likewise, the emergence of a new function from redundant 'spandrels'—with no function at all (Gould and Lewontin, 1979)—could be approached starting with zero weights for all the functions (in a particular subset of the technology), some of which would become positive when the function is activated and when the technology is purposed towards this new function.

A second important issue is the generation of weights that activate and deactivate functions out of and in the latent state. A simple approach is to generate weights randomly in the simulation itself. A second alternative is to estimate weights from real data, such as the network of patent classes, and use them in the simulation. According to standard classification systems, technological classes broadly identify a technology's *existing* functions and uses (USPTO, 2012). On the basis of the co-occurrence of patent classes, the links between classes and their strength can be calculated (Yayavaram and Ahuja, 2008) to identify those functional links that are more common. In this regard, functional links should be thought of as phenomena-based, that is, some functions are more likely to co-occur than others (e.g. the 'screw' and 'open a door' functions of a screwdriver with respect to the 'screw' and 'fly' functions). Therefore, functional links can be seen as part of a large—and evolving—network of functions with a topological structure that defines what functions are more often linked to others. As already mentioned, it would be interesting to exploit this type of topological information to estimate empirically the likelihood that a weight will be activated and then use this information to initialize the simulation; in this way, the activation of a function out of its latent state—when w_i becomes positive—would depend on empirically based topological information.

Unprestateable evolution

As we argued above and further discuss here, all the versions of the NK—and of landscapes in general—are problematic for the modelling of radical novelty owing to the inherently unprestateable nature of new functions and opportunities, whose emergence is continual and highly contextual

(Felin et al., 2014; Felin et al., 2016). Nevertheless, we see them as part of the recent attempts to map the 'topology of the possible' (Fontana and Schuster, 1998; Stadler et al., 2001) under the assumption that evolution is not fully unbounded but canalized into trajectories of 'evolvability' even though landscapes and 'phase spaces' are not pre-stateable (Wagner and Altenberg, 1996). Therefore, evolution is inherently poised towards the 'adjacent possible' (Kauffman, 2000).

The bottom line is that NK landscapes and phase spaces are inherently limited in the contexts of technological evolution characterized by generative processes, such as those of new functions and uses, technologies, and products. The limitations are not of the 'NP type', meaning that search (of new functions and uses) cannot be performed in polynomial time owing to the high dimensionality of the problem, complexity, and bounded rationality (Rivkin, 2000). It is rather a matter of 'frame', which refers to the 'problematic nature of explaining the full task set of activities and *possible* functionalities and uses for operating in the world' (Felin et al., 2014: p. 5). For example, a screwdriver can be used not only for screwing but also for opening a door, killing a predator, and so on (Longo et al., 2012). Without knowing the context in which an artefact can be used, all possible functions and uses are indefinite and *cannot* be listed *a priori* or cannot be assigned a probability; given that the uncertainty is fundamental, 'not only do we not know what will happen—we also do not know what *can* happen' (Felin et al., 2014: p. 6). Overall, the landscape is not fixed *ex ante* but changes continually owing to the emergence of new functions. As shown in Figure 5.6, the landscape grows and changes on a continual basis along the genotype and phenotype dimensions: as new components and functions are gradually added to the system, the cube of possible configurations is transformed into more complex hypercubes, and the number of fitness axes grows.

How can one model emergent novelty then? A new set of mathematical tools seems necessary to capture the emergent richness of unprestateable evolution. A first possibility is the abovementioned weighted function approach (Altenberg, 1996; Frenken, 2006) and its possible extensions. For example, we could model weight activation as a function of the (expanding) dimensionality of the context that enables new functions and uses, that is $p(w_i = 1) = f(N)$. Another possibility is the novel approach of Gavetti et al. (2017), which allows the analysis of endogenous 'shaping' or niche construction of the environment. However, these approaches are not equipped to model the dynamic of important evolutionary phenomena such as speciation, the unboundedness or infinite dimensionality of the possible functions, or functional activation via context expansion. Accordingly, two other approaches

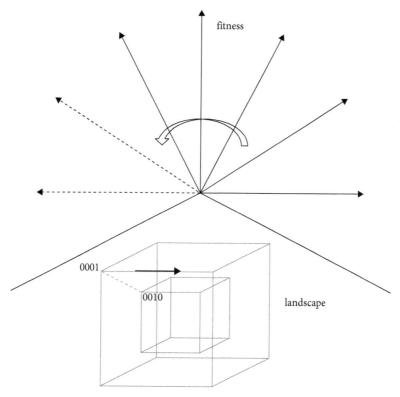

Figure 5.6 Functional emergence in the NK setting

are briefly outlined in the next two sections. The first approach is based on the so-called 'holey landscapes' and is particularly fit for modelling the dynamics of speciation (Gavrilets, 1997). The second approach is less conservative because it fully departs from landscapes and embraces quantum formalism, thus accommodating unboundedness and functional expansion via contextual interaction (Gabora et al., 2013).

Holey landscapes

Holey landscapes were introduced by Gavrilets (1997) and can be considered as the current revolution in landscape modelling (Pigliucci and Kaplan, 2006). Following the early intuitions of Wright (1932), the development of Kauffman (1993) of a general theory of evolution and the extensions of Altenberg (1996), the approach of holey landscapes emphasizes—and aims to overcome—the limitations of fitness landscapes, particularly with regard to the modelling of speciation (Gavrilets, 2009) and possibly exaptation.

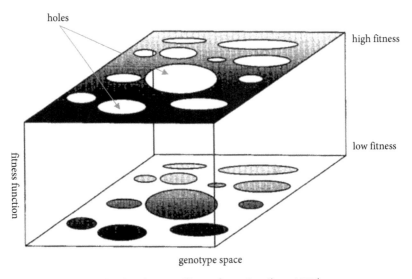

Figure 5.7 Gavrilets' holey landscapes (figure from Gavrilets, 1997)

As Figure 5.7 illustrates (see Gavrilets, 1997), holey landscapes have a qualitatively different type of structure because they consist of a surface of high and relatively flat fitness filled with holes of very low fitness rather than a rugged surface of peaks and valleys similar to that of classical fitness landscapes.

The main objective of classical fitness landscapes is to explain how adaptation happens under the influence of forces such as recombination, mutation, and selection (Gavrilets, 1997). In this line of work, much less emphasis has been placed on the problem of speciation. Moreover, when trying to address speciation, modelling builds on underlying 'shifting balance' assumptions (Wright, 1932); that is, a population has to cross a valley when shifting from one peak to another—where we assume that this shift subsumes a process of differentiation, thus leading to new species. The fundamental premise of the holey approach is the high dimensionality of spaces due to the astronomical number of possible genotypes. However, we cannot expect all genotypes 'to have different fitnesses—there should be a lot of redundancy in the genotype-to-fitness relationship, so that different genotypes must have similar fitnesses' (Gavrilets, 2009: p. 55). This explains a flatter surface (than that assumed by rugged landscapes) called 'neutral' surface, which is filled with holes of low fitness. In fact, there is an explicit link with the idea of 'neutral evolution', according to which there is a considerable number of mutations that have little or no effects on fitness values (Kimura, 1968).

How does speciation fit in? While adaptation can be seen as jumping from a hole up to the neutral surface, speciation can be seen as the path on the neutral surface leading 'to a genetic state separated from its initial state by a hole' (Gavrilets, 2009: p. 60). In other words, speciation is like walking and finding oneself on the other side of the hole. As we can see in the three-dimensional representation below (Gavrilets, 2009), there is clear analogy with speciation processes, such as those based on allopatric mechanisms, which occur when the two populations (p1 and p2) of the same species become isolated from each other (e.g. due to a geographic fracture that separates two lands); that is, the exchange of genetic information stops, and the two populations become two separated species owing to reproductive isolation (Mayr, 1954) (Figure 5.8).

The interesting aspect of holey landscapes is that they are fit for modelling different types of speciation beyond the allopatric case, thus helping us improve our understanding of the different cases, drivers, and dynamics of speciation (Gavrilets, 2009). In summary, the holey approach consists of modelling how the populations of evolving entities (such as biological entities or, in our case, technologies) fragment and thus cluster themselves on the different ridges of the neutral surface.

Moving to the technological setting, we identify a genotype with a technology that consists of a configuration of components expressed by a vector $\overline{X} = [1_1, 1_2, 1_3, \ldots]$, where $1_i = \{0,1\}$ for i=1, 2...N, and N is the number of

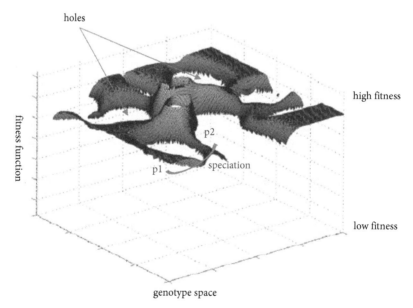

Figure 5.8 Gavrilets' holey landscapes: speciation dynamics (figure from Gavrilets, 2009)

components. Without any loss of generality, each technology is (again) represented with a string of zeros and ones. The key objective of holey landscapes is to simulate the genetic divergence between subpopulations (of technologies), which is the basis of speciation when a certain distance threshold is reached. A first fundamental requisite is defining the distance measure between subpopulations, which results (through averaging) from the distance between individual technologies given by the following:

$$\text{dist}_{\bar{X}_1\bar{X}_2} = \sum_{i=1}^{N} (1_{i,\bar{X}_1} - 1_{i,\bar{X}_2})^2,$$

where $\text{dist}_{\bar{X}_1\bar{X}_2}$ is the distance between technologies $\bar{X}_1$ and $\bar{X}_2$, $1_{i,\bar{X}_1}$ is the component/locus i of technology $\bar{X}_1$, $1_{i,\bar{X}_2}$ is the component/locus i of technology $\bar{X}_2$, and N is the number of components/loci of the technology (Gavrilets, 1999).

Therefore, the distance is the number of components/loci at which the two technologies differ among each other. A second requisite is specifying a threshold for the distance among individual technologies, which determines the fitness landscape according to the following formula:

$$f(\text{dist}_{\bar{X}_1\bar{X}_2}) = \begin{cases} 1 \text{ for } \text{dist}_{\bar{X}_1\bar{X}_2} \leq T \\ 0 \text{ for } \text{dist}_{\bar{X}_1\bar{X}_2} \geq T \end{cases}$$

where $f(\text{dist}_{\bar{X}_1\bar{X}_2})$ is the fitness of the pair $\bar{X}_1$ and $\bar{X}_2$ as a function of the distance between $\bar{X}_1$ and $\bar{X}_2$, respectively, and T is the threshold value (Gavrilets, 1999).

The idea is that when $\bar{X}_1$ and $\bar{X}_2$ are different at less than T components/loci, they have a fitness of one (high fitness, in the figures), that is, they are connected among each other by the neutral surface. Conversely, when $\bar{X}_1$ and $\bar{X}_2$ are different at more than T components/loci, they have a fitness of zero (low fitness, in the figures), that is, there is a hole between them. This creates a neutral surface filled with holes and thus a holey landscape. The basic setting of the simulation consists of initializing a population of strings, evolving the population through a process of mating that creates offspring, and modelling how the distance between subpopulations—and thus speciation, and the holey landscape itself—unfolds, in function of several parameters. This is, of course, a very simplified review; thus, we refer to Gavrilets (1999) for further details. However, what is important to stress is the ability of holey landscapes to model the dynamics of speciation (and related evolutionary phenomena), whereas the NK is more fit for modelling adaptive processes.

Beyond landscapes: towards a quantum formalism?

One important limitation of the NK modelling approach, in all its forms, is the difficulty of capturing the unboundedness (infinite dimensionality) of the functional space, modelling how new functions emerge as the technology interacts with a changing context, and, in general, dealing with 'potentiality' in evolutionary theory. A new possible approach that is less conservative because it fully departs from the landscape logic (and from biology itself) is based on quantum formalism. Quantum formalism is part of the generalization attempts of quantum theory outside physics and is based on the mathematical apparatus of infinite-dimensional Hilbert spaces and non-Bayesian probability (Busemeyer and Bruza, 2012). An example (and possible source of inspiration) is the quantum model proposed by Gabora et al. (2013) for exaptation, which has a high potentiality in terms of all the possible, infinite, functions of a technology and is highly contextual in terms of their process of activation. As stated by Gabora et al. (2013), a novel (quantum) logic is necessary to model the dynamics of evolving systems and phenomena such as exaptation, which 'presents a formidable challenge to efforts to describe biological phenomena using a classical...mathematical framework' (p. 1).

The key message of quantum theory is that a subatomic entity (such as an electron) behaves both as a particle and as a wave, and that the type of behaviour depends on whether the entity is subject to a measurement process or not (i.e. whether it is observed or not). When the entity is not observed, it behaves as a smeared path similar to a wave forming on a lake after a stone is thrown in. In such a state, the entity is in 'superposition' and is governed by Schrödinger's equation, which captures potentiality and assigns different probabilities of finding the entity at different possible positions. When the entity is subject to observation, this produces a 'collapse' of the wave out of the state of potentiality, that is, the entity is found at a given position. Overall, 'the transition from the "possible" to the "actual" [i.e. from superposition to collapse] is absolutely necessary here and cannot be omitted from the interpretation of quantum theory' (Heisenberg, 1958: p. 137). This is evident in the double-slit setting, which is the most important and replicated experiment of quantum theory (Kumar, 2008).

A key insight is that quantum theory is not only about the nature of the physical world. In fact, the formal apparatus of quantum theory has been applied in multiple fields outside physics. These applications are known as 'generalized quantum theory' or 'quantum-like frameworks' (Khrennikov, 2010). Examples can be found in finance, game theory, and semantic analysis, but also in management (Lord et al., 2015) and decision-making (Busemeyer and Bruza, 2012), among other fields. The common denominator of these approaches is the adoption of a particular mathematical formalism. This formalism is based on Hilbert spaces with multiple (and, possibly, infinite) dimensions that capture the multiple potentialities of the modelled entity, combined with the violation of the Bayesian probabilistic apparatus, which occurs when the entity is in a state of potentiality. Similar to Gabora et al. (2013), our setting of interest is technology (i.e. the modelled entity is a technology rather than a physical particle). Similar to previous approaches, the technology has multiple latent functions that, in quantum terms, can be seen as superpositions. The technology interacts with a context that, in quantum terms, can be seen as a measurement device (or an observer) that produces the collapse on a single function out of the superposition, thus enabling exaptation via a process of continual emergence.

More specifically, we define a technology as a configuration of components expressed by $\overline{X}$. The technology has a number of latent functions that is potentially infinite and is indicated by $\acute{f}$. We define a multidimensional Hilbert space as a set of basis vectors:

$$\left|f_1\right\rangle, \ \left|f_2\right\rangle, \left|f_3\right\rangle \ldots \left|f_f\right\rangle$$

which are orthogonal because they represent mutually exclusive events.

In our setting, basis vectors represent the elementary outcomes of functional activation such as 'the function of technology $\overline{X}$ is f_1', 'the function of technology $\overline{X}$ is f_2', and so on. A second element of the Hilbert space is the modelled entity, the technology itself, or a cognitive system perceiving the different affordances/functions of the technology, represented by a system vector $\left|\overline{X}\right\rangle$ inside the multidimensional space that is superposed among the possible functions. Therefore, basis vectors $\left|f_1\right\rangle, \ \left|f_2\right\rangle, \left|f_3\right\rangle \ldots \left|f_f\right\rangle$ 'represent the alternate elemental events and outcomes that can be obtained by a system' (Lord et al., 2015: p. 284), that is, *superpositions*. The system vector $\left|\overline{X}\right\rangle$ represents the system itself, which eventually *collapses*, under contextual influence, on one of the elementary outcomes. It is important to note that basis vectors represent elementary outcomes, although subspaces can be

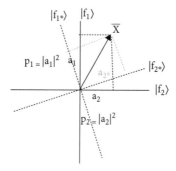

Figure 5.9 Modelling exaptation with the quantum formalism

used to represent more complex outcomes (e.g. a technology with more functions active at the same time and that, therefore, do not mutually exclude each other). A third important element is the relationship between basis vectors and the system vector, which is expressed by the following linear superposition:

$$|\overline{X}\rangle = \sum_j a_j |f_j\rangle,$$

where the amplitudes $a_1, a_2, a_3 \ldots a_j$ represent the contribution of each basis vector to the system vector and reflect the probability of each elementary outcome (function), which is given by $p_i = |a_i|^2$. A simple example of this approach is a technology $\overline{X}$ with two latent functions $|f_1\rangle$ and $|f_2\rangle$ (Figure 5.9).

As shown in Figure 5.9, the emergence of function 2 from the latent state can be modelled as the collapse of the system vector $\overline{X}$ on the basis vector $|f_2\rangle$, with the probability given by the square of the module of the amplitude a_2, which is the projection of $\overline{X}$ on the $|f_2\rangle$ axis. An interesting aspect of the quantum formalism is the possibility to model the dynamic of superposition and collapse with respect to different bases, such as the second base represented by the dotted lines. The second base, which is translated with respect to the first base, can be interpreted as a different cognitive system 'perceiving' the same technology (hence the context changes, where this implies a different base). Alternatively, we can see it as the same cognitive system perceiving the same technology but in a different situation (again, the context changes). As the figure indicates, when considered with respect to the second basis, the collapse of the system vector $\overline{X}$ on the dotted basis vector $|f_{2*}\rangle$ occurs with a higher amplitude a_{2*} with respect to a_2. In other words, the likelihood of function 2's activation changes depending on the context that we are considering. For instance, for a simple screwdriver $\overline{X}$ with functions f_1 'screw in a screw' and f_2 'kill a predator', assuming that the normal base refers to a 'house' context and the dotted base to a 'jungle' context, function f_2 is more likely when the context shifts from house to jungle.

Although speculative, the quantum formalism can be the basis for modelling and simulating some particular aspects of exaptation that cannot be easily addressed with landscape methods, particularly the latent potentiality of a technology in functional spaces that are intrinsically infinite-dimensional and the role of contexts in activating new functions, which the quantum formalism sees as collapses out of the superposition state. It is important to emphasize here the cognitive side of exaptation, which has its basis in the perception of multiple functions, uses, and affordances of technologies and objects (Felin et al., 2016). Instead of simply focusing on a technology as the superposed quantum-like entity, a possible approach is to model directly the cognitive and perceptual aspects. In this regard, the literature on quantum cognition has found only very few applications in studying technological evolution (see Gabora et al., 2013). Similar to other extensions of the quantum formalism, quantum cognition is also based on the apparatus of Hilbert spaces and non-Bayesian probability.[3] Overall, the quantum formalism could represent an additional approach for simulating exaptation and other evolutionary phenomena. However, some important limitations remain, such as the impossibility to pre-state the basis vectors of the Hilbert space or the set of activating contexts and the impossibility to define their probabilities. As Felin et al. (2014) emphasized, evolution is not governed by classical laws. Although the quantum approach marks a significant departure from classical assumptions, some aspects remain intrinsically difficult to capture.

History-friendly modelling

The evolutionary literature adopting a computational approach is quite variegated, with different models looking at different levels of analysis and addressing different questions. A systematic review goes beyond the scope of this chapter. Thus, we focused only on a specific family of computational models that are particularly suitable for studying the new evolutionary theories discussed in the book. Accordingly, we discussed the family of fitness

---

[3] For further details on quantum cognition and quantum-like models, we refer to Bruza et al. (2015), Busemeyer and Bruza (2012), and Wang and Busemeyer (2013).

landscapes (Kauffman, 1993) that previous research has adopted at the micro-level to analyse several questions, such as the *generative* mechanisms responsible for the emergence of novelty via the adaptation of complex technologies. However, *once* novelty has emerged, these micro-level approaches are less appropriate for modelling *how* novelty translates into radical emergence or the evolution (including the shakeout) of an industry or sector. Therefore, a meso-level approach is necessary for a deeper understanding of these phenomena.

A well-established computational approach in evolutionary theory is the use of so-called 'history-friendly' models (Malerba et al., 1999; Malerba and Orsenigo, 2002; Malerba et al., 2008; Malerba et al., 2016; Engler et al., 2020). A key feature of the history-friendly approach to simulation is that the formal model used in the simulation is grounded in a verbal description and 'appreciative theory' of the historical details. The main objective of this approach is to 'capture the gist of the appreciative theory put forth by analysts of the history of an industry or a technology, and thus to enable its logical exploration' (Malerba et al., 1999: p. 5). As noted by Malerba et al. (2016), industrial evolution is extremely complex because it is characterized by 'persistent heterogeneity' in terms of entry/exit dynamics, life cycles, and trajectories, which in turn reflects the persistent variety of routines, practices, and ways of doing things observed at any particular point in time (Nelson and Winter, 1982). Owing to this persistent heterogeneity, history-friendly approaches aim to model the evolution of industries case by case rather than by extracting general patterns on a cross-industry basis. In particular, history-friendly approaches seek to isolate the key variables that may explain an industry's observed pattern, and then build an explanatory model. On the basis of this model, the next step consists of reconstructing the historical dynamic of the industry via simulations to test the model's ability to replicate the observed pattern and modelling what happens when some of the key variables are altered or removed. By using historical events and details to calibrate the simulation's parameters, history-friendly models provide an intuitive understanding of the realized historical narrative and a platform for generating theoretically meaningful alternative narratives. As such, history-friendly approaches are particularly useful for modelling, on an *ex post* basis, some of the complex dynamics reviewed in the previous chapters. A possible application that we see as potentially fruitful is the exaptive-based emergence of new dominant designs leading to industry upheaval or emergence on the basis of the processes analysed in Chapter 3. Similar to the other approaches proposed in this chapter, we leave these developments to future research.

References

Altenberg, L. 1996. B2.7.2 NK fitness landscapes. In Back, T., Fogel, D., and Michalewicz, Z. (eds.). *The handbook of evolutionary computation*. Oxford University Press.

Andriani, P. and Carignani, G. 2014. Modular exaptation: a missing link in the synthesis of artificial form. *Research Policy*, 43(9): 1608–20.

Baumann, O., Schmidt, J., and Stieglitz, N. 2019. Effective search in rugged performance landscapes: a review and outlook. *Journal of Management*, 45(1): 285–318.

Bruza, P.D., Wang, Z., and Busemeyer, J.R. 2015. Quantum cognition: a new theoretical approach to psychology. *Trends in Cognitive Sciences*, 19(7): 383–93.

Busemeyer, J.R. and Bruza, P.D. 2012. *Quantum models of cognition and decision*. Cambridge University Press.

Engler, D., Cattani, G., and Porac, J. 2020. Studying the incubation of a new product market through realized and alternative histories. *Strategy Science*, forthcoming.

Ethiraj, S.K. and Levinthal, D. 2004. Modularity and innovation in complex systems. *Management Science*, 50(2): 159–73.

Felin, T., Kauffman, S., Koppl, R., and Longo, G. 2014. Economic opportunity and evolution: beyond landscapes and bounded rationality. *Strategic Entrepreneurship Journal*, 8(4): 269–82.

Felin, T., Kauffman, S., Mastrogiorgio, A., and Mastrogiorgio, M. 2016. Factor markets, actors and affordances. *Industrial and Corporate Change*, 25(1): 133–47.

Fleming, L. and Sorenson, O. 2001. Technology as a complex adaptive system: evidence from patent data. *Research Policy*, 30(7): 1019–39.

Fontana, W. and Schuster, P. 1998. Shaping space: the possible and the attainable in RNA genotype-phenotype mapping. *Journal of Theoretical Biology*, 194(4): 491–515.

Frenken, K. 2006. *Innovation, evolution and complexity theory*. Edward Elgar.

Frenken, K. and Mendritzki, S. 2012. Optimal modularity: a demonstration of the evolutionary advantage of modular architectures. *Journal of Evolutionary Economics*, 22(5): 935–56.

Gabora, L., Scott, E.O., and Kauffman, S. 2013. A quantum model of exaptation: incorporating potentiality into evolutionary theory. *Progress in Biophysics and Molecular Biology*, 113(1): 108–16.

Ganco, M. 2017. NK model as a representation of innovative search. *Research Policy*, 46(10): 1783–800.

Gavetti, G. 2012. Toward a behavioral theory of strategy. *Organization Science*, 23(1): 267–85.

Gavetti, G. and Levinthal, D. 2000. Looking forward and looking backward: cognitive and experiential search. *Administrative Science Quarterly*, 45(1): 113–37.

Gavetti, G., Helfat, C.E., and Marengo, L. 2017. Searching, shaping, and the quest for superior performance. *Strategy Science*, 2(3): 194–209.

Gavrilets, S. 1997. Evolution and speciation on holey adaptive landscapes. *Trends in Ecology and Evolution*, 12(8): 307–12.

Gavrilets, S. 1999. A dynamical theory of speciation on holey landscapes. *The American Naturalist*, 154(1).

Gavrilets, S. 2009. High-dimensional fitness landscapes and speciation. In Pigliucci, M., and Müller, G.B. (eds.). *Evolution—the extended synthesis*. MIT Press.

Gould, S.J. and Lewontin, R.C. 1979. The spandrels of San Marco and the Panglossian paradigm: a critique of the adaptationist programme. *Proceedings of the Royal Society of London*.

Gould, S.J. and Vrba, E.S. 1982. Exaptation—a missing term in the science of form. *Paleobiology*, 8(1): 4–15.

Heisenberg, W. 1958. *Physics and philosophy*. Harper.

Kauffman, S. 1993. *The origins of order*. Oxford University Press.

Kauffman, S. 2000. *Investigations*. Oxford University Press.

Khrennikov, A.Y. 2010. *Ubiquitous quantum structure: from psychology to finance*. Springer.

Kimura, M. 1968. Evolutionary rate at the molecular level. *Nature*, 217: 624–6.

Kumar, M. 2008. *Quantum: Einstein, Bohr and the great debate about the nature of reality*. Icon Books Ltd.

Levinthal, D. A. 1997. Adaptation on rugged landscapes. *Management Science*, 43(7): 934–50.

Longo, G., Montevil, M., and Kauffman, S. 2012. No entailing laws, but enablement in the evolution of the biosphere. In *Proceedings of the Genetic and Evolutionary Computation Conference*.

Lord, R.G., Dinh, J.E., and Hoffman, E.L. 2015. A quantum approach to time and organizational change. *Academy of Management Review*, 40(2): 263–90.

Malerba, F., Nelson, R., Orsenigo, L., and Winter, S. 1999. 'History-friendly' models of industry evolution: the computer industry. *Industrial and Corporate Change*, 8(1): 3–40.

Malerba, F. and Orsenigo, L. 2002. Innovation and market structure in the dynamics of the pharmaceutical industry and biotechnology: towards a history friendly model. *Industrial and Corporate Change*, 11(4): 667–703.

Malerba, F., Nelson, R., Orsenigo, L., and Winter, S. 2008. Vertical integration and disintegration of computer firms: a history-friendly model of the co-evolution of the computer and semiconductor industries. *Industrial and Corporate Change*, 17(2): 197–231.

Malerba, F., Nelson, R.R., Orsenigo, L., and Winter, S.G. 2016. *Innovation and the evolution of industries: history friendly models*. Cambridge University Press.

Marengo, L. and Pasquali, C. 2012. How to get what you want when you do not know what you want: a model of incentives, organizational structure, and learning. *Organization Science*, 23(5): 1298–310.

Mayr, E. 1954. Geographic speciation in tropical echinoids. *International Journal of Organic Evolution*, 8(1): 1–18.

Nelson, R.R. and Winter, S.G. 1982. *An evolutionary theory of economic change.* Harvard University Press.

Pigliucci, M. and Kaplan, J. 2006. *Making sense of evolution: the conceptual foundations of evolutionary biology.* University of Chicago Press.

Rivkin, J.W. 2000. Imitation of complex strategies. *Management Science*, 46(6): 824–44.

Simon, H.A. 1955. A behavioral model of rational choice. *Quarterly Journal of Economics*, 69(1): 99–118.

Simon, H.A. 1962. The architecture of complexity. In *Proceedings of the American Philosophical Society.*

Stadler, B., Stadler, P.F., Wagner, G., and Fontana, W. 2001. The topology of the possible: formal spaces underlying patterns of evolutionary change. *Journal of Theoretical Biology*, 213(2): 241–74.

USPTO, 2012. *Handbook of classification.* Washington, DC.

Wagner, G.P. and Altenberg, L. 1996. Complex adaptations and the evolution of evolvability. *Evolution*, 50(3): 967–76.

Wang, Z. and Busemeyer, J. 2013. A quantum question order model supported by empirical tests of an a priori and precise prediction. *Topics in Cognitive Sciences*, 5(4): 689–710.

Wright, S. 1932. The roles of mutations, inbreeding, crossbreeding and selection in evolution. *Proceedings of the 11th International Congress of Genetics.*

Yayavaram, S. and Ahuja, G. 2008. Decomposability in knowledge structures and its impact on the usefulness of inventions and knowledge-base malleability. *Administrative Science Quarterly*, 53(2): 333–62.

6

From Trees to Networks

Technological Evolution from the Complexity Angle

Gino Cattani and Mariano Mastrogiorgio

Patent data in innovation research: beyond localness

In Chapter 5, we proposed new simulation approaches to model evolutionary phenomena such as exaptation. Some studies have already approached exaptation via simulation (Villani et al., 2007), whereas other studies have modelled related phenomena, such as the interplay of luck and foresight, by using fractal geometry (Winter et al., 2007). An alternative route is empirical. However, capturing a complex phenomenon such as exaptation is not easy, and a key challenge is to 'identify appropriate—and possibly widely shared—methodological approaches' (Andriani and Cattani, 2016: p. 127). One possibility is to conduct longitudinal case studies and analyse the micro-dynamics of technological evolution in depth (Cattani, 2006). Another possibility is to quantify the phenomenon via large-sample studies to give an answer to questions such as 'what percentage of innovations is due to exaptation?...Is the exaptation process more relevant in certain industries than in others?' (Andriani and Cattani, 2016: p. 128).

A defining characteristic of exaptation is the functional shift of an existing artefact (e.g. a technology, resource, or capability). The same artefact can be co-opted into a completely different function than the one for which it was originally selected. This new function corresponds to a new application domain that is unanticipated, unplanned, or unprestateable. An evolutionary theory on 'the emergence of novelty must explicitly account for what causes the "functional shift" of an existing artefact, i.e. the functional discontinuity that is central to the notion of exaptation' (Andriani and Cattani, 2016: p. 118). The first challenge is mapping the functions of a technology over time; that is, creating a longitudinal database of those functions. The second challenge is understanding whether the functional shift was indeed unanticipated. This

Gino Cattani and Mariano Mastrogiorgio, *From Trees to Networks: Technological Evolution from the Complexity Angle*
In: *New Developments in Evolutionary Innovation: Novelty Creation in a Serendipitous Economy.* Edited by: Gino Cattani and Mariano Mastrogiorgio, Oxford University Press (2021). © Gino Cattani and Mariano Mastrogiorgio.
DOI: 10.1093/oso/9780198837091.003.0006

is harder to establish because it requires one to determine what exactly the people (e.g. inventors) involved in the development of a new technology were thinking when certain decisions were made and when certain initiatives were undertaken. In showing how the invention of fibre optics for long-distance telecommunication applications at Corning was exaptive in nature, Cattani (2006) emphasizes the importance of having 'access to internal memos/documents dating back to the period when Corning first learned about the new investment opportunity, explored its feasibility, and decided to start the first laboratory experiments' (Cattani, 2006: p. 294). In case one cannot access original memos or documents, alternative approaches must be considered.

A first approach relies on the exploitation of pharmaceutical databases, such as DrugDex (see Andriani et al., 2017). However, the main shortcoming of this approach is that the results are context-specific, and it is difficult to generalize them to other industries. A second approach is to use patent data. Patent data span several industries, they have been widely employed in innovation research, and their richness seems to pose few limits to the modelling of evolutionary phenomena. As indicated by Andriani and Cattani (2016), one possibility is to measure exaptation by using patent citations to the focal patents coming from different technological classes as a proxy for what might correspond to possible functional shifts (see Mastrogiorgio and Gilsing, 2016). However, owing to the inherent difficulty of establishing a lack of intentionality in patent citations, patent data should be triangulated with other data sources that contain more fine-grained information, such as patent claims, patent file wrappers, scientific publications, or news articles. This will require expanding the toolbox with text mining and machine learning techniques. By means of these techniques, it is possible to detect newly emerging patterns in patent citations and determine whether they prefigure the functional shifts of existing technologies that were not foreseen in the original patent claims. A step in this direction is already underway in patent research (Nameroff et al., 2004).

Another possibility is to change the way patents are analysed. In essence, a patent is a legal document that protects a novel and non-obvious technology, with respect to the prior art upon which the technology builds. 'Building on prior art' means that patents cite each other, thus forming a vast, complex and evolving *network* of patent citations, as illustrated in Figure 6.1 (Mastrogiorgio, 2014).

Most of the current studies on innovation rely on patent-based measures that exploit information within the citation network only at the local level. One example are the standard measures of forward (and backward) citations,

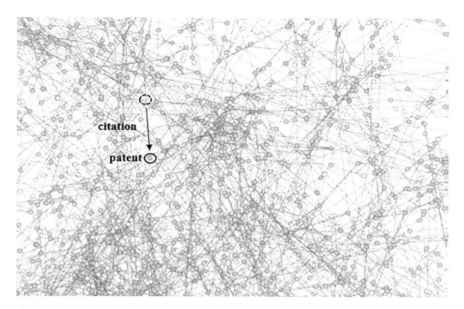

Figure 6.1 Patent data as complex citation networks

which only consider the direct citations received (or made) by a given patent. In other words, standard measures take a given 'node' in the citation network and only consider what is in its immediate vicinity. However, this approach ignores that patents are cited by other patents, which in turn are cited by other patents, and so on. Standard measures do not incorporate the information contained in the wider network of direct *and* indirect citations. However, from an evolutionary point of view, it is more appropriate to approach patent citation networks from a global, rather than local, perspective. As noted in a previous chapter, an important insight of a Woesian perspective is that evolution reveals a reticulate (network) structure owing to the coexistence of horizontal transfer and vertical inheritance of functional modules (Carignani et al., 2019). Accordingly, we must see technological evolution as the complex unfolding of multiple trajectories, with jumps taking place back and forth along a given trajectory and between trajectories.

It is interesting to note that, thanks to the advances in research on complex graphs (Newman, 2010; Solé et al., 2013), a radical change in patent analysis seems to be underway in evolutionary literature, where a network-oriented stream is slowly emerging (Barberá Tomás et al., 2011; Fontana et al., 2009; Martinelli, 2012; Martinelli and Nomaler, 2014; Mina et al., 2007; Stuart and Podolny, 1996; von Wartburg et al., 2005). Despite their potential, network approaches have not yet received enough attention and (to our knowledge) have not been used to model punctuated equilibrium, speciation, and technological exaptation. The aim of this chapter is to propose some very general ideas, with the hope of inspiring future empirical research.

Network approaches to technological evolution

As argued in the previous section and in Chapter 2, patent data can be examined in network terms where nodes and links correspond, respectively, to patents and citations. From a network perspective, standard measures assume a very specific meaning. For instance, the commonly used measure of 'forward citations' corresponds to an index of 'in-degree network centrality' that measures the local importance of a node in a network. As Fontana et al. (2009) argued, although the use of local measures is certainly intuitive, 'one may also suggest that this exercise ought to be integrated with a study of the whole "connectivity structure" of the network in question' (p. 7). As discussed above, the network approach consists of taking into account not only direct citations but also indirect citations (i.e. the larger network structure). Although indirect citations may be less relevant in social networks, they are certainly important in terms of their informative content in technological networks. In fact, the simple idea of technological trajectory is based on the assumption that we are considering some sort of lineage of subsequent technologies that build on each other. Indirect citations allow the identification of trajectories and their degree of change and evolution over time because the whole network grows owing to the appearance of new patents. These evolving trajectories can be used to illustrate several things, such as the process of lineage development via vertical transfer (adaptation) or, more importantly, the emergence of new lineages via the horizontal transfer of modules and reactivation of old lineages (Carignani et al., 2019). By using a network lens, technological evolution can be modelled as a process littered with vertical and horizontal shifts of modules across different application domains that resurrect extinct technologies, reactivate technological dead ends, or repurpose old technologies for new uses and functions via *exaptation*. As indicated by Kelly (2010) and consistent with the evolution of cornets (Tëmkin and Eldredge, 2007) and a Woesian model of evolution (Carignani et al., 2019), technological evolution looks like a 'spreading, recursive network of pathways that often double back to dead ends' (p. 50).

Drawing from 'connectivity analysis' (Barberá Tomás et al., 2011; Fontana et al., 2009; Martinelli, 2012; Martinelli and Nomaler, 2014; Mina et al., 2007; Stuart and Podolny, 1996; von Wartburg et al., 2005), we outline some ideas for modelling the evolutionary phenomena at the core of this book. To this

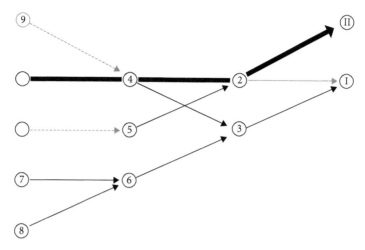

Figure 6.2 Identifying paths in a complex citation network with 'connectivity analysis'

end, we consider the stylized patent citation network in the figure. The first property is directedness. A citation among two patents has a direction (represented by a unidirectional arrow) that expresses a link to 'prior art' between the two patents (i.e. one of the two patents—the citing one—builds on the prior art on which the other patent is based). This means that technological knowledge flows from the cited to the citing patent. As we can see in Figure 6.2, patent 2 cites patents 4 and 5 (i.e. technological knowledge flows from patents 4 and 5 to patent 2).

For our purposes, citations must be seen as pure technical links among patents; therefore, citing a patent just indicates that 'the knowledge in the latter patent was in some way useful for developing the new knowledge described in the citing patent' (Verspagen, 2007: p. 6). A second property of a patent citation network is its binary nature (i.e. it has a 1/0 nature) depending on the presence/absence of a citation between two patents. A third property is the absence of cycles because patents can only cite those patents that were granted previously. On the basis of these properties, three types of patents can be identified in a patent citation network: startpoints, endpoints, and intermediates (Martinelli, 2012). Startpoints (e.g. 7, 8, and 9) identify where the paths start; endpoints (e.g. I and II) identify where the paths end; intermediates (i.e. 2, 3, 4, 5, and 6) identify where the paths pass through.

There is a class of algorithms that can be used to identify all paths in a patent citation network. Although the number of patents and citations in a patent citation network can be in the order of millions, these algorithms are highly efficient because they can quickly identify all the paths and conduct several types of analyses. An example is the so-called 'Search Path Count'

(SPC) algorithm. SPC is easily implementable in Pajek software, is based on a breadth-first-search algorithm, and consists of a topological sorting of the patent citation network and calculation of the weight for *each* citation in the patent citation network (De Nooy et al., 2018). The weight of a citation is a function of the number of network paths, as defined above, that pass through it: a higher number corresponds to a higher weight. For a patent, SPC also counts how many times the patent lies on all the paths between all the patents of the citation network under consideration. Therefore, SPC transforms a binary network into a weighted network, where the weights capture the importance of citations and patents in a technological path or trajectory. On the basis of the thickness of the weights, it is possible to extract technological paths, such as the thick grey line in the previous figure, and map them as they evolve over time due to network growth via the addition of new patents. This is the idea at the core of the so-called 'main path' analysis, which has been recently applied to several industries, such as telecommunications (Martinelli, 2012) and medical devices (Barberá Tomás et al., 2011) among others. The shortcoming of this approach is the extraction of just one single path (or a few) out of the network. This explains why the approach has been mainly used for small patent networks that typically belong to the same technological class or industry.

Main paths, islands, and the genetic approach

There are three possibilities to model exaptation, speciation dynamics, and horizontal transfer in network terms: 'main path' analysis, 'islands' analysis, and the 'genetic approach'. Figure 6.3 illustrates how a patent citation network evolves over time. This specific network is a subset of the entire US patent system because it contains only patents (and relative citations)

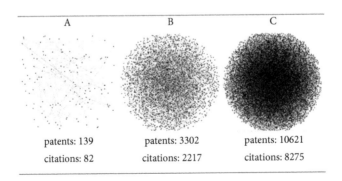

Figure 6.3 A growing complex citation network

assigned to technological classes in the biotech and pharmaceutical industry (see Mastrogiorgio, 2014). Panel A includes patents granted in 1975, whereas panels B and C *also* include patents granted in 1976 and 1977 (and their relative citations), respectively. As we can see, the network quickly grows in size and becomes increasingly complex even if it consists only of a small subset of the US patent system.

Moreover, as the network grows, it exhibits the features of complex systems, with citation weights following power-law statistical distributions, which are typically associated with the emergence of a large cluster of connected patents (see Mastrogiorgio, 2014). Networks with these features are known as 'scale-free' networks (Newman, 2010). Interestingly, power-law distributions have also been observed in the case of exaptation (Andriani et al., 2017). This suggests that the analysis of patent citation networks can complement in-depth case-based studies in tracing evolutionary phenomena such as exaptation, speciation, or Woesian dynamics.

The first approach is the 'main path' analysis (Martinelli, 2012) (see Figure 6.4), in which a network of patents is seen as a system of channels through which technological knowledge flows through citations and patents. The citations and patents through which most of the knowledge flows (as expressed in high citation weights) may form one or several large channels, which are known as 'main paths' in the connectivity analysis literature (Martinelli, 2012: p. 135) and correspond to what others define as technological trajectories (Dosi, 1982). Technological advances may take the form of continual accumulation along a trajectory or a discontinuity that radically reshapes an existing trajectory and may result in the emergence of a new technological 'paradigm' (Dosi, 1982). These discontinuities are often represented by patents that disappear from the main path (as the overall network

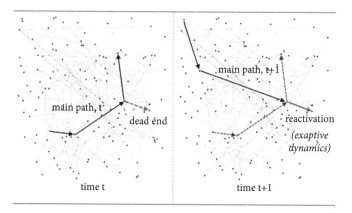

Figure 6.4 The main path approach

grows in size) and become 'dead ends' (Barberá Tomás et al., 2011: p. 475). However, they may reappear on the same path or even *new* paths in *new* domains via a process of reactivation for novel functions and uses.

Corning's invention of Gorilla Glass, which is currently used as cover glass for portable electronic devices such as mobile phones, portable media players, and television screens, is an apt illustration of this process. In the early 1960s, Corning embarked on what was then called 'Project Muscle' in an effort to 'pursue and refine a set of techniques for strengthening glass' (Graham and Shuldiner, 2001: p. 260). At the time, three different glass strengthening approaches were known: thermal strengthening (i.e. tempering), layering of glasses with different coefficients of thermal expansion and ion exchange, or post-forming chemical treatment. Corning focused on improving the latter two approaches by inventing (and patenting) a strengthened glass called 'Chemcor'. Initially, no clear application for Chemcor was identified. Although Corning looked for a variety of different uses for Chemcor, it pursued two applications more aggressively in the 1960s. First, Corning tried to develop chemically strengthened lenses for safety eyewear. Compared with existing tempered eyewear, the use of chemically strengthened lenses bore the promise of stronger and lighter eyewear. However, in addition to cost considerations, scratching chemically tempered lenses could cause them to explode, thereby proving hazardous. Considering that lens manufacturers refused to use Chemcor, Corning decided to abandon the idea of using Chemcor in the safety eyewear market.

Chemcor then seemed like a good fit for car windscreens. Chemically strengthened windscreens were used on Javelins, which were made by American Motors, but the high costs discouraged most car manufacturers— also considering that other glassmakers had significantly improved the laminated glass that car manufacturers had been using since the 1930s. As a result, after pitches to Ford Motors and other carmakers failed, Corning shut down Project Muscle and Chemcor, which was known internally as 0317. This project was shelved in September 1971 until a more practical application could be found. The opportunity to resurrect Chemcor emerged in 2005 before Apple had even entered the picture. Following Motorola's release of the Razr V3, a flip phone that featured a glass screen instead of the typical high-impact plastic, Corning examined whether a 0317-like glass could be revived and applied to devices such as cell phones and watches. The old Chemcor samples were as thick as 4 mm, but Corning thought they could be made thinner. After some market research, executives believed that the company could even make a little money out of this specialty glass. The project was codenamed Gorilla Glass.

In February 2007, Steve Jobs asked Corning CEO Wendell Weeks if Corning could make 1.3 mm-thin, chemically strengthened glass in six months. This type of glass had never been created, much less manufactured before. By the end of March, Corning was closing in on its formula, but it also needed to manufacture it. To meet Apple's deadline, Corning decided to adapt and troubleshoot a process the company was already using that was capable of producing massive quantities of thin, pristine glass in a matter of weeks. To this end, the fusion draw process, which Corning invented in 1959 and developed in the 1960s, appeared as the only viable solution. Resorting to its fusion-capable factory in Harrodsburg (Kentucky), Corning started production in May 2007. The first patent for a glass to be used as cover plate for mobile electronic devices was filed by Corning on 31 July 2007, and this patent was granted on February 23, 2010 (US patent 7,666,511). By using main path analysis, we could trace out the technological roots of this patent and show how one of the key technological antecedents was Corning's patent 3,524,737, which was granted to Corning on 18 August 1970, for its invention of Chemcor.

In general, main path analysis may prove useful for modelling exaptation and other evolutionary phenomena, such as the horizontal transfer of 'functional modules' (Carignani et al., 2019). To this end, it should be extended to a multi-domain setting (e.g. patents assigned to multiple technological classes) rather than being applied to a single domain as extant research tends to do. The analysis could also be used to shed light on the interdependencies between horizontal transfer and technological paradigm shifts.

A second approach is the 'islands' analysis (see Figure 6.5), which consists of splitting a network into subnetworks called islands. An island is a

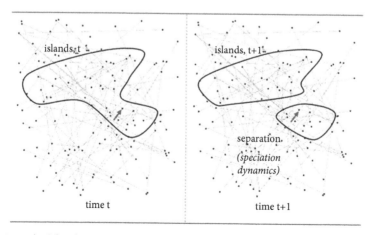

Figure 6.5 The island approach

subnetwork of patents connected through citations that have a higher weight than the citations among patents *outside* the island. By weights, we mean the citation weights defined above or weights of a slightly different nature; therefore, the island is a cluster with high connectivity (Batagelj et al., 2006). An island looks like a local peak whose height is a function of the weights' values. The entire network can be seen as a landscape that *evolves* and changes as it grows in size with the addition of new patents. The islands approach could be particularly useful for modelling evolutionary dynamics such as technological speciation in changing landscapes. As discussed earlier, speciation is induced by the macro context via geological (or similar) shocks (e.g. a fracture splits a peninsula and turns it into two islands) (Gould, 2007). In our setting, islands clearly have a technological rather than a geological nature, and the objective is to capture cases of *technological* speciation, such as when a patent (or a group of patents) first appears in an island and then, as the whole network evolves, eventually becomes part of a different island. This dynamic can be caused by several underlying processes, such as the deployment of a technology or module to a new domain where the selection criteria and resources of this domain, in turn, may foster the emergence of a new lineage (Levinthal, 1998). Although the approach seems promising for modelling certain aspects of speciation dynamics, it must be integrated with qualitative and case-based analyses (Cattani, 2006) because the underlying processes are inherently complex and nuanced and cannot be inferred from simply relying on patent data. Similar arguments apply to main path analysis.

A third approach is the 'genetic approach' to knowledge persistence developed by Martinelli and Nomaler (2014). This approach could be particularly useful for studying Woesian dynamics because patents can be used to trace the transfer of functional modules. As discussed in a previous chapter, the Woesian model assumes that the choice of the artefact as the evolutionary unit of analysis (the correspondent of a biological organism) is not always appropriate because the artefact is made up of separable functional modules. The horizontal transfer of a functional module can trigger radical innovation, as illustrated by the inception of the turbojet revolution (Carignani et al., 2019). Horizontal transfer is the first stage of a multistage process (i.e. the acquisition phase) when the genetic material is transferred from a lineage to create new ones; the transferred material is then subject to the forces of retention, selection, fixation, and amelioration (Carignani et al., 2019). The Woesian model illustrates the coexistence of horizontal and vertical forces, through which modules—and technological knowledge, broadly speaking— spread and persist within the larger technological system. The 'genetic

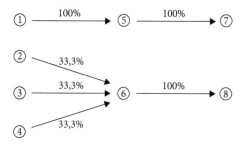

Figure 6.6 The genetic approach (figure adapted from Martinalli and Nomaler, 2014)

approach' (Martinelli and Nomaler, 2014) is a method that was specifically designed for studying how technological knowledge spreads and persists in large patent networks. The method is also part of the 'connectivity analysis' literature (Barberá Tomás et al., 2011; Fontana et al., 2009; Martinelli, 2012; Mina et al., 2007; Stuart and Podolny, 1996; von Wartburg et al., 2005), but its main objective is to develop a *patent-level* indicator of technological relevance. The genetic approach draws from population genetics and Mendelian gene inheritance (Cavalli-Sforza et al., 1994). As Martinelli and Nomaler (2014) argued, although population geneticists 'trace our (geographical) origins by looking at genetic mutation in today's population', the genetic approach decomposes 'the technological content of today's patents into the technological contribution of previous ones' (p. 624).

The genetic approach is illustrated in Figure 6.6 (adapted from Martinelli and Nomaler, 2014), which reproduces a very simple patent citation network composed of four startpoints (1, 2, 3, and 4), two intermediates (5 and 6), and two endpoints (7 and 8). Patent 5 is the only one to cite patent 1, and patent 7 is the only one to cite patent 5 (technological knowledge flows in the opposite direction, as indicated by the arrows). The technological knowledge embodied in patent 5 comes entirely from patent 1, and the technological knowledge embodied in patent 7 comes entirely from patent 5 and, by implication, from patent 1. This means that technological knowledge *persists* in the system. By contrast, patent 6 cites patents 2, 3, and 4, which implies that the technological knowledge embodied in patent 6 comes one-third from patent 2, one-third from patent 3, and one-third from patent 4. Patent 8 cites patent 6, which implies that the technological knowledge embodied in patent 8 comes entirely from patent 6 and, by implication, one-third from patents 2, 3, and 4, respectively.

Overall, patent 7 is an invention that builds on prior art that persists more in the patent system (because it is the only source) compared to the case of patent 8, which, on the contrary, builds on prior art that originates from different sources and tends to persists less. According to the genetic approach, the intersection of lineages is part of the underlying (and widespread) process of cumulative recombination of inherited knowledge into new artefacts, during which 'knowledge is recombined and, by definition, is transformed into something different and therefore new' (Martinelli and Nomaler, 2014: p. 628). The genetic approach is a multistep method that assigns a persistence index to each patent in a network. The approach is new and could require adjustments. However, it could be a starting point for describing Woesian dynamics in technology by using large sample data to measure the intensity of horizontal and vertical transfer in a patent citation network, in terms of distributional properties of patent-level persistence indexes, and of their temporal dynamic, as the network grows in size via the appearance of new patents.

Summing up, future research may explore the applicability of the previous approaches—main path, islands, genetic approach—to the study of technological exaptation, speciation dynamics, and horizontal transfer of functional modules. To this end, 'connectivity analysis' looks promising because technological evolution exhibits a networked structure. Despite their potential, connectivity approaches have not yet received significant attention in mainstream innovation research. As Wartburg et al. (2005) argued, 'the use of patents and patent statistics as indicators of technological progress stands for both a long tradition *and* a controversial discussion about the value of patents as indicators of technological progress' (p. 1591, emphasis added). In particular, the single-stage or local approach to patent citations seems to be inadequate for revealing more complex patterns in technological evolution and should be integrated with a multistage, network-based approach to patent data.

Networks, economic complexity, and disequilibrium

Patent networks can be used to shed light on some key issues at the centre of the book, such as economic disequilibrium via unprestateable evolution driven by complex networks. As mentioned at the beginning of the book, it is not possible to pre-state all the possible functions of an artefact (e.g. a technology) resulting from its interaction with the changing contexts of use (Felin et al., 2016). As Koppl et al. (2015) argued, the continual (and unprestateable) emergence of new functions for existing artefacts is a function of 'cambiodiversity', which refers to the increasing size, heterogeneity, and complexity of our universe of material objects. For instance, it is the appearance of cans that gave rise to the new functions of a screwdriver (e.g. 'opening the can'). Greater cambiodiversity drives functional expansion, which in turn is a source of disequilibrium (Koppl et al., 2015) due to inherent unprestateability (Longo et al., 2012):

$$\text{Cambiodiversity} \rightarrow \text{functional expansion} \rightarrow \text{disequilibrium}$$

Therefore, we should expect disequilibrium to originate from an increasingly complex and *networked* technosphere, as illustrated by the evolution of patent citation networks.

The patent network approach can bring new insights to the emerging research on complexity economics, whose main contribution to the evolutionary tradition is to see disequilibrium emerge from the underlying complex structure of the economy, of which 'networks are an essential ingredient' (Beinhocker, 2007: p. 141). Some studies in complexity economics are indeed studying how the complexity of a country's economy, inferred from the 'product space' (i.e. the network of countries to which the country exports and from which it imports) affects economic variables, such as growth (Hidalgo et al., 2007). Hidalgo (2015) underlined how economic wealth resides in the growth of a complex order and, in particular, in the information incorporated in the product space and technological space that connects technologies together. In fact, patent networks have also started to become part of these research efforts (Morrison et al., 2017) but not yet from the neo-evolutionary lens proposed here.

A key insight of the theoretical biologist Stuart Kauffman is the idea that life itself started from chemical networks: when these networks reached a certain threshold of connectedness, the emergence of new reactions was prompted (Kauffman, 1993). An interesting but often-overlooked feature of networks is the intrinsic novelty potential embedded in them as they grow in size and degree of connectedness. A network is made up of nodes and links between them. When the network grows and the number of connections exceeds the number of nodes, it acquires the typical characteristics that underlie different forms of complex organization: the emergence of giant clusters and statistical distributions of power laws, which can also be found in the patent system (Mastrogiorgio, 2014). The novelty potential embedded in these complex networks is clearer when we observe them from a Boolean perspective (Beinhocker, 2007). In a Boolean network, a node can be in one of two states (zero or one) and be activated (i.e. it becomes one) as a function of predefined rules that typically involve adjacent nodes. For example, the focal node x becomes one if both nodes y *and* z are equal to one; otherwise, it remains inactive. This is the so-called AND rule that, together with other basic rules like OR, NOT, and NAND, is at the basis of the Boolean logic in different forms of computation. Therefore, from a Boolean perspective, complex networks can be seen not only as repositories of information but also as 'computational engines' that generate novelty. In this regard, a very simple Boolean network with only 100 nodes has such an extremely large number of possible configurations that it would take the world's fastest computer almost 600 million years to explore all of them (Beinhocker, 2007). Therefore, there is significant potential for novelty even in a very simple network. We believe that the evolutionary mechanisms examined in this book, as well as the empirical approaches that have been proposed to study them, could enhance our understanding of *how* this novelty emerges from the adjacent space of unexplored possibilities (Kauffman, 2000).

References

Andriani, P. and Cattani, G. 2016. Exaptation as a source of creativity, innovation, and diversity in evolutionary sciences: introduction to the special section. *Industrial and Corporate Change*, 25(1): 115–31.

Andriani, P., Ali, A., and Mastrogiorgio, M. 2017. Measuring exaptation and its impact on innovation, search and problem-solving. *Organization Science*, 28(2): 320–38.

Barberá Tomás, D., Jiménez Sáez, F., and Castelló, I. 2011. Mapping the importance of the real world: the validity of connectivity analysis of patent citation networks. *Research Policy*, 40(3): 473–86.

Batagelj, V., Kejžar, N., Černe, S., and Zaveršnik, M. 2006. Analyzing the structure of U.S. patents network. In Batagelj, V., Bock, H., Ferligoj, A., and Žiberna, A. (eds.). *Data science and classification*. Springer.

Beinhocker, E.D. 2007. *The origins of wealth: evolution, complexity, and the radical remaking of economics*. Harvard Business Review Press.

Carignani, G., Cattani, G., and Zaina, G. 2019. Evolutionary chimeras: a Woesian perspective of radical innovation. *Industrial and Corporate Change*, 28(3): 511–28.

Cattani, G. 2006. Technological preadaptation, speciation and emergence of new technologies: how Corning invented and developed fiber optics. *Industrial and Corporate Change*, 15(2): 285–318.

Cavalli-Sforza, L., Menozzi, P., and Piazza A. 1994. *The history and geography of human genes*. Princeton University Press.

De Nooy, W., Mrvar, A., and Batagelj, V. 2018. *Exploratory social network analysis with Pajek*. Cambridge University Press.

Dosi, G. 1982. Technological paradigms and technological trajectories: a suggested interpretation of the determinants and directions of technical change. *Research Policy*, 11(3): 147–62.

Felin, T., Kauffman, S., Mastrogiorgio, A., and Mastrogiorgio, M. 2016. Factor markets, actors and affordances. *Industrial and Corporate Change*, 25(1): 133–47.

Fontana, R., Nuvolari, A., and Verspagen, B. 2009. Mapping technological trajectories as patent citation networks. An application to data communication standards. *Economics of Innovation and New Technology*, 18(4): 311–36.

Giuri, P., Mariani, M., Brusoni, S., Crespi, G., Francoz, D., Gambardella, A., Garcia-Fontes, W., Geuna, A., Gonzales, R., Harhoff, D., Hoisl, K., Lebas, C., Luzzi, A., Magazzini, L., Nesta, L., Nomaler, O., Palomeras, N., Patel, P., Romanelli, M., and B.Verspagen 2007. Inventor and invention processes in Europe. Results from the PatVal-EU survey. *Research Policy*, 36(8): 1107–27.

Gould, S.J. 2007. *Punctuated equilibrium*. Belknap Press.

Graham, M. and Shuldiner, A. 2001. Corning and the military: Innovation in an era of permanent mobilization. In *Corning and the craft of innovation*. Oxford University Press.

Hidalgo, C. 2015. *Why information grows. The evolution of order, from atoms to economies*. Basic Books.

Hidalgo, C.A., Klinger, B., Barabasi, A.L., and Hausmann, R. 2007. The product space conditions the development of nations. *Science*, 317: 482–7.

Kauffman, S. 1993. *The origins of order*. Oxford University Press.

Kauffman, S.A. 2000. *Investigations*. Oxford University Press.

Kelly, K. 2010. *What technology wants*. Viking Press.

Koppl, R., Kauffman, S., Felin, T., and Longo, G. 2015. Economics for a creative world. *Journal of Institutional Economics*, 11(1): 1–31.

Levinthal, D.A. 1998. The slow pace of rapid technological change: gradualism and punctuation in technological change. *Industrial and Corporate Change*, 7(2): 217–47.

Longo, G., Montevil, M., and Kauffman, S. 2012. No entailing laws, but enablement in the evolution of the biosphere. In *Proceedings of the Genetic and Evolutionary Computation Conference*.

Martinelli, A. 2012. An emerging paradigm or just another trajectory? Understanding the nature of technological changes using engineering heuristics in the telecommunications switching industry. *Research Policy*, 41(2): 414–29.

Martinelli, A. and Nomaler, Ö. 2014. Measuring knowledge persistence: a genetic approach to patent citation networks. *Journal of Evolutionary Economics*, 24(3): 623–52.

Mastrogiorgio, M. 2014. *New insights on technological evolution*. Unpublished PhD dissertation.

Mastrogiorgio, M. and Gilsing, V. 2016. Innovation through exaptation and its determinants: the role of technological complexity, analogy making and patent scope. *Research Policy*, 45(7): 1419–35.

Mina, A., Ramlogan, R., Tampubolon, G., and Metcalfe, J.S. 2007. Mapping evolutionary trajectories: applications to the growth and transformation of medical knowledge. *Research Policy*, 41(2): 414–29.

Morrison, G., Buldyrev, S.V., Imbruno, M., Alonso Doria Arrieta, O., Rungi, A., Riccaboni, M., and Pammolli, F. 2017. *Nature Scientific Reports*, article 15332.

Nameroff, T.J., Garant, R.J., and Albert, M.B. 2004. Adoption of green chemistry: an analysis based on U.S. patents. *Research Policy*, 33(6–7): 959–74.

Newman, M. 2010. *Networks*. Oxford University Press.

Solé, R.V., Valverde, S., Rosas Casals, M., Kauffman, S.A., Farmer, D., and Eldredge, N. 2013. The evolutionary ecology of technological innovations. *Complexity*, 18(4): 15–27.

Stuart, T.E. and Podolny, J.M. 1996. Local search and the evolution of technological capabilities. *Strategic Management Journal*, 17(S1): 21–38.

Tëmkin, I. and Eldredge, N. 2007. Phylogenetics and material cultural evolution. *Current Anthropology*, 48(1): 146–53.

Verspagen, B. 2007. Mapping technological trajectories as patent citation networks: a study on the history of fuel cell research. *Advances in Complex Systems*, 10(1): 93–115.

Villani, M., Bonacini, S., Ferrari, D., Serra, R., and Lane, D. 2007. An agent-based model of exaptive processes. *European Management Review*, 4(3): 141–51.

von Wartburg, I., Teichert, T., and Rost, K. 2005. Inventive progress measured by multi-stage patent citation analysis. *Research Policy*, 34(10): 1591–607.

Winter, S.G., Cattani, G., and Dorsch, A. 2007. The value of moderate obsession: insights from a new model of organizational search. *Organization Science*, 18(3): 403–19.

7

The Search Function and Evolutionary Novelty

Teppo Felin and Stuart Kauffman

Introduction

Search is a pervasive feature of biological and economic systems. Animals forage for food and economic actors search for value or opportunities. Search is a central component of many aspects of organism behaviour and evolution, including problem-solving, information processing, learning, and innovation. In an important sense, 'search is a ubiquitous property of life' (Hills et al., 2015: p. 46).

But search is often problematic and hard. Environments 'teem' with potential things of which organisms—humans included—might become aware. This includes varied things like stimuli or cues, objects, or sources of food. The teeming nature of environments means that environments cannot fully be represented, exhausted, or accounted for—making search difficult. The outcomes of search can be precarious given environmental uncertainty and ambiguity. Searching through environments is often highly resource-intensive, as well as cognitively and computationally taxing.

In this chapter, we address this hard problem of search. We specifically discuss the role of question-answer probing in simplifying and enabling search. We argue that a generalized form of question-answer probing provides a key mechanism for explaining not only mundane forms of search, but also for explaining the emergence of novelty. Organisms use search images and functional search to simplify this process by directing their awareness towards potential solutions. This form of probing essentially reduces the search space, but it counterintuitively also expands the set of possibilities. Instead of focusing on environmental structure, computation, information processing, and the nature of stimuli or cues—as is done in existing work (e.g. Anderson, 2013; Kahneman, 2003; Gershman et al., 2015; Gigerenzer and Gaissmaier, 2011; Oaksford and Chater, 2007)—we focus on

Teppo Felin and Stuart Kauffman, *The Search Function and Evolutionary Novelty* In: *New Developments in Evolutionary Innovation: Novelty Creation in a Serendipitous Economy*. Edited by: Gino Cattani and Mariano Mastrogiorgio, Oxford University Press (2021). © Teppo Felin and Stuart Kauffman. DOI: 10.1093/oso/9780198837091.003.0007 the nature of organisms and their directed queries. We build on insights from biology and perception science, and discuss the role of organism probing in uncovering and realizing new functions and possibilities in environments. Organism-specific questions provide a proximate and generative mechanism that does not rely on computation, information processing, or deterministic or reductionist forms of explanation. This form of search essentially makes the adjacent possible salient, by drawing out and revealing new functional uses and unveiling novelty both in biological and economic environments.

Passive environments and organisms in economics and biology

Evolutionary biology has been highly influential within the domain of economics, as well as in the broader social sciences (Alchian, 1950; Aldrich et al., 2008; Nelson and Winter, 2002). Environmental selection is seen as the unifying master mechanism for explaining competition and survival at the level of firms and industries. As argued by Winter (1987) many decades ago, 'natural selection and evolution should not be viewed as concepts developed for the specific purposes of biology and possibly appropriable for the specific purposes of economics, but rather as elements of the framework of a new conceptual structure that biology, economics and other social sciences can comfortably share' (p. 617). Evolutionary arguments are said to provide universal, organism-independent (rather than organism or species-specific) and ultimate (rather than proximate) conceptions for understanding biological and economic evolution (Hodgson and Knudsen, 2010; Nelson, 2006).

The overall emphasis in both evolutionary biology and evolutionary economics has been on environmental selection and long-run evolution (cf. Mayr, 1982; Polanyi, 1968; Nelson and Winter, 2002). The evolution of economic entities has focused on passive and macro mechanisms (variation-selection-retention), at the expense of more active, proximate, and organism-specific ones (cf. Felin et al., 2014; Kauffman, 2019). Central issues about organism nature and the emergence of novelty are often sidelined, given the emphasis on population-level dynamics. This argument has also been made by others across the biological and physical sciences. For example, the biologist Patrick Bateson (2017) notes that 'the picture of the external hand of natural selection doing all the work is so compelling that it is easy to regard organisms as if they were entirely passive in the evolutionary process' (p. 105; also see Noble and Noble, 2017). In his book *What is Life?*, Erwin Schrödinger (1944) points out that 'popular expositions of Darwin's theory are apt to lead to a gloomy and discouraging view on account of the apparent passivity of the organism in the process of evolution' (p. 106). These problems have also been echoed by others more recently (e.g. Niemann, 2014; Longo et al., 2015; Noble and Noble, 2018; Odling-Smee et al., 2003; Vladar et al., 2017).

The environment-oriented view of evolution has influenced economic arguments about the nature of firm behaviour and markets (e.g. Alchian, 1950; also see Winter, 1964). This point was made by Edith Penrose (1952) a number of decades ago, in her response to Armen Alchian's (1950) advocacy of blind evolution, competition, and natural selection as the central mechanisms in the context of economics. Penrose persuasively argues that the economics that focuses on natural selection relies on evolutionary and biological arguments that largely attend to *external* factors that are outside the control of economic actors themselves—leaving little room for agency, choice, purpose, novelty, or any form of motivation or other organism-specific factors. As put by Penrose (1952), 'paradoxically, where explicit biological analogies crop up in economics, they are drawn exclusively from that aspect of biology which deals with the non-motivated behavior of organisms or in which motivation does not make any difference' (p. 808). Market forces simply, automatically, operate themselves—like a machine. These types of mechanistic conceptions are also directly paralleled in evolutionary biology (Day, 2011; cf. Vladar et al., 2017). Variation is largely accidental and serendipitous, and competition and natural selection provide the key mechanisms for explaining market behaviour. Again, evolutionary economics has of course made important contributions (Nelson and Winter, 2002). However, it has largely engaged with passive and environmental mechanisms, at the expense of more active, choice-related ones (for a debate on these issues, see Hodgson and Knudsen, 2011; Winter, 2011).

The emphasis on the environment is also mirrored in the contemporary focus on the *physical* and *material* aspects of environments and reality. For example, the literature on judgment and decision-making builds directly on psychophysics (or so-called inverse optics: Hoffman et al., 2015), where environments and visual scenes are captured by attending to their 'physical properties'—the 'actual properties of the object of judgment' (Kahneman, 2003; for a review, see Felin et al., 2017). In turn, the literature on ecological rationality and heuristics emphasizes environmental cues (Gigerenzer and Gaissmaier, 2011; Todd and Brighton, 2016). The focus is on the amount of environmental information and cues, and on sorting through these cues in different ways (Crupi et al., 2018; Fawcett et al., 2014; Gigerenzer and Gaissmaier, 2011; Miller, 1953; Rahnev and Denison, 2018). Salience is given by the nature of environmental cues, rather than the nature of organisms (Chater et al., 2018; Hoffrage et al., 2015).

These approaches focus on the so-called bottom-up, physical aspects of reality, and on their role in shaping and determining judgment and perception. From this perspective, vision is seen in computational terms (Marr, 1982; cf. Hoffman et al., 2015). Vision is a function of actual physical stimuli and cue characteristics: organisms and humans see and record what is in front of them (Oaksford and Chater, 2007). The organism itself only plays a role in mechanistic terms, like a passive camera, which computes, absorbs, and captures the data in front of it (Kingdom and Prins, 2016; cf. Chater et al., 2018). This is the foundation of many popular conceptions of judgment and reasoning that emphasize optimality and computational rationality (e.g. Gershman et al., 2015), including Bayesian and related approaches. It is also the basis of the ongoing optimism about the possibilities associated with artificial intelligence (Griffiths et al., 2015; Simon, 1990). Once optimality and rationality has been defined, then we can also point out deviations from this optimality. This has led to a large literature on suboptimality, blindness, bias, and boundedness (Chabris and Simons, 2010; Rahnev and Denison, 2018; Kahneman, 2011; Simon, 1955), a focus that is now pervasive across the economic, psychological, and cognitive sciences (for a review, see Felin et al., 2017).

These models are reductionist in the sense that they seek to extract, capture, and exhaust reality via the physical stimuli and cues that constitute any given visual scene or environment. This of course is an impossible task (cf. Koenderink, 2012). These approaches seek scientific objectivity *without* appealing to the perceiving organism itself, as this is said merely to introduce bias and distortion. The models are organism-*general*. Scene statistics, physical stimuli, and cues—their nature, size, number, redundancy (see Gigerenzer and Gaissmaier, 2011; cf. Rahnev and Denison, 2018)—are given primacy. Some models postulate a god-like ideal observer that optimally captures what is in front of it (e.g. Geisler, 2011; Kersten et al., 2004). Once identified, this ideal is used to point out deficiencies and biases on the part of the perceiving organisms. Discrepancies from optimality and rationality are used to specify boundedness—as put by Simon (1979), 'rationality is bounded when it falls short of omniscience' (p. 356; for further background, see Felin et al., 2017). In sum, these represent organism-independent models that try to capture or categorize environments based on the nature of the stimuli or cues (Gigerenzer and Goldstein, 1996; Todd and Brighton, 2016). Each of the above models offers different cognitive tools for dealing with search, through bias reduction, heuristic information processing, and so forth.

Thus far—specifically in this section of the chapter—we have said very little about search. This is because the notion of search is either too passive, automatic, or overly environment-focused in much of the above work. For example, neoclassical conceptions of markets essentially assume that search is instantaneous—it simply happens (for a review, see Chater et al., 2018: pp. 818–21). Markets are seen as efficient. This approach assumes that the phase space of market activity (the environment) can be fully represented (Kauffman, 2016). There are of course semi-efficient versions of markets that allow for short-term arbitrage opportunities (Bray and Savin, 1986), though these diffuse quickly and are rare. The models are explicitly tuned to avoid so-called free lunches. Or to use another popular metaphor: there simply are no $500 bills to be found on sidewalks (Akerlof and Yellen, 1985; cf. Evans and Honkapohja, 2005). The price mechanism automatically sorts through possibilities and best uses. Put in evolutionary terms, there is a macro selection-mechanism, which serves as a global search function of sorts. Economic opportunities are snuffed out by assuming omniscience and computational omnipotence on the part of the actors or the system as a whole. Although the computational complexity of the macro selection-mechanism is taken into account, it does allow for a 'perpetual maladaptive disequilibrium' (Kaznatcheev, 2019; Roughgarden, 2010). But in general, any notion of deliberate, organism-level search or emergent novelty is largely dismissed as serendipity or random noise. That said, the idea of bounded rationality of course is deeply linked with the idea of search (Simon, 1956). In the next sections, we discuss the organism-specific problems with these variations of understanding search and evolutionary novelty (e.g. Gigerenzer and Gaissmaier, 2011).

Teeming environments and organism-specificity

The above models of environments—whether evolutionary ones or ones focused on perception and judgment—inherently cannot account for novelty. This is because their underlying assumptions about the nature of organisms and environments are problematic. First, it is essential to grapple fully with the fact that environments 'teem' with an indefinite number of possible things and thus it is impossible to capture or represent them exhaustively and omnisciently. Omniscient models of environments—featuring computational or perfect representation—cannot help us understand novelty. As we will discuss, they mis-specify the nature of the search problem. And the second, essential recognition is that environments are organism- or species-specific, with radical consequences for how we think about search and novelty. We discuss both of these points next, as they in turn provide the foundation of our subsequent discussion of organism-specific probing, search, and the emergence of evolutionary novelty.

Any environment—visual scene, situation, surrounding, or context—features an innumerable number of things. If one asks 'How many things are in this room?', the question is systematically vague and unanswerable. We might of course list various obvious things, but even this quickly becomes complicated. After all, what constitutes a 'thing'? We might readily agree that the chair in front of us is a thing. But is the distance between the chair and the fireplace a thing? Or for that matter, is the distance between the chair and the moon a thing? What about the luminance, colour, or visible electromagnetic radiation of objects in the room? And is the crack in the wooden top of the table a thing? The crack in the table complicates things, as not only are there objects but also there are varied possible uses and functions. Thus the question 'How many things are there in this room?' is radically expanded by the implied 'A thing for what purpose or use?' question. After all, the crack in the table, just as anything else, might be used in different ways. For example, the crack might be used to wedge in the power cord running from the electric coffee pot on the table to the floor, and so protect the coffee pot on the table from being pulled off the table. Or the crack might be used by an insect to avoid detection. In short, the crack is an affordance that can be used for any number of different purposes (Kauffman 2008; Felin et al., 2016). Thus the set of things, uses, and affordances in any environment is unlistable and indefinite. Environments (objects, stimuli, and things) are hard to pin down exhaustively and objectively.

Note that Bayesian notions of 'reading' environments are also not useful for the above scenario. Bayesian approaches focus on environmental stimuli and cues that are recorded and updated by some actor or organism (e.g. Chater et al., 2010; Eckstein et al., 2006; Hoffrage et al., 2015; Kersten et al., 2004). But the problem is that there is no *ex ante*, task-independent way to decide what represents an initial or useful cue, stimulus, or data point in the first place (Felin et al., 2017). Put differently, there is no definition of what constitutes the relevant contents of priors or the specific locus of what is being updated (Chater et al., 2018; Koenderink, 2016). Humans encounter teeming environments and visual scenes with indefinite stimuli and cues, and the specific ones that become salient, relevant, and useful depend on the organism and problem at hand. We develop this point more carefully in the next section.

The notion of teeming environments becomes most evident especially when we consider the idea of function and use. In the context of evolution, the set of possible, adjacent functions and uses is indefinite (Kauffman, 2003). There is no physical way to account for the set of possible uses—as illustrated by the crack in the table—for any given object, stimulus, or point of data. And any visual scene or environment features an indefinite number of possible things (again, compounded by the problem of interaction and possible use and function) that one might attend to or be aware of. There are of course more common or obvious things and uses. But even the idea of obviousness—as we will discuss later—is highly organism-, problem-, and situation-dependent (Chater et al., 2018). Obviousness is, more often than not, only evident in retrospect.

The generic word 'environment' masks this type of specificity and environmental munificence. Environment has become a catch-all term for explaining behaviour and survival. But the idea of an environment needs to be unpacked. Many existing models of science—whether in psychology, biology, or economics—presume that the key objects or variables of the environment can indeed be extracted and represented, in the form of some kind of landscape, state, or phase space. Again, this has, for example, been an influential way to model markets and rational expectations (e.g. Arrow, 1986; Muth, 1961). While this can certainly be useful for some types of closed, physical systems (Nolte, 2010), it is important to recognize that representing a static, closed system is not true to the actual nature of the environments inhabited by organisms or economic actors. The upside of this impossibility (of fully representing an environment or visual scene) is that it provides the underlying foundations for addressing the role of organisms in generating novelty. Scholars, economists included, have recently begun to wrestle with the idea of closed versus more open-ended phase spaces and their implications for understanding the emergence of novelty (e.g. Buchanan, 2014; Felin et al., 2014; Karni and Vierø, 2013).

Our second point is that environments are organism-specific. This point, while seemingly mundane and obvious, has radical consequences. Most models of search, evolution, and environments are organism-general or organism-independent (Chater et al., 2018; cf. Henderson et al., 2009). But our argument is that environments and novelty can only be understood by understanding organisms themselves, and their active probing of, and interactions and encounters with, their specific environments. As summarized by Goldstein (1963), 'environment first arises from the world *only when* there is an ordered organism' (p. 88, emphasis added).

The organism-specific nature of environments was recognized by some early ethologists and comparative biologists, such as Jakob von Uexküll. He argued that 'every animal lives in a world specific to it, different from that of its neighbors' (von Uexküll, 2010: p. 639). Each organism exists in its own *Umwelt* or surroundings, where certain species-specific factors are visible and salient to it: 'every animal is surrounded with different things, the dog is surrounded by dog things and the dragonfly is surrounded by dragonfly things' (von Uexküll, 2010: p. 117). To illustrate, Clarke et al. (2017) recently summarized the varied sensory capacities of bees in their environments (their unique vision and electroreception when foraging), which differ radically from other organisms. Bees interact with flowers in remarkably complex ways, through varied forms of signalling and electroreception. But existing work on organism search and environments tends to take a unitary approach to understanding environments, without any focus on this type of species-specificity (Caves et al., 2019). Environments feature species-specific stimuli that 'light up' or 'pop out' for the organism in question, amongst the indefinite variety of other stimuli and objects present in any scene. Male stickleback fish are highly attuned to red splotches or marks of a certain size, thus even attacking inanimate objects that happen to feature an appropriately sized red spot (Tinbergen, 1963). Some stimuli are supernormal in the sense that they are irresistibly attractive to particular species (Barrett, 2010; see Alcock, 1972, 1975; Dawkins and Krebs, 1979). For example, the beetle *Julodimorpha bakervelli* nearly went extinct in Australia as the male beetle found the colouring and curvature of discarded beer bottles irresistible and sought to copulate with the bottles rather than females of its own species (Gwynne and Rentz, 1983).

In some sense, the *Umwelt* or surroundings of organisms can partly be seen as perceptual interfaces that structure the desired interactions with the environment, without representing it directly (that is, where the desired interactions are those that maximize fitness: Hoffman, Singh and Prakash, 2015). Such evolved interfaces are not always localized to the individual, but can also be social interfaces that allow for useful delusions (Kaznatcheev, Montrey and Shultz, 2014). For example, an organism might misperceive its payoffs in an evolutionary game in such a way that by acting 'selfishly' to maximize its perceived utility, the organism will actually maximize its inclusive fitness rather than its individual fitness. But our most important point here is that the concept of an organism-specific surroundings highlights that environments are specific and scarcely singular.

The species-specificity of perceptual worlds might be further illustrated with a brief example, as this conception of environments provides an important background foundation of our subsequent arguments. Take the tick and its surroundings and environment (Randolph, 2014; Uexküll. 2010). Ticks are small, 3–5mm arachnids and parasites that feed on the blood of hosts, such as mammals, birds, and reptiles. Many tick sub-species do not have eyes, or they have extremely poor vision. But the tick has a sensory surrounding of its own. Ticks 'quest' (or search) for hosts by using their chemosensory organ, called Haller's organ, which allows them to sense the olfactory presence of chemicals (butyric acid or carbon dioxide), as well as temperature and infrared light. Ticks perch themselves on high ground, such as on branches or bushes, and wait for potential hosts to pass by. When there is a co-occurrence of certain chemicals, such as carbon dioxide emitted by the host breathing, and the right temperature (body temperature of mammals), the tick drops from its perch and latches onto the host. Thus the tick environment is highly specific (Randolph, 2014). It is of course hard to know what it phenomenologically feels like to be a tick, a bat (Nagel, 1974), or any other animal. Specific forms of sentience are a function of species-specific factors, and the nature of the sensory organs that the organism possesses. That said, while much of organism behaviour might be explained in genetic and mechanistic terms, it is not possible to account for organisms in solely deterministic ways (cf. Noble and Noble, 2018). There is a generative and emergent remainder to be explained.

The above two points—that environments teem with potential stimuli, cues, and objects (that are impossible to exhaustively represent) and that species have specific environments and surroundings—provide the foundation on which we build our notion of question-answer probing, search, and evolutionary novelty. The two points above serve as the enabling conditions for explaining the emergence of novelty. They are necessary but not sufficient. These ideas map onto the idea of the adjacent possible (Kauffman, 2003). But they require an active, searching, probing, and choosing organism—suggesting a form of consciousness (an awareness-of). That is, the two facts about teeming environments and species-specific surroundings require an animating mechanism that goes beyond a simple stimulus-response relationship. After all, the above points could also be used to make the point that organisms are machines that simply respond to their specific environments. But organisms are not simplistic machines (Goodwin and Dawkins, 1995; cf. Monod, 1971). A more organism-specific, choice-theoretic, and directed approach is needed to explain the emergence of novelty, beyond mere random chance.

It is worth noting that while our informal notion of question-answer probing differs across organisms, we argue that it also offers a *general* mechanism for explaining evolutionary novelty. Here we build on a biological tradition that says that organisms in an important sense 'have agency and make choices' within their environments (Noble and Noble, 2018: p. 5; also see Kauffman and Clayton, 2006; Kauffman 2000; Longo et al., 2015). Although what this agentic and choice-theoretic activity looks like across species varies substantially, the similarity can be seen in its problem-oriented, exploratory, and directed nature.

By mentioning agency or choice, we do not necessarily aim to raise philosophical issues about the nature of free will or the so-called hard problem of consciousness. Instead we simply focus on the perceptual and vision-oriented factors that shape organism search and behaviour in environments, and which enable the emergence of novelty. Our focus here might be seen as related to small-c-forms of consciousness, defined simply as awareness-of something: being conscious *of* a specific stimulus or cue, or a specific object or thing, or a use or function. We steer clear of capital-c-types of consciousness (Chalmers, 1996) that focus on awareness of, say, one's self, or awareness of other minds, or awareness of something transcendental. Our focus in this chapter is on more mundane, everyday forms of consciousness: awareness (or not) of everyday things around us. However, we do think that this small-c form of consciousness also provides the basis for understanding capital-c types of consciousness, including the emergence of novelty.

An implicit upshot of our arguments is that scholars studying consciousness have been overly focused on the *physical* and the *material*. For example, a prominent philosopher of consciousness, David Chalmers (1996), argues that 'a theory of consciousness will have more in common with a theory in physics than a theory in biology'. We fundamentally disagree. We think the organism-specific *biology* discussed here is absolutely fundamental to truly understanding consciousness. Philosophers focused on the objective representation of physical realities are missing the point (e.g. Block, 2011; Burge, 2010, 2014). Reducing consciousness to inverse optics or psychophysics (Kingdom and Prins, 2016), the recording or measurement of environmental stimuli or cues, is wrong-headed because it sidelines the probing organism itself. We instead side with physicists who have emphasized the fundamental role of consciousness in the physical universe, whether we speak of organisms, observers, or observation at the quantum or cosmological levels (Eddington, 1928; Ellis, 2005; Heisenberg, 1971; Wheeler, 1990; Wilczek, 2016).

Our mundane, small-c sense of consciousness (awareness-of something, like an object) has fundamental consequences, as it is not reducible to the physical or material. We concur with Schrödinger (1944) who argued that 'consciousness cannot be accounted for in physical terms. For consciousness is absolutely fundamental. It cannot be accounted for in terms of anything else' (p. 21; see also Polanyi, 1958). We believe that the visual, perceptual, and search-oriented mechanisms discussed in this chapter are quite proximate to consciousness. But, that said, our overall focus is not philosophical per se. Rather, we emphasize the everyday mundane activities of perception and behaviour on the part of organisms as they encounter their surroundings, and on the novelty that emerges as organisms, in essence, probe and query their environments.

The role of search images and functional search

One of the problems we have referred to throughout this chapter is the vastness of environments and search spaces, the number of cues and stimuli, and the problem of how to process them. The concept of bounded rationality (Simon, 1955) emerged precisely from the recognition that organisms, humans included, face overwhelming amounts of potential information and that they lack the computational or perceptual capacities for dealing with this (cf. Kahneman, 2003). Environmental search is also an essential concept and metaphor in the context of biology, for example, in the literature on animal foraging (e.g. Griffin and Guez, 2014; Pyke et al., 1977) and related models of organism search (Abbott et al., 2015; Fawcett et al., 2014; Hills et al., 2015; Simon, 1990). In the context of economics and strategy, the problem of search as information processing (and information overload) is seen as akin to the problem of NP completeness in computer science. Managers and organizations face overwhelming amounts of information and data, and processing it all simply is not computationally possible. For example, others have recently looked at how some environments are too 'hard' for any organism or evolutionary search strategy to be optimal (Kaznatcheev, 2019). Our favoured approach for search, however, is not focused on environmental processing, or even the representation of cues or stimuli. Nor is it focused on the computational problem of sorting through cues.

We instead focus on the directed nature of search and how varied organism-specific and exploratory strategies in effect simplify search. We do so by first discussing the more mundane, moment-by-moment factors that shape organism search, perception, and awareness, and then discuss the larger-scale implications of these arguments for the emergence and evolution of novelty.

Imagine an organism in some environment. As discussed above, the environment of the organism features an indefinite number of potential stimuli, cues, and objects. The first, essential point is that what the organism sees or recognizes (or can recognize) is species-specific. Perceptual salience and organism awareness is determined *not* by what is there (as suggested by psychophysics) per se, but first by what the organism *is*, and by its aforementioned *Umwelt* or surroundings. But there are also important, *directed* aspects to organism perception and awareness. Namely, organisms come to environmental encounters motivated *by* and searching *for* something, beyond passively responding to stimuli. These organism-specific motivational and search states—and idea of searching-for-something—change the nature of the search problem. They change the search problem from one of brute computation and information processing to something more targeted and specific.

The notion of searching-for is aptly captured by the idea of a species-specific *Suchbild*—a German word for a search image that guides organism perception and awareness (Uexküll, 2010; cf. Chater et al., 2018). The search image is shaped by the nature of the organism and the different drives, motivations, and interests that it might have at any given moment, for things like food, reproduction, or shelter. The organism's search image shapes what is salient and visible to it at any given moment. For example, many species of frog specifically look for movement when hunting for locusts or crickets. If the prey does not move (even if the locust is right under the frog's nose), the frog does not recognize or see it (Ewert, 2004). Search images thus direct organism awareness towards highly specific stimuli and features of the environment, allowing organisms to readily ignore any number of other things. Thus the task of visual processing is not computational (Marr, 1982) or oriented towards serial processing. Rather, visual recognition is driven by the *ex ante Suchbild* or search image of the organism. The concept of a search image essentially simplifies search. It also provides a powerful way to understand perception, vision, and search in the context of humans.

To offer a casual example, imagine you have lost your house keys. The rooms in your house, and perhaps your yard, feature an indefinite number of varied objects, cues, and stimuli that serve as the search space. This search space is extremely large. So, how do you find the keys? One approach for solving this problem might be some form of brute, serial processing of visual cues and objects. That is, you might individually consider (look at and inspect) each item that you happen to encounter in your immediate (local) surroundings and then make a decision about whether the item in question represents your keys: 'Are these my keys?...No...Are these my keys?...No...Are these my keys?…No…' and so forth. This type of serial processing and search would of course be extremely costly and time-consuming.

Instead of brute computation and serial processing, search is radically simplified by having a key search-image in our minds as we visually scan our surroundings. Since we know what we are looking for, we can quickly bypass (without processing or recognizing) any number of irrelevant stimuli and objects. The search image of a key—the thing we are searching for—allows us to readily disregard, skip, and ignore most things within our visual field, and to attend to problem-relevant stimuli or cues. For the most part we do not even become aware of or consider irrelevant items, unless they have key-like features. Awareness thus is given by the search-*for*-something that we have in mind.

With a search image, the search space is in effect significantly reduced. While this might appear obvious, it is explicitly not recognized by most of the prominent models of perception (for a discussion, see Chater et al., 2018). Namely, the search-for approach is fundamentally different from models of attention and information processing that focus on cues and their aggregation (Gigerenzer and Gaissmaier, 2011) or approaches that focus on natural assessments, such as the stimulus size or colour (Kahneman, 2003). Even the literature on search in vision science is highly focused on stimulus-related characteristics and features (Wolfe and Utochkin, 2019), such as detecting target objects or features amongst similar distractions. These models are built bottom-up, from the physical stimuli themselves (Treisman, 1998: p. 50). Salience in these forms of psychophysics is given by environment- or cue-driven characteristics, such as stimulus thresholds, stimulus features, similarity, and size (Kingdom and Prins, 2016). But cataloguing stimuli does not meaningfully address the issue of relevance, that is, what an organism might be searching for. The same can be said for Shannon-type conceptions (Shannon, 1948) of information: they lack a mechanism for accounting for meaning. Or put differently, the idea of information lacks contextual relativity and meaning that is inherent to the search-for idea. Information is an emergent outcome of the query rather than something given by the *ex ante* statistical probabilities of a visual scene or environment. The queries themselves, in essence, add information to the search.

The search for lost keys is also significantly simplified—that is, the search space is reduced—by some kind of theory that one might have about where the keys were (mis-)placed and lost in the first place (cf. Chater et al., 2018: pp. 817–18). We might think back to which rooms we visited during the prior hour, where we were sitting, or what we were doing when we lost the keys. The lost keys may not even be readily visible. But a hunch that we lost them while sitting in our favourite chair in the living room can allow us to find them in the crevice of the chair. Thus the search space and search problem is vastly reduced by both the search image of the keys *as well as* a conjecture, expectation, hunch, and hypothesis about where the keys might be found.

Granted, this example of looking for lost keys may seem quite mundane. But it provides a glimpse into a more generalized process. This mundane search-for notion supplies us with the underlying raw material for explaining the emergence of novelty as well. This is especially the case in an organism's exploratory probes that take the form of *looking-for-a-function*, that is, looking for an object or tool to serve a specific use or purpose (cf. Uexküll, 2010).

To illustrate, an organism may search for something to take shelter under, to protect itself, say, from an overhead predator or inclement weather. The set of possible objects and things in the environment that might satisfy this function—objects that are shelter-like—can be innumerable. For an ant, shelter might be found under a rock or leaf, under another animal, in a crevice, and so forth. An organism's functional search—'looking-for-something-to-x-under/with'—could include any number of things: searching or looking for something to throw (something throw-'able'), something to hide behind, something to communicate with, something to attract with, something to open or dig with, and so forth. The organism-object or organism-function interactions are indefinite and hard to pre-state. For example, in the context of a predator attacking, a stone might be useful if the organism can grip it, if it can throw it hard enough with sufficient accuracy, depending on the nature and size of the predator. An organism might postulate and test what happens if they behave or use a certain object as a tool in a specific way. In his *The Mentality of Apes* (1925), the psychologist Wolfgang Köhler found that apes engaged in highly creative and planned behaviours as they sought to solve problems, such as trying to reach bananas well out of their reach (by using tools). Animals more generally have been shown to engage in a wide variety of innovation and instrumental problem-solving (Amici et al., 2019; Audet and Lefebvre, 2017; Fragaszy and Liu, 2012; Griffin and Gues, 2014; Morand-Ferron et al., 2016) and an astounding array of tool use (Fragaszy and Mangalam, 2018; Sanz et al., 2013).

For any given organism in any given environment, the set of possible answers to functional questions is extremely large. Objects feature different affordances for different organisms (Felin et al., 2016; Kauffman, 2019). A small leaf might be shelter-like for an ant but not for a large rodent. Thus anatomical and embodied aspects of the organism (size, shape, colouring, etc.)—as well as the capabilities of the organism (ability to move or sense, capacity to grip or carry, etc.)—also play a role in the range of functional possibilities of objects in the environment. Most importantly, the idea of functional search and associated problem-solving yields a greater number of possible solutions and affordances (in short, novelty) than the aforementioned search image, which focuses organism search on *a particular* answer or outcome. Functional search—the organism looking for a specific function—has the possibility of revealing new uses and possibilities. Functional search is essentially the mechanism behind the realization of adjacent possibilities.

The search for functional uses can be further illustrated with a quick example from a human context. Say you are working at your computer in your office and are pestered by a fly. In the absence of a fly swatter, you might look around for an object to serve the swatting function: something-to-swat-with. A nearby magazine or book might do the job, or perhaps an article of clothing. Even the keyboard might work, or perhaps your shoe. Functional search opens up possibilities that are latent in objects within one's environment. Functional search can lead to novelty as organism-directed queries interact with the set of surrounding objects, with possible, *dormant* uses and functions. Note that the functional use of an object cannot be accounted for in any type of reductionist way. The use or function only becomes salient in response to a question or problem. As discussed by Kauffman (2016), the set of possible uses for anything (e.g. a screwdriver) is indefinite—that is, there is no orderable list. Our contribution here is to point out that these novel uses emerge—the adjacent possible becomes more salient and realizable—in response to the organism-specific search to solve problems and find uses.

The possible uses of objects for varied purposes simply cannot be anticipated. For analytic convenience, economics makes the assumption that we in fact can, in rough and abstract form, capture all functional uses and even order them (Felin et al., 2014). Prices serve an important function here. But the search for functional use offers a mechanism for the emergence of novelty and value. Consider Xerox Parc in the late 1970s. The company had developed innumerable technologies, which were showcased to different technology companies, venture capitalists, and interested parties. The technologies, however, became meaningful and salient in response to the problem-solving of Steve Jobs and his team of engineers at Apple (cf. Hiltzik, 2000; Rolling, 1998). In short, they were looking for a functional use: something-to-make-computers-easy-to-use-and-interface-with. They identified a set of technologies (graphic-user interface, mouse, bit-mapping) at Xerox as a solution to this question-answer probe (Felin and Zenger, 2017). The functional search led to the identification and realization of something useful, as well as the creation of new value. This type of functional search and emergent use of objects more generally provides a mechanism for explaining cultural and technological evolution (cf. Gabora, 2019).

Now, while we have focused on the power of search images and functional search, these mechanisms are not without their limitations and attendant costs. Cognitive psychologists have highlighted how intently focusing on something can lead to so-called 'inattentional blindness' (Chabris and Simons, 2010). In their famous gorilla study, Simons and Chabris (1999) asked experimental subjects to watch a video clip and to count the number of basketball passes they observe. Meanwhile, a person in a gorilla suit walks across the scene. Given that subjects are so focused on the task at hand (looking for basketball passes), a significant number of them never see the gorilla. In some sense, the search image of basketball passes (or the question: how many basketball passes?) causes people to miss something significant and obvious. This overall idea—that humans are 'blind to the obvious'—has become a central building block of the cognitive revolution in decision making and behavioural economics (see Kahneman, 2011; Chater, 2018). From our perspective, there is of course no question that humans and other organisms can miss things in their surroundings. We necessarily have to focus, as a full accounting of our surroundings and environments is impossible. This is obvious. But the more profound issue, from our perspective, is how to address the various organism-specific factors that direct awareness and attention in the first place (cf. Felin et al., 2019). We argue that search images provide a powerful explanation of this, along with the role of other organism-directed factors such as theories, along with various forms of questioning and problem-solving.

In fact, the exploratory search of organisms, whether searching for images or functional uses, can readily be summarized as a form of question-answer probing. Search consists of a question and proto-hypothesis on the part of the organism. The question (and implied answer) shapes what the organism looks for, becomes aware of, and sees, in an environment that teems with indefinite possible objects, cues, and uses. The question shapes which stimuli become salient, or which objects might be deemed useful for some purpose. Importantly, questions and answers are tightly coupled. Questions presume an answer, a sense of what the organism is looking for, what it will see and recognize, and what it will be satisfied with as a solution to its query. An organism visually scans its environment (or traverses or moves within space), and the stimuli that light up are the ones that answer the question (or functional use) the organism has put forward. It is worth repeating: there is no possible way to account for this type of targeted search activity on the basis of trial and error (specifically, of the random variety), nor on the basis of some kind of *ex ante*, obvious, physical environment. Certainly, luck and serendipity can play a role. But a probing organism is needed for the realization and recognition of novelty. Even the idea of adjacent possibilities (Kauffman, 2003) only comes alive with this form of probing. Organisms elicit new functionalities and uses through their targeted search.

It is impossible to offer any kind of reductionist, physical explanation for this type of search, and more generally for the possible use of objects in environments (Felin et al., 2014). There is no physics or chemistry for explaining function (Ellis, 2005): functions and emergent uses are not reducible. This is aptly illustrated by a brief story by Michael Polanyi (1970: p. 970, emphasis added):

> Some time ago, on returning to England from America, I found that I had unwittingly picked up and brought with me an object that looked like an instrument of some kind. I handed it around to many people, but they could not tell what it was. Once more back in America I was told that the thing was designed to make two holes simultaneously in a can of beer. *No physical chemical examination of the object could have revealed this fact*, for the conception of opening cans of beer forms no part of physics or chemistry. Physicists and chemists could have identified every possible configuration of the curious object, if its shape were due to the forces intrinsic to its substance, but no form of the material deliberately shaped for a practical purpose can be accounted for in terms of physics and chemistry. This applies equally to all mechanisms functioning as parts of a living being; they cannot be represented by the principles of physics or chemistry.

In sum, question-answer probes provide the cognitive 'software' for manipulating and interacting with physical environments. Organism-directed factors—like search images and search-for-functions—provide an interface that shapes organism awareness and yields emergent novelty (new uses, functions, and niches). This activity more generally can include other (closely overlapping) forms of organism-directed query such as what-if and yes-no questions (cf. Wheeler, 1990). But the essential point is that these processes are necessarily initiated through some form of organism-directed probing and query. Or, as summarized by Wheeler (1990), 'No question? No answer!' (p. 310).

A side note: science and life as problem-solving

In an important sense we are saying that *life itself is a directed form of proto-scientific probing*. Or, as put by Popper (1991), 'all life is problem-solving'. Just like scientists, varied organisms have questions—hunches, problems, hypotheses, and expectations—that direct their awareness and behaviour into the unknown and the possible. Life finds new ways of doing things, new problems and solutions, new ways of being and becoming, in response to exploratory probing. Much novelty of course might emerge from accidents and serendipity. But even accidents require a probing organism that recognizes (or acts on) an anomalous outcome and a possibility worth harnessing (cf. Noble, 2018). Thus there are interesting links between the question-answer notion and scientific observation more generally.

Scientists encounter teeming environments (nature or reality) just like any other organism. As we have discussed, these environments feature indefinite data, cues, stimuli, and information. These data however are not meaningful or even recognizable without some kind of question or theory. To provide a casual illustration, experiences of gravitation (for example, of apples falling) are a readily observable, common occurrence. But it was only with Newton's theory and question that this observation took on new meaning and relevance. There is no brute-force computation, big data, or Bayesian method to extract this information. And it was only with Einstein's theory that Eddington knew what data to look for when he verified the theory of relativity. Scientific observation then is a motivated (rather than passive) activity that directs us towards the relevant data and their meaning and interpretation. In fact, things are only observed and salient in response to specific questions, as guided by theories. As put by Einstein, 'whether you can observe a thing or not depends on the theory which you use. It is the theory which decides what can be observed' (Polanyi, 1971: p. 604; also see Salam, 1990).

The relevant stimuli, data, observations, objects, and measurements are not somehow automatically recognized or extracted from a theory-independent reality. Seeing something as data or information requires active questioning and probing. As put by Heisenberg (1971), 'what we observe is not nature itself, but nature exposed to our method of questioning'. At a high level, this applies to both scientists exploring the nature of reality and organisms exploring and probing their environments. Proto-questions are a generalized mechanism through which reality emerges and reveals itself. Questions expand the consciousness-of possibilities in the sense of enabling organisms to become aware of new, heretofore unseen, or unrecognized things and uses in their surroundings. Furthermore, theories also enable the creation of tools and apparatuses for identifying the right evidence and data.

If one's conception of science is based on strict materialism and reductionism—just the so-called visible facts and data—then the importance of, or even need for, this type of organism-directed probing and conjecture can be hard to accept. Science has sought to expunge any form of agency, mind, and life out of the equation (Monod, 1971; cf. Polanyi, 1968). Materialist and reductionist arguments remain the implicit background assumption of much of science (often for good reason). But this focus on the material has come at a cost. The focus on the 'material world has been constructed at the price of taking the self, that is, the mind, out of it, removing it' (Schrödinger, 1958). As noted by others, consciousness and mind are inevitable and essential even for the hardest of sciences (Eddington, 1928; Wilczek, 2016). There is no omniscient way to read or observe the world (Chater et al., 2018; Nagel, 1989). Without a subject, that is, without an active probing organism (e.g. for functions and uses), we can hardly explain the emergent growth and novelty we observe all around us. That said, this seeming subjectivity does not mean that there are no objective facts. Rather, this subjectivity in fact provides the enabling conditions for explaining the objective world and the key mechanisms for explaining the emergence of new facts.

The importance of the organism and active probing is captured in debates about the primacy of theory versus the primacy of data. The problem of trying to focus on just the data was recognized by Charles Darwin. The English naturalist Edwin Lankester publicly criticized Darwin for not publishing 'facts alone'. In response to this criticism, Darwin wrote to a friend:

> It made me laugh to read of [Lankester's] advice or rather regret that I had not published *facts alone*. How profoundly ignorant he must be of the very soul of observation. About 30 years ago there was much talk that Geologists ought *only to observe and not theorise*; and I well remember someone saying, that at this rate a man might as well go into a gravel-pit and count the pebbles and describe their colours. How odd it is that everyone should not see that *all observation must be for or against some view*, if it is to be of any service.   (1861, italics added)

In all, there are important parallels between scientific observation and more mundane, everyday perception and awareness on the part of organisms. Both are motivated by something, looking *for* something. Environments cannot be attended to without this sort of about-ness and direct-ness. Organisms and scientists have something in mind when engaging with and encountering the world. Description always comes from a point of view. As summarized by Tinbergen (1963), 'description is never, can never be, random; it is in fact highly selective, and selection is made with reference to the problems, hypotheses and methods the investigator has in mind' (p. 6). So whether we are talking about an organism mundanely interacting with its surroundings and environment, or a scientist measuring and exploring the world, both are driven by active probing on the part of organisms.

Search and novelty: implications for economics and innovation

Search on landscapes has provided a powerful metaphor and tool for explaining evolutionary behaviour and innovation, whether in the context of biological organisms (e.g. Kauffman and Weinberger, 1989) or economic actors (e.g. Kauffman, 1993; Levinthal, 1997; Gavetti and Levinthal, 2000). In the economics and management literatures, this research has offered varied solutions for how economic agents might identify and find value. Search strategies have included mechanisms such as distant search, the power of analogies and association, modular problem-solving, problem representations, and so forth (e.g. Baumann et al., 2019; Ganco and Hoetker, 2009; Gavetti, 2012). The idea of distant search and recombination has also been a prominent theme in the context of studying innovation and creativity with patent data (e.g. Ahuja and Morris Lampert, 2001; Fleming and Sorensen, 2001; Kneeland et al., 2020). The vast combinatorial possibilities of technologies and innovation have also been an important focus (Sole et al., 2013). Recent research has more generally looked at how 'different search strategies' can be useful in 'different environments' (Csaszar and Levinthal, 2016). Roughly similar intuition can also be found in the judgment and decision making literature, which seeks to match environmental characteristics with different types of heuristics (Artinger et al., 2015; cf. Bingham and Eisenhardt, 2011). This research has offered important insights about search and innovation.

   In this chapter, we have offered a contrasting, organism-focused view of search, with implications for innovation and economic activity. Rather than specify an *ex ante* environment and offering insights on optimal search strategies or heuristics, we start with organisms themselves. Our focus is on organism-specific search and on how this shapes the emergence of adjacent possibilities and environments (cf. Kauffman, 2003). At a high level, the traces of this type of organism- or *firm*-specificity can implicitly be found in the existing literature. For example, the very concept of a firm is, of course, firm-specific. That is, as discussed by Coase (1937), an entrepreneur replaces the market's price mechanism in the coordination and 'direction of [some] resources'. Therefore, firms are founded by economic actors for specific purposes and reasons, by entrepreneurs who decide which transactions to engage in, which investments to make and why, whom to hire, and so forth. All of these decisions presume a firm-specific point of view or theory about how to create value (Felin and Zenger, 2017; Van den Steen, 2017). This might be linked to the search literature and the idea of a firm's 'preferred direction' (Winter et al., 2007). Importantly, firm-specificity can be seen as a type of *Suchbild* or search image that directs unique awareness and attention towards potentially valuable, unseen assets, or new uses for objects. The search for specific functions, coupled with the impossibility of accounting for all functional uses of objects and assets (Felin et al., 2016), means that economic actors can and do in fact identify and create value, even in seemingly efficient markets. Thus our conception of search challenges the idea that factor markets are efficient (cf. Denrell et al., 2003; Felin et al., 2016).

The existing strategy and economics literature has also placed a strong emphasis on search in the form of information gathering, information processing, and environmental scanning (e.g. Elenkov, 1997; Hwang, 1993; Makadok and Barney, 2001; Verrecchia, 1982). While these approaches might have their place, our approach seeks to change the environment-organism relationship to an organism-environment one (Gigerenzer and Gaissmaier, 2011; Todd and Brighton, 2007). The difference between these two may seem subtle or artificial (due to interactions). But the decision of whether we start an analysis with the environment or the organism is essential (cf. Goldstein, 1963), as this choice will directly shape which mechanisms are seen as essential. A focus on environmental scanning places the emphasis squarely on 'reading' the environment correctly, whereas an organism-first approach focuses on the specific (and unique) search-for solutions and functions. The latter approach, which was advocated by us in this chapter, begins with the premise that there is no scanning or informational processing without some form of organism and *ex ante*, targeted question, or firm-specific search. This argument is born out of existing research in perception science (Chater et al., 2018; Felin et al., 2019). Therefore, what is modelled or represented *ex ante* is the organism and not the environment. Or more specifically, the focus is on the representation held by the searching organism—but not the organism's representation of the environment, rather their representation of the relevant question-answer. As we have emphasized throughout this chapter, this shift has radical implications for how we understand both evolutionary novelty and economic value. In all, we think that the notion of organism- and firm-specificity with regard to search can open up new possibilities for understanding strategy, innovation, and the emergence of economic novelty.

Finally, one additional stream of research deserves attention, as it relates to our arguments about functional search and novelty. This is the literature on pre-adaptations and exaptation in the context of economic environments and innovation. For example, Cattani (2006; see also Andriani and Cattani, 2016) highlights how technological pre-adaptations of firms can find surprising and novel uses that could not have been anticipated. Andriani et al. (2017) explicitly measure this process of exaptation by looking at how drugs find new, unanticipated applications in the pharmaceutical industry. In short, the focus of this literature is on how technologies or products end up having new and novel uses that are hard to anticipate *ex ante*. We concur that this is an important driver of the emergence and evolution of technologies and innovation. In this chapter, however, we focus on another central mechanism—that is, deliberate functional search and its role in uncovering novelty and value. Thus, we start with a 'teeming' environment and discuss how deliberate functional search—on the part of organisms and economic actors—can reveal new functions and uses for objects and technologies. That is, firms might deliberately search to solve specific problems and thus uncover value in technologies, value that previously was not evident or obvious to others (Felin and Zenger, 2016). Luck undoubtedly can play a role here as well. Von Hippel and Von Krogh (2016) in fact discuss how economic actors might stumble onto novelty, without any form of *ex ante* problem formulation or deliberate search. Undoubtedly, this happens. But in this chapter we have focused on more deliberate search mechanisms. That said, certainly more work is needed on the respective contingencies of relying on deliberate versus more luck-oriented approaches to search and novelty, and the respective implications of this for value creation and appropriation by firms need to be studied.

Conclusion

In this chapter, we have focused on the hard problem of search. We challenge the existing focus on environments in evolutionary theorizing, whether in the context of biology or economics. We specifically focus on organism-specific search and the role this plays in the emergence of evolutionary novelty. Organisms' (or organizations') search images, problem-solving, and functional search are essential in realizing adjacent possibilities in uncertain environments. We call for a shift from computational, information processing-oriented approaches to more organism-specific ones. Developments in biology and perception science provide an opportunity to attend more carefully to the active, directed role that organisms and economic actors play in shaping and realizing environments. Overall, we think that the organism-centred arguments from biology, rather than the rigid and deterministic methods of physics, offer a fruitful way forward for understanding evolutionary innovation.

Acknowledgements

This chapter has benefited from interactions with George Ellis, Artem Kaznatcheev, Jan Koenderink, and Todd Zenger. We would like to thank the volume editors Mariano Mastrogiorgio and Gino Cattani for their feedback. We would also like to thank Pertti Felin for proofreading an earlier version of this manuscript. We received useful feedback from two presentations: a related presentation at the Santa Fe Institute in August 2019 and a presentation at the Oxford University Novelty workshop in September 2019. Any mistakes are our own.

References

Abbott, J.T., Austerweil, J.L., and Griffiths, T.L. 2015. Random walks on semantic networks can resemble optimal foraging. *Psychological Review*, 122(3): 558–69.

Ahuja, G. and Morris Lampert, C. 2001. Entrepreneurship in the large corporation: a longitudinal study of how established firms create breakthrough inventions. *Strategic Management Journal*, 22(6–7): 521–43.

Akerlof, G.A. and Yellen, J.L. 1985. Can small deviations from rationality make significant differences to economic equilibria? *American Economic Review*, 75(4): 708–20.

Alchian, A.A. 1950. Uncertainty, evolution, and economic theory. *Journal of Political Economy*, 58(3): 211–21.

Alcock, J. 1972. The evolution of the use of tools by feeding animals. *Evolution; International Journal of Organic Evolution*, 26(3): 464–73.

Alcock, J. 1975. *Animal behaviour: an evolutionary approach*. Oxford University Press.

Aldrich, H.E., Hodgson, G.M., Hull, D.L., Knudsen, T., Mokyr, J., and Vanberg, V.J. 2008. In defence of generalized Darwinism. *Journal of Evolutionary Economics*, 18(5): 577–96.

Amici, F., Widdig, A., Lehmann, J., and Majolo, B. 2019. A meta-analysis of inter-individual differences in innovation. *Animal Behaviour*, 155: 257–68.

Anderson, J.R. 2013. *The architecture of cognition*. Psychology Press.

Andriani, P., Ali, A., and Mastrogiorgio, M. 2017. Measuring exaptation and its impact on innovation, search and problem solving. *Organization Science*, 28(2): 320–38.

Andriani, P. and Cattani, G. 2016. Exaptation as source of creativity, innovation, and diversity: introduction to special issue. *Industrial and Corporate Change*, 25(1): 115–31.

Arrow, K.J. 1986. Rationality of self and others in an economic system. *Journal of Business*, 59(S4): 385–99.

Artinger, F., Petersen, M., Gigerenzer, G., and Weibler, J. 2015. Heuristics as adaptive decision strategies in management. *Journal of Organizational Behavior*, 36(S1): S33–S52.

Audet, J.N. and Lefebvre, L. 2017. What's flexible in behavioral flexibility? *Behavioral Ecology*, 28(4): 943–7.

Barrett, D. 2010. *Supernormal stimuli: how primal urges overran their evolutionary purpose*. WW Norton & Company.

Bateson, P. 2017. *Behaviour, development and evolution*. Open Book Publishers.

Baumann, O., Schmidt, J., and Stieglitz, N. 2019. Effective search in rugged performance landscapes: a review and outlook. *Journal of Management*, 45(1): 285–318.

Bingham, C.B. and Eisenhardt, K.M. 2011. Rational heuristics: the 'simple rules' that strategists learn from process experience. *Strategic Management Journal*, 32(13): 1437–64.

Block, N. 2011. The higher order approach to consciousness is defunct. *Analysis*, 71(3): 419–31.

Bray, M.M. and Savin, N.E. 1986. Rational expectations equilibria, learning, and model specification. *Econometrica*, 54(5): 1129–60.

Buchanan, M. 2014. Great leap outwards. *Nature Physics*, 10(4): 243.

Burge, T. 2010. *Origins of objectivity*. Oxford University Press.

Burge, T. 2014. Perception: where mind begins. *Philosophy*, 89(3): 385–403.

Cattani, G. 2006. Technological pre-adaptation, speciation, and emergence of new technologies: how Corning invested and developed fiber optics. *Industrial and Corporate Change*, 15(2): 285–318.

Caves, E.M., Nowicki, S., and Johnsen, S. 2019. Von Uexküll revisited: addressing human biases in the study of animal perception. *Integrative and Comparative Biology*, 59(6): 1451–62.

Chabris, C. and Simons, D. 2010. *The invisible gorilla: and other ways our intuitions deceive us*. Random House.

Chalmers, D.J. 1996. *The conscious mind: in search of a fundamental theory*. Oxford University Press.

Chater, N. 2018. *The mind is flat: the illusion of mental depth and the improvised mind*. Penguin Books.

Chater, N., Felin, T., Funder, D.C., Gigerenzer, G., Koenderink, J.J., Krueger, J.I., Noble, D., Nordli, S.A., Oaksford, M., Schwartz, B., Stanovich, K.E., and Todd, P.M. 2018. Mind, rationality, and cognition: an interdisciplinary debate. *Psychonomic Bulletin and Review*, 25(2): 793–826.

Chater, N., Oaksford, M., Hahn, U., and Heit, E. 2010. Bayesian models of cognition. *Wiley Interdisciplinary Reviews. Cognitive Science*, 1(6): 811–23.

Clarke, D., Morley, E., and Robert, D. 2017. The bee, the flower, and the electric field: electric ecology and aerial electroreception. *Journal of Comparative Physiology A*, 203(9): 737–48.

Coase, R.H. 1937. The nature of the firm. *Economica*, 4(16): 386–405.

Crupi, V., Nelson, J.D., Meder, B., Cevolani, G., and Tentori, K. 2018. Generalized information theory meets human cognition: introducing a unified framework to model uncertainty and information search. *Cognitive Science*, 42(5): 1410–56.

Csaszar, F.A. and Levinthal, D.A. 2016. Mental representation and the discovery of new strategies. *Strategic Management Journal*, 37(10): 2031–49.

Dawkins, R. and Krebs, J.R. 1979. Arms races between and within species. *Proceedings of the Royal Society of London. Series B, Biological Sciences*, 205(1161): 489–511.

Day, T. 2011. Computability, Gödel's incompleteness theorem, and an inherent limit on the predictability of evolution. *Journal of the Royal Society. Interface/the Royal Society*, 9(69): 624–39.

Denrell, J., Fang, C., and Winter, S.G. 2003. The economics of strategic opportunity. *Strategic Management Journal*, 24(10): 977–90.

Eckstein, M.P., Drescher, B.A., and Shimozaki, S.S. 2006. Attentional cues in real scenes, saccadic targeting, and Bayesian priors. *Psychological Science*, 17(11): 973–80.

Eddington, A. 1928. *The nature of the physical world*. Cambridge University Press.

Elenkov, D.S. 1997. Strategic uncertainty and environmental scanning: the case for institutional influences on scanning behavior. *Strategic Management Journal*, 18(4): 287–302.

Ellis, G.F. 2005. Physics, complexity and causality. *Nature*, 435(7043): 743.

Evans, G.W. and Honkapohja, S. 2005. An interview with Thomas J. Sargent. *Macroeconomic Dynamics*, 9(4): 561–83.

Ewert, J.P. 2004. Motion perception shapes the visual world of amphibians. In Prete, F.R. (ed.). *Complex worlds from simpler nervous systems*. The MIT press.

Fawcett, T.W., Fallenstein, B., Higginson, AD, Houston, A.I., Mallpress, D.E., Trimmer, P.C., and McNamara, J.M. 2014. The evolution of decision rules in complex environments. *Trends in Cognitive Sciences*, 18(3): 153–61.

Felin, T., Felin, M., Krueger, J.I., and Koenderink, J. 2019. On surprise-hacking. *Perception*, 48(2): 109–14.

Felin, T., Kauffman, S., Koppl, R., and Longo, G. 2014. Economic opportunity and evolution: beyond landscapes and bounded rationality. *Strategic Entrepreneurship Journal*, 8(4): 269–82.

Felin, T., Kauffman, S., Mastrogiorgio, A., and Mastrogiorgio, M. 2016. Factor markets, actors and affordances. *Industrial and Corporate Change*, 25(1): 133–47.

Felin, T., Koenderink, J., and Krueger, J.I. 2017. Rationality, perception, and the all-seeing eye. *Psychonomic Bulletin and Review*, 24(4): 1040–59.

Felin, T. and Zenger, T.R. 2016. Strategy, problems and a theory of the firm. *Organization Science*, 27(1): 222–31.

Felin, T. and Zenger, T.R. 2017. The theory-based view: economic actors as theorists. *Strategy Science*, 2(4): 258–71.

Fleming, L. and Sorenson, O. 2001. Technology as a complex adaptive system: evidence from patent data. *Research Policy*, 30(7): 1019–39.

Fragaszy, D. and Liu, Q., 2012. Instrumental behavior, problem-solving, and tool use in nonhuman animals. *Encyclopedia of the Sciences of Learning*, 1579–82.

Fragaszy, D.M. and Mangalam, M. 2018. *Tooling. Advances in the Study of Behavior*. Academic Press, Cambridge.

Gabora, L. 2019. Creativity: linchpin in the quest for a viable theory of cultural evolution. *Current Opinion in Behavioral Sciences*, 27: 77–83.

Ganco, M. and Hoetker, G. 2009. NK modeling methodology in the strategy literature: bounded search on a rugged landscape, In Bergh, D.D. and Ketchen, D.J. (eds.). *Research methodology in strategy and management*. Emerald Group Publishing.

Gavetti, G. 2012. Perspective—toward a behavioral theory of strategy. *Organization Science*, 23(1): 267–85.

Gavetti, G. and Levinthal, D. 2000. Looking forward and looking backward: cognitive and experiential search. *Administrative Science Quarterly*, 45(1): 113–37.

Geisler, W.S. 2011. Contributions of ideal observer theory to vision research. *Vision Research*, 51(7): 771–81.

Gershman, S.J., Horvitz, E.J., and Tenenbaum, J.B. 2015. Computational rationality: a converging paradigm for intelligence in brains, minds, and machines. *Science*, 349(6245): 273–8.

Gigerenzer, G. and Gaissmaier, W. 2011. Heuristic decision making. *Annual Review of Psychology*, 62: 451–82.

Gigerenzer, G. and Selten, R., 2001. Rethinking rationality. In Gigerenzer, G. and Selten, R. (eds.) *Bounded rationality: the adaptive toolbox*. The MIT press.

Gigerenzer, G., Todd, P.M., and ABC Research Group, 1999. *Simple heuristics that make us smart*. Oxford University Press.

Gigerenzer, G. and Goldstein, D.G. 1996. Reasoning the fast and frugal way: models of bounded rationality. *Psychological Review*, 103(4): 650–69.

Goldstein, K. 1963. *The organism*. The MIT Press.

Goodwin, B. and Dawkins, R. 1995. What is an organism? A discussion. In Thompson, N.S. (ed.). *Perspectives in ethology*. Plenum Press.

Griffin, A.S. and Guez, D. 2014. Innovation and problem solving: a review of common mechanisms. *Behavioural Processes*, 109(B): 121–34.

Griffiths, T.L., Lieder, F., and Goodman, N.D. 2015. Rational use of cognitive resources: levels of analysis between the computational and the algorithmic. *Topics in Cognitive Science*, 7(2): 217–29.

Gwynne, D.T. and Rentz, D.C.F. 1983. Beetles on the bottle: male buprestids mistake stubbies for females (Coleoptera). *Australian Journal of Entomology*, 22(1): 79–80.

Heisenberg, W. 1971. *Physics and beyond: encounters and conversations.* Harper Collins.

Henderson, J.M., Malcolm, G.L., and Schandl, C. 2009. Searching in the dark: cognitive relevance drives attention in real-world scenes. *Psychonomic Bulletin and Review*, 16(5): 850–6.

Hills, T.T., Todd, P.M., Lazer, D., Redish, A.D., Couzin, I.D., and Cognitive Search Research Group 2015. Exploration versus exploitation in space, mind, and society. *Trends in Cognitive Sciences*, 19(1): 46–54.

Hiltzik, M.A. 2000. *Dealers of lightning: Xerox PARC and the dawn of the computer age.* Harper Business.

Hodgson, G.M. and Knudsen, T. 2010. *Darwin's conjecture: the search for general principles of social and economic evolution.* University of Chicago Press.

Hodgson, G.M. and Knudsen, T. 2011. Poverty of stimulus and absence of cause: some questions for Felin and Foss. *Journal of Institutional Economics*, 7(2): 295–8.

Hoffman, D.D., Singh, M., and Prakash, C. 2015. The interface theory of perception. *Psychonomic Bulletin and Review*, 22(6): 1480–506.

Hoffrage, U., Krauss, S., Martignon, L., and Gigerenzer, G. 2015. Natural frequencies improve Bayesian reasoning in simple and complex inference tasks. *Frontiers in Psychology*, 6: 1473.

Hwang, H.S. 1993. Optimal information acquisition for heterogenous duopoly firms. *Journal of Economic Theory*, 59(2): 385–402.

Kahneman, D. 2003. Maps of bounded rationality: psychology for behavioral economics. *American Economic Review*, 93(5): 1449–75.

Kahneman, D. 2011. *Thinking, fast and slow.* Farrar, Straus and Giroux.

Karni, E. and Vierø, M.L. 2013. 'Reverse Bayesianism': a choice-based theory of growing awareness. *American Economic Review*, 103(7): 2790–810.

Kauffman, S. 1996. *At home in the universe: the search for the laws of self-organization and complexity.* Oxford University Press.

Kauffman, S. 2003. Molecular autonomous agents. *Philosophical Transactions. Series A, Mathematical, Physical, and Engineering Sciences*, 361(1807): 1089–99.

Kauffman, S. 1993. *The origins of order: self-organization and selection in evolution.* Oxford University Press.

Kauffman, S. 2016. *Humanity in a creative universe.* Oxford University Press.

Kauffman, S. 2019. *A world beyond physics: the emergence and evolution of life.* Oxford University Press.

Kauffman, S. and Clayton, P. 2006. On emergence, agency, and organization. *Biology and Philosophy*, 21(4): 501–21.

Kauffman, S. and Weinberger, E.D. 1989. The NK model of rugged fitness landscapes and its application to maturation of the immune response. *Journal of Theoretical Biology*, 141(2): 211–45.

Kaznatcheev, A. 2019. Computational complexity as an ultimate constraint on evolution. *Genetics*, 212(1): 245–65.

Kaznatcheev, A., Montrey, M., and Shultz, T.R., 2014. Evolving useful delusions: subjectively rational selfishness leads to objectively irrational cooperation. *arXiv preprint arXiv:1405.0041*.

Kersten, D., Mamassian, P., and Yuille, A. 2004. Object perception as Bayesian inference. *Annual Review of Psychology*, 55: 271–304.

Kingdom, F.A.A. and Prins, N. 2016. *Psychophysics: a practical introduction.* Academic Press.

Kneeland, M., Schilling, M.A., and Aharonson, B. 2020. Exploring uncharted territory: knowledge search processes in the origination of outlier innovation. *Organization Science*, 31(3): 535–795.

Knill, D.C. and Richards, W. 1996. *Perception as Bayesian inference.* Cambridge University Press.

Koenderink, J.J. 2012. Geometry of imaginary spaces. *Journal of Physiology-Paris*, 106(5–6): 173–82.

Koenderink, J. 2014. The all-seeing eye. *Perception*, 43(1): 1–6.

Koenderink, J. 2016. To bayes or not to bayes.... *Perception*, 45(3): 251–4.

Kohler, W. 1925. *The mentality of apes.* Harcourt, Brace, Incorporated.

Levinthal, D.A. 1997. Adaptation on rugged landscapes. *Management Science*, 43(7): 934–50.

Longo, G., Montévil, M., Sonnenschein, C., and Soto, A.M. 2015. In search of principles for a theory of organisms. *Journal of Biosciences*, 40(5): 955–68.

Lorenz, K. 1973. *Behind the mirror: a search for a natural history of human knowledge.* Brace Jovanovich, Harcourt.

Makadok, R. and Barney, J.B. 2001. Strategic factor market intelligence: an application of information economics to strategy formulation and competitor intelligence. *Management Science*, 47(12): 1621–38.

Marr, D., 1982. *Vision: a computational investigation into the human representation and processing of visual information.* Henry Holt and Co. Inc.

Mayr, E. 1982. *The growth of biological thought: diversity, evolution, and inheritance.* Harvard University Press.

Miller, G.A. 1953. What is information measurement? *American Psychologist*, 8(1): 3–11.

Monod, J. 1971. *Chance and necessity: an essay on the natural philosophy of modern biology.* Vintage Book Company.

Morand-Ferron, J., Cole, E.F., and Quinn, J.L. 2016. Studying the evolutionary ecology of cognition in the wild: a review of practical and conceptual challenges. *Biological Reviews of the Cambridge Philosophical Society*, 91(2): 367–89.

Muth, J.F. 1961. Rational expectations and the theory of price movements. *Econometrica*, 29(3): 315–35.

Nagel, T. 1974. What is it like to be a bat? *The Philosophical Review*, 83(4): 435–50.

Nagel, T. 1989. *The view from nowhere.* Oxford University Press.

Nelson, R. 2006. Evolutionary social science and universal Darwinism. *Journal of Evolutionary Economics*, 16(5): 491–510.

Nelson, R.R. and Winter, S.G. 2002. Evolutionary theorizing in economics. *Journal of Economic Perspectives*, 16(2): 23–46.

Niemann, H.J. 2014. *Karl Popper and the two new secrets of life: including Karl Popper's Medawar lecture 1986 and three related texts.* Mohr Siebeck.

Noble, D. 2016. *Dance to the tune of life: biological relativity.* Cambridge University Press.

Noble, D. 2018. Central dogma or central debate? *Physiology*, 33(4): 246–9.

Noble, R. and Noble, D. 2017. Was the watchmaker blind? Or was she one-eyed? *Biology*, 6(4): 47.

Noble, R. and Noble, D. 2018. Harnessing stochasticity: how do organisms make choices? *Chaos*, 28(10): 106309.

Nolte, D.D. 2010. The tangled tale of phase space. *Physics Today*, 63(4): 33–8.

Oaksford, M. and Chater, N. 2007. *Bayesian rationality: the probabilistic approach to approach to human reasoning.* Oxford University Press.

Odling-Smee, F.J., Laland, K.N., and Feldman, M.W. 2003. *Niche construction: the neglected process in evolution.* Princeton University Press.

Penrose, E. 1952. Biological analogies in the theory of the firm. *American Economic Review*, 42(5): 804–19.

Polanyi, M. 1957. Problem solving. *British Journal for the Philosophy of Science*, VIII(30): 89–103.

Polanyi, M. 1958. *Personal knowledge.* Routledge.

Polanyi, M. 1968. Life's irreducible structure: live mechanisms and information in DNA are boundary conditions with a sequence of boundaries above them. *Science*, 160(3834): 1308–12.

Polanyi, M. 1970. Science and man. *Proceedings of the Royal Society of Medicine*, 63(9): 969–76.

Polanyi, M. 1971. Genius in science. *Archives de Philosophie*, 34: 593–607.

Popper, K. 1991. *All life is problem solving.* Routledge.

Pyke, G.H., Pulliam, H.R., and Charnov, E.L. 1977. Optimal foraging: a selective review of theory and tests. *The Quarterly Review of Biology*, 52(2): 137–54.

Rahnev, D. and Denison, R.N. 2018. Suboptimality in perceptual decision making. *Behavioral and Brain Sciences*, 41(e223): 1–66.

Randolph, S.E. 2014. Ecology of non-nidicolous ticks. *Biology of Ticks*, 2: 3–38.

Rolling, J.M. 1998. No protection, no progress for graphical user interfaces. *Marquette Intellectual Property Review*, 2(1): 157–94.

Roughgarden, T. 2010. Computing equilibria: a computational complexity perspective. *Economic Theory*, 42(1): 193–236.

Salam, A. 1990. *Unification of fundamental forces*. Cambridge University Press.

Sanz, C.M., Call, J., and Boesch, C. 2013. *Tool use in animals: cognition and ecology*. Cambridge University Press.

Schrödinger, E. 1944. *What is life?* Cambridge University Press.

Schrödinger, E. 1958. *Mind and matter*. Cambridge University Press.

Shannon, C.E. 1948. A mathematical theory of communication. *Bell System Technical Journal*, 27(3): 379–423.

Simon, H.A. 1955. A behavioral model of rational choice. *The Quarterly Journal of Economics*, 69(1): 99–118.

Simon, H.A. 1956. Rational choice and the structure of the environment. *Psychological Review*, 63(2): 129–38.

Simon, H.A. 1964. On the concept of organizational goal. *Administrative Science Quarterly*, 9(1): 1–22.

Simon, H.A. 1979. Rational decision making in business organizations. *American Economic Review*, 69(4): 493–513.

Simon, H.A. 1979. *Models of thought*. Yale University Press.

Simon, H.A. 1980. Cognitive science: the newest science of the artificial. *Cognitive Science*, 4(1): 33–46.

Simon, H.A. 1981. *Sciences of the artificial*. The MIT Press.

Simon, H.A. 1985. Human nature in politics: the dialogue of psychology with political science. *American Political Science Review*, 79(2): 293–304.

Simon, H.A. 1990. Invariants of human behavior. *Annual Review of Psychology*, 41(1): 1–19.

Simon, H.A. 1991. Organizations and markets. *Journal of Economic Perspectives*, 5(2): 25–44.

Simons, D.J. and Chabris, C.F. 1999. Gorillas in our midst: sustained inattention blindness for dynamic events. *Perception*, 28(9): 1059–74.

Solée, R.V., Valverde, S., Casals, M.R., Kauffman, S.A., Farmer, D., and Eldredge, N. 2013. The evolutionary ecology of technological innovations. *Complexity*, 18(4): 15–27.

Tinbergen, N. 1963. On aims and methods of ethology. *Zeitschrift für Tierpsychologie*, 20(4): 410–33.

Todd, P.M. and Brighton, H. 2016. Building the theory of ecological rationality. *Minds and Machines*, 26(1–2): 9–30.

Todd, P.M. and Gigerenzer, G. 2007. Environments that make us smart: ecological rationality. *Current Directions in Psychological Science*, 16(3): 167–71.

Treisman, A. 1998. The perception of features and objects. *Visual Attention*, 8: 26–54.

Van den Steen, E. 2016. A formal theory of strategy. *SSRN Electronic Journal*, 63(8): 2616–36.

Van den Steen, E. 2017. A formal theory of strategy. *Management Science*, 63(8): 2397–771.

Verrecchia, R.E. 1982. Information acquisition in a noisy rational expectations economy. *Econometrica*, 50(6): 1415–30.

Vladar, H.P., Santos, M., and Szathmáry, E. 2017. Grand views of evolution. *Trends in Ecology and Evolution*, 32(5): 324–34.

Von Hippel, E. and Von Krogh, G. 2016. Identifying viable need-solution pairs: problem solving without problem formulation. *Organization Science*, 27(1): 207–21.

Von Uexküll, J. 2010. *A foray into the worlds of animals and humans*. University of Minnesota Press.

Wheeler, J.A. 1990. Information, physics, quantum: the search for links. In Zurek, W.H. (ed.). *Complexity, entropy, and the physics of information*. Addison-Wesley.

Wilczek, F. 2016. *A beautiful question: finding nature's deep design*. Penguin.

Winter, S.G., 1964. Economic 'natural selection' and the theory of the firm. *Yale Economic Essays*, pp. 225–72.

Winter, S.G. 1987. Natural selection and evolution. In Eatwell, J., Milgate, M., and Newman, P. (eds.). *Allocation, information and markets*. Palgrave Macmillan.

Winter, S.G. 2011. Problems at the foundation? Comments on Felin and Foss. *Journal of Institutional Economics*, 7(2): 257–77.

Winter, S.G., Cattani, G., and Dorsch, A. 2007. The value of moderate obsession: insights from a new model of organizational search. *Organization Science*, 18(3): 403–19.

Wolfe, J.M. and Utochkin, I.S. 2019. What is a preattentive feature? *Current Opinion in Psychology*, 29: 19–26.

8

Extended Cognition and
The Innovation Process

Antonio Mastrogiorgio, Enrico Petracca, and Riccardo Palumbo

Introduction

The idea that innovation processes are enabled by propositional knowledge, which is also called 'epistemic base', is a central assumption of many works in the innovation tradition (see Mokyr, 2010). Such an assumption is supported by abundant evidence showing that knowledge breadth and depth affect radical innovations (Dewar and Dutton, 1986; Zhou and Li, 2012). Although propositional knowledge seems to be an important factor for innovating, many innovations can hardly be considered mere applications of existing knowledge. Future innovations arising from extant epistemic bases are more than simple projections of those epistemic bases insofar as they are hard to identify *ex ante*. Most works in the innovation tradition tend to focus on macro-level phenomena concerning the relation between scientific knowledge, industry, and the institutional background (Etzkowitz and Leydesdorff, 2000; Lundvall and Borrás, 2005) or meso-level phenomena concerning knowledge transfer (Argote and Ingram, 2000) and absorptive capacities in organizations (Cohen and Levinthal, 1990); this often at the expense of a deeper understanding of the individual-level cognitive dynamics involved in the innovation process and the role of knowledge (broadly conceived) in it.

When retracing the individual-level cognitive dynamics of innovation processes, we soon realize that unpredictability is the rule rather than the exception. Anecdotal evidence on the difficulty of prediction is abundant: 'I predict the internet will go spectacularly supernova and in 1996 catastrophically collapse' (Robert Metcalfe, founder of 3Com, 1995); 'Fooling around with alternating current is just a waste of time. No one will use it, ever' (Thomas Edison, 1889); 'There's no chance that the iPhone is going to get any significant market share' (Steve Ballmer, former CEO of Microsoft

Antonio Mastrogiorgio, Enrico Petracca, and Riccardo Palumbo, *Extended Cognition and The Innovation Process*
In: *New Developments in Evolutionary Innovation: Novelty Creation in a Serendipitous Economy.* Edited by: Gino Cattani and
Mariano Mastrogiorgio, Oxford University Press (2021). © Antonio Mastrogiorgio, Enrico Petracca, and Riccardo Palumbo.
DOI: 10.1093/oso/9780198837091.003.0008

Corp., 2007); 'Television won't be able to hold on to any market it captures after the first six months. People will soon get tired of staring at a plywood box every night' (Darryl Zanuck, 20th Century Fox, 1946). The predictions of experts on future innovations in their field of knowledge are often astonishingly wrong. However, although such predictive difficulties are, as we shall see, intrinsic to the logic of innovation, laypeople are often surprised by such blunders. Laypeople's attitude to rationalize may be the outcome of the 'hindsight bias', as they tend, *ex post*, to consider predictable what is not predictable (Roese and Vohs, 2012; Hoffrage and Pohl, 2003). The result is that what is (*ex ante*) actually unpredictable for experts is (*ex post*) allegedly predictable for laypeople.[1]

This type of unpredictability is one of the many things that biological and technological evolution have in common (Kauffman, 2000). Just as biological evolution is often characterized by discontinuities (Gould and Eldredge, 1977), the technological development of modern and contemporary ages also seems to be largely 'punctuated'. Evolutionarily speaking, what will occur in the proximate future is an 'adjacent possible' that is enabled and constrained by the current state of the world (Kauffman, 2000) in a manner that is unpredictable and not law-entailed (Longo et al., 2012). Economic evolution is largely creative and non-reducible to such an extent that it can hardly be bounded to causal laws and formally modelled (Koppl et al., 2015). Economic opportunities are not just 'searched' in a pre-existing landscape but rather emerge via *exaptations*, revealing new uses of existing technologies, products, and resources (Gould and Vrba, 1982) and resulting from perceptions of new affordances of existing artefacts (Felin et al., 2014, 2016).

The objective of this chapter is to explore the cognitive and behavioural factors involved in exaptive innovation processes. As we discuss in this contribution, the last three decades of advancements in cognitive and behavioural sciences provide an insightful theoretical framework for analysing innovation processes under new lenses. We will refer to the general notion of 'embodied cognition' (Wilson, 2002), and particularly to the notion of 'extended cognition' (Clark and Chalmers, 1998; Clark, 2008a). The fact that innovation processes cannot be predicted, generalized, or even

---

[1] Interestingly, this type of micro-level unpredictability of innovation is often reflected in the methodology of innovation studies. The micro-level dynamics of innovation processes is often investigated by means of case studies in which, by definition, the possibility of generalization is limited owing to the uniqueness and complexity of innovation phenomena and the presence of idiosyncratic factors. Moreover, the presence of an evolutionary selection bias (i.e. the fact that unsuccessful cases are often not observable) makes the systematic investigation of innovation processes even more problematic. Therefore, the history of technological innovations often results in a retrospective repertoire of successful cases. Case studies on failures are certainly common (e.g. Tripsas and Gavetti, 2000; Smith and Alexander, 1999), but the history of technological innovations is mainly written by the winners and often reveals an *ex post* hindsight bias that, in turn, reveals how technological developments were, *ex ante*, truly unpredictable.

reduced to formal models supports the hypothesis that innovation processes are constitutively embodied in the contingent interaction between individuals and artefacts and cannot be understood outside of the dimension of *practicality* and procedural knowledge. As we will see, this emphasis on practicality sheds new light on the individual-level cognitive dynamics of innovation processes while at the same time allowing us to revisit some key topics of the evolutionary tradition, such as routines in organizational innovation (see Nelson and Winter, 1982) and resources as the basis of firm heterogeneity (see Barney, 1991).

Theoretical background

The extended cognition hypothesis

Since the late 1980s, a significant amount of theoretical and experimental research has challenged the general assumption that cognitive processes are based on information-processing, which consists of the symbolic manipulation of internal representations of the external environment (see Gomila and Calvo, 2008). Such a new domain of research, flourishing under the name *embodied cognition*, has been originally intended as a paradigmatic change in the cognitive and behavioural sciences (see Wheeler, 2014), as it emphasizes the constitutive dependence of cognitive processes on the sensory-motor system and the morphological traits of the human body. Far from providing a unitary and internally coherent set of assumptions, embodied cognition is a vast programme of research characterized by a plurality of approaches (see Wilson, 2002; Clark, 2008b), which are often denoted by different labels such as 'distributed cognition', 'situated cognition', and 'embedded cognition', emphasizing specific aspects of the general hypothesis that cognition is embodied. Such a plurality is demonstrated by the wide spectrum of contributions, from experimental evidence on how specific body features and actions affect specific cognitive tasks (for a review, see Schwarz and Lee, 2018) to theoretical debates addressing the embodied nature of entire cognitive faculties (e.g. the hypothesis that numerical processing is not abstract but modality-dependent; see Kadosh and Walsh, 2009). Recently, the label '4E cognition' (Newen et al., 2018) has been introduced to express that the new turn in cognitive science is better described by the four pillars (the 4Es) of 'embodied', 'embedded', 'enacted', and 'extended' cognition.

Among the different threads on embodiment, this contribution will focus on 'extended cognition'. Although the precursors of extended cognition can be found in pragmatism (James, 1907), phenomenology (Merleau-Ponty, 1945), and situated robotics (Brooks, 1991), the extended cognition hypothesis is today mostly linked to the names of philosophers Andy Clark and David Chalmers. In a seminal contribution introducing the notion of 'extended mind', Clark and Chalmers (1998) argued that cognitive processes are not bound to what goes on in the head but are *extended* to the environment as they are (under certain conditions) constitutively coupled to the resources provided by the environment, its artefacts, and the interaction with them. A famous example by Clark and Chalmers of how cognition is extended to environmental artefacts concerns the case of *memory*. Consider an individual named Otto, who is suffering from Alzheimer's disease. Like most of the patients suffering from memory impairment, Otto uses a notebook in which he takes note of a number of relevant pieces of information and consults it when needed: the notebook is his (only) memory device. Now consider a healthy person named Inga who has no memory issues. Assuming that Otto and Inga have to go separately to an exhibition at MoMA on 53rd Street in New York, Otto could only use his notebook to find the address, whereas Inga would likely simply rely on her 'internal' memory. Now, Otto's notebook and Inga's hippocampal neurons can be considered equivalent from a functional point of view. Otto and Inga both trust their sources and use them to reach their goal regardless of the material substrate. The notion of extended mind is based on the so-called 'parity principle': if a part of the world is functionally equivalent to an internal cognitive process, then it should be considered cognitive as well. Clark and Chalmers (1998) indeed stated the following: 'If, as we confront some task, a part of the world functions as a process which, *were it done in the head*, we would have no hesitation in recognizing as part of the cognitive process, then that part of the world *is* (so we claim) part of the cognitive process' (p. 8).

Before going on with the characterization of the extended cognition hypothesis, it is important to clarify what extended cognition is not. Most importantly, it is not a hypothesis on the adaptation of a cognitive content (e.g. heuristics) to the structure of task environments (Newell and Simon, 1972; Gigerenzer and Selten, 2002). A fundamental aspect of extended cognition is that it does not focus on the content of cognitive processes but on their working mechanisms, that is, it advances a theory of how the vehicles of cognition spread out into the world (and are not just bound to internal resources, such as the brain). As stated by Clark (2005), 'It is important…to maintain a distinction between vehicles and contents. Possessing a contentful mental state is most plausibly a property of a whole active system (perhaps in some historical and/or environmental context). Within that system, certain enduring material aspects may play a special role in enabling the system to possess (whether occurrently or dispositionally) a given mental state. These material aspects are the vehicle of the content' (p. 1) (see also Lyre, 2018).

From its introduction in 1998, the extended mind hypothesis has faced a number of critiques and subsequent restatements (for an updated account of the research on the extended mind, see Gallagher, 2018). One criticism concerns the so-called 'coupling-constitution fallacy', according to which what is coupled with cognition (i.e. causally determining a cognitive outcome) does not in principle mean that it also 'constitutes' cognition (Adams and Aizawa, 2010; Aizawa, 2010). According to this criticism, what is inside the head—the 'mark of the cognitive'—cannot be equated to what is in the world. Such critiques (for Clark's replies, see Clark, 2008a) have led the extended cognition hypothesis to slightly change. Indeed, the idea that external resources should be functionally equivalent to internal ones in order to extend the mind (as emphasized by the 'parity principle') is a rather restrictive requirement and, in the evolution of the hypothesis, has been identified with the *first wave* of extended cognition research. The *second wave* of extended cognition emphasizes instead the idea of 'complementarity'. External resources do not always substitute for internal ones but can play other roles and integrate with them (Sutton, 2010). In other words, the focus of the second wave is on 'functional integration' rather than on 'functional equivalence': the mind is extended by external resources when the coupling between internal and external resources creates a new cognitive entity in its own right that is *more* than individuals' cognition alone. In the specific view of Menary (2007, 2010a), there is 'cognitive integration' when organisms physically manipulate the environment so as to modify their cognitive niche and transform their cognitive capacities. Finally, the *third wave* of extended cognition considers cognitive processes beyond the coupling between individuals' resources and narrowly-understood artefacts (e.g. Otto's notebook) to encompass also the social, institutional, and cultural dimensions (Gallagher, 2013). This approach also advocates a more radical interactionist perspective on the coupling between individuals and environments. Kirchhoff and Kiverstein (2019: pp. 15–23) have recently identified four pillars of the third-wave approach to extended cognition. According to them, extended cognition entails the following: i) dynamic singularities and no fixed properties of cognitive processes, ii) flexibility of the boundaries of the mind, iii) distributed cognitive assembly of cognitive processes, and iv) diachronic constitution of cognition. The third wave is often considered strictly connected to an approach in the philosophy of mind known as 'enactivism' (Gallagher, 2018; Gallagher and Allen, 2018).

Overall, extended cognition is a fast-moving and far-from-consolidated domain of inquiry. Possible intersections with other prominent hypotheses in cognition and neurosciences—among which there is the hypothesis of *predictive processing* (for an overview, see Clark, 2013)—are being currently explored and seem promising (see Kirchhoff, 2018). In the following paragraph, we will discuss how cognitive extendedness can be an insightful framework for understanding cognitive processes in the real world of artefacts and resources.

Off-loading, epistemic manipulation, and the transformative approach

The first wave of extended cognition originally introduced by Clark and Chalmers has been mostly related to the notion of off-loading. Off-loading means that the environment can do the cognitive work in place of individuals (Risko and Gilbert, 2016). The case of Otto shows that off-loading may be 'constitutive', that is, the system composed by Otto and his notebook can be considered as a cognitive system of its own, altogether constituting Otto's cognition. The case of Inga represents instead a milder notion of off-loading. Inga may use her notebook to ease her memory load, but in this way Inga's cognition seems to be just 'enabled' by the notebook (and not constituted by it), as she does not necessarily need it to perform her cognitive activity. Stated as such, the case of cognitive enabling is more common than constitution. People usually use external devices to off-load their cognitive load even if they do not—strictly speaking—need it. Entire environments can be used or even designed to off-load people's cognition (Kirsh, 1995). Less trivially, beyond tools in individuals' 'peripersonal' space, institutional architectures can also be said to off-load individuals' cognition (Clark, 1997). In any case, the difference between Otto and Inga's cases shows that cognitive off-loading is not always conceptually easy to define and circumscribe; many complex cognitive processes involve off-loading but are not restricted to it. Moreover, the notion of off-loading can misleadingly convey the idea that off-loading entails a merely passive attitude, in which agents entirely outsource their cognitive load onto the environment without any engagement with it.

A number of extended cognitive processes in the real world are better and more saliently conceptualized as cases of functional integration rather than functional equivalence (Sutton, 2010; Menary, 2010b). Consider once more Inga's case. We know that Inga is a mathematician and that she uses pen and paper to do her maths, like the majority of her colleagues. Not surprisingly,

Inga not only finds that approaching maths problem with pen and paper is easier, but she would say that many ideas would never come to her mind without pen and paper (Zhang, 1997). As for the system consisting of Inga and pen and paper, we could hardly say that pen and paper play the same function of Inga's neurons. Rather, they enhance Inga's cognition. The new cognitive system that integrates Inga's internal resources and pen and paper is *more* than Inga's cognition alone.

Manipulation, particularly the physical manipulation of tools and artefacts in the real world, is a key ingredient of cognitive integration. Consider the case of the jigsaw puzzle. It would be inconceivable to solve a jigsaw puzzle only by means of cognitive effort, that is, by mentally rotating and assembling its pieces. If one is asked to solve the jigsaw puzzle, one soon realizes that physical manipulation is necessary: no human cognitive resource would be enough to solve the puzzle without physically juxtaposing the pieces or without the possibility to go forward through trial and error. This is because our perceptual apparatus alone could not discriminate between slightly different shapes of the tiles. The fundamental epistemic role played by manipulation can be emphasized by using the distinction between 'epistemic' and 'pragmatic' action introduced by Kirsh and Maglio (1994). This distinction maintains that 'pragmatic' action is a kind of action that puts an agent closer to her goal, whereas an 'epistemic' action is an action performed to enhance our epistemic state and cognitive capacities. The manipulation of artefacts, as in the case of the tiles of a jigsaw puzzle, is a process that we often perform 'epistemically', that is, to extract information from the artefacts that would never be available otherwise.

Cognitive extension can go beyond the cases just considered. The third wave of extended mind opens up new possibilities for cognitive extension. Extension, as we have seen, may involve objects that are not only seen as off-loading tools but also as constituents of a novel system in which manipulation creates new cognitive and epistemic possibilities. Norman (1993) goes beyond this view by looking at cognition-enhancing objects such as Otto's notebook (which he calls 'epistemic artefacts') (see also Sterenly, 2004) from a systemic and cultural point of view. He focuses on the entire and complex system of interactions between humans and epistemic artefacts emphasizing the mutually transformative processes that interaction entails. Malafouris (2013) has recently introduced the notion of 'material engagement' to address these transformative relationships by focusing on the level of material culture. From this point of view, epistemic artefacts not only help new cognitive and epistemic possibilities to emerge (as sorts of 'transactional objects'); they also serve the purpose of building cognitive niches (Sterenly, 2004), and can embody stratified knowledge and even entire worldviews. Not all epistemic artefacts, so to say, are created epistemically and cognitively equal. Pen and paper are not the same thing as an electronic microscope or a quantum collider, as they enable specific cognitive processes differing in terms of vehicles, contents, and epistemic reach. Zooming out from the domain of objects, Clark (1997) broadens the scope of extendedness by showing that institutions can also be understood as off-loading devices. In turn, the third wave of extended mind maintains that the relationship between individuals and institutions cannot be understood as a mere case of off-loading but that mutually transformative relationships are the rule in the socio-institutional and cultural environments (Hutchins, 2008; Gallagher, 2013).

In the next section, we discuss the exaptive innovation process from the extended cognition point of view. If we accept, even loosely, the idea that artefacts coupled with individuals play a distinctive and irreducible cognitive and epistemic role, we then realize that we can, and even should, reconceptualize entirely the cognitive processes involved in innovation.

The exaptive innovation process in an extended perspective

According to well-known definitions, incremental innovations are 'minor improvements or simply adjustments in current technology' (Dewar and Dutton, 1986: p. 1423), and radical innovations 'are fundamental changes that represent revolutionary changes in technology. They represent clear departures from existing practice' (ibid.). While incremental innovations are usually thought to be based on *adaptive* processes involving linear and incremental improvements of existing artefacts and resources, recent studies emphasize the role of *exaptive* processes (Gould and Vrba, 1982) at the root of radical innovations. The idea is that a number of radical innovations actually come into being as new applications of existing artefacts and resources originally developed for different purposes (Andriani et al., 2017; Andriani and Cattani, 2016; Cattani, 2006; Dew et al., 2004). If we endorse the idea that many innovations are simply due to functional shifts (or to partial functional redeployments), then we must recognize that the 'grand narratives of science and innovation' are only part of the innovation story (and not necessarily the most salient one). The so-called 'jugaad' innovations (Radjou et al., 2012) are a case in point: they are novel, original, and impactful redeployments of available artefacts and resources, often of marginal importance (e.g. using recycled plastic bottles as rudimentary air coolers to refresh rooms without electricity). Importantly, these functional shifts are not simply made by design but are the outcome of users' shift in use (Faulkner and Runde, 2009).

Ecological psychology offers a number of insights for understanding the exaptive innovation process following James Gibson's approach: 'Ask not what's inside your head, but what your head's inside of.' This approach emphasizes the role of environments in cognitive phenomena and provides a theoretical framework that is able to conceptualize the emergence of new uses of existing artefacts in terms of perception-action dynamics. How living beings perceive their environment is species-specific and depends on their body morphology and on the specificities of their perception-action apparatus; that is, perception is sensitive to specific environmental traits in which the bodies and the perceptual apparatuses have evolved (the species-specific adaptive process is known as *Umwelt*: see von Uexküll, 1957, and Felin and Kauffman in this volume). In this context, 'affordances' are defined as the traits of the environment that allow species-specific actions for organisms (Gibson, 1977). As such, affordances can be understood as 'potentials' to the extent that they invite a range of possible actions (Norman, 1988) and, for this very reason, are able to trigger innovation when new actions are explored (Felin et al., 2016).

Innovating through artefacts

As we have discussed, the manipulation of artefacts is not only pragmatic but, even more importantly for studying innovation, epistemic. Physicist Richard Feynman did not just write down on paper the mathematical ideas he had previously and independently formulated in his head. He worked through pen and paper, and, as he said, his ideas could not have come into existence without the help of those artefacts (Clark, 2008, p. xxv). We argue that Feynman's case is not an exception but the rule. In creative activities in general, thinking through artefacts is fundamental and, sometimes, the only way to innovate.

Lorenzo Magnani has extensively studied discovery processes, which he labels 'abductive processes' (Magnani, 2009). Within abductive processes, he has focused in particular on what he calls 'manipulative abduction', which is defined as the cognitive process 'that happens when we are thinking through doing and not only, in a pragmatic sense, about doing' (Magnani, 2004: p. 442). Manipulative abduction is another way to call what we have already defined above 'epistemic manipulation'. Both terms convey the idea that manipulations not only enable but sometimes also constitute cognitive processes. Solutions to problems, discoveries, new ideas, and so on, could not come into being without such manipulations. It has been shown that insights leading to problem-solving are strictly dependent on the physical manipulation of the task environment and that the effectiveness of such insights increases with the degree of embodiment of the manipulation (see Vallée-Tourangeau et al., 2016). Real world examples of the fundamental role of manipulation are ubiquitous. Architects use 3D models to elicit potentials hidden in their original projects (Kirsh, 2010). Designers and mechanical engineers use prototypes to explore problems and find solutions. Painters create the very instant they interact with the surface of the canvas.

Given these examples, the view that artefact manipulation is just a phase of the innovation process that ideally moves from the conception phase to the realization phase is empirically untenable. The traditional sequence of idea generation, development, and realization (Eppinger and Ulrich, 2015) not only simplifies but somehow misrepresents the actual nature of innovation processes. The shift in cognitive science from an information-processing to an 'embodied' and 'situated' approach originally started in the 1980s by acknowledging that human cognition does not generally implement plans of action (Petracca, 2017). The anthropologist of technology Lucy Suchman found that plans are not just preconceived courses of action that are then executed. For instance, people learning to use technological objects do not read the instruction manual and then just apply the prescriptions. In many cases, the plan of action unfolds through the action and interaction with the technological object; therefore, action and interaction become the plan itself (Suchman, 1987). Even in cases that apparently fit the standard view of product innovation, working with artefacts is crucial for exploring the possibilities of a product. In R&D laboratories, prototypes are not merely intended as the materialization of abstract design. Cattani (2006) discusses Corning's invention of optical fibres and shows that Corning 'conducted its R&D without anticipating its subsequent importance for developing fiber optics', adding that 'it was during this phase that Corning (unintentionally) created the conditions' (p. 299) for market success. Prototypes and experiments do not just sequentially follow an allegedly pure ideation stage, but in many crucial examples transform the ideation stage itself.

Hence, it is crucial to change our traditional view of how innovation processes are actually instantiated. From the epistemic point of view, we suggest considering the test and realization stages within the same analytical boundary as the ideation stage. Consider the case of a laboratory testing the effectiveness of a certain drug that was originally intended to cure a specific pathology. If we conceived the test as a mere exercise in falsification or confirmation of the original idea, we would not be able to go beyond the originally intended purposes in terms of mere dichotomy: it works/it doesn't work for that pathology. However, if we conceived the experimentation as an investigation into the full potential of that drug, we might realize that the active principle could work for different (and sometimes seemingly unrelated) pathologies than the one for which it was originally designed (Andriani et al., 2017). This open approach would allow whoever is in charge of the innovation enterprise to exploit serendipitous mechanisms (Merton and Barber, 2004). Notice that we do not need to change the actual manipulations but rather the way we look at them. In other words, the shift lies in the mindset through which agents conceive of the manipulation phase. Manipulations and tests can be intended as 'shadow tools' for exploring new possibilities rather than simply testing prespecified uses. In the real world, epistemic manipulations are not alternative to pragmatic manipulations but work with them synergistically. Looking at them as two radically different concepts may prevent us from conceiving of them as opportunities to explore new possibilities.

Affordable innovations

Sarasvathy (2001) emphasizes the importance of effectuation logic (intended as an alternative to causal explanation) in entrepreneurship. According to effectuation theory, entrepreneurs start from what they have, namely, the artefacts and resources in their possession, and not from what they aim for. They search for goals given existing means instead of searching for means able to 'cause' the given goals (as suggested in classical approaches to entrepreneurship). This view is consistent with the idea that innovators, in general, manipulate the resources in their possession to explore new possibilities of innovation instead of starting from pre-existing, unsatisfied needs and then innovating to satisfy those needs. Following this logic, opportunities are not just discovered or exploited but are created (for a discussion, see Alvarez and Barney, 2007). Such an act of creation often relies on the possibility of uncovering novel 'affordances' for resources available to the innovator (Felin et al., 2016; Soler and Santacana, 2013). The identification of novel affordances, understood as new uses for artefacts currently used for a certain set of functions, rests on the conceptualization of artefacts as epistemic means of creation. Functions are not ontological and exclusive properties of the artefacts, but properties attributed by people who interact with them, be they designers or users (Faulkner and Runde, 2009). In the words of the father of the concept of affordance, James Gibson (1986), 'the fact that a stone is a missile does not imply that it cannot be other things as well. It can be a paperweight, a bookend, a hammer, or a pendulum blob' (p. 126).

The ability to generate original and appropriate solutions, which is a constitutive ingredient of creativity (Sternberg and Lubart, 1999), has often been investigated by measuring the level of 'divergent thinking' (e.g. Guilford 1967). Divergent thinking occurs because artefacts are not cognitively represented and categorized in terms of necessary and sufficient conditions. Human cognition does not categorize artefacts in terms of complete descriptors of their features but in terms of their 'family resemblance' with a prototype (Wittgenstein, 1953; Rosch, 1975). Given that artefacts cannot be defined by a complete list of features, new affordances can be perceived, in a situated manner, depending on ecological pressures. Accordingly, creativity can be reconceptualized in ecological and situated terms depending on underlying actions, artefacts, and affordances (Glăveanu, 2013).

The ecological and situated arguments discussed in this paper allow us to hypothesize that a number of creative processes are artefact-specific. Many innovations indeed emerge via reasoning processes enabled by specific artefacts. Let us go back to the case of mathematical invention and consider, as an illustration of the idea of artefact specificity, the 'invention' of Euclidean geometry. We could argue that there is an artefact specificity between the development of Euclidean geometry and the two-dimensional substrate (such as papyri sheets) on which it was developed. The ecological roots of Euclidean geometry lie in the two-dimensional flat surfaces of papyrus sheets on which geometry was originally ideated. In other words, Euclidean geometry becomes possible (and is thus 'affordable', in Gibson's terms) when two-dimensional surfaces, such as an old papyrus or a modern paper (or even a salt-writing tray), are involved in geometrical reasoning. Speculatively, if we had instead studied geometry on different surfaces, e.g. elliptic or hyperbolic surfaces, we would have perhaps developed different constructs and different sorts of geometrical knowledge. Two parallel lines (in Euclidean geometry) curve away or towards each other in hyperbolic or elliptic geometry, respectively. In this regard, the paper sheet is more than a neutral artefact for the representation of mathematical constructs (Lakoff and Núñez, 2000).

The dynamic interplay between internal and external factors is a fundamental tenet of extended cognition. The brain, the body, and environments are dynamically interwoven so that cognitive processes are continuously shaped and reshaped. Such dynamic interplay is consistent with the notion of 'dynamic singularity', i.e. 'a continuous and complex dynamic system... with feedback loops that...have external as well as internal orbits' (Hurley, 1998: p. 333). A ceramist working on a potter's wheel is a good example: the brain, hands, arms, eyes, and wet clay are so interwoven that the process is constantly unfolding over short time scales (Kirchhoff, 2018). From this perspective, there is no analytical priority of specific constituents, such as the brain, the body, or the artefact. As a result of this integration, the cognitive process cannot be separated from the artefact that is taking shape. Accordingly, referring to what we discussed above, the innovation process can be (re)conceptualized by adopting a *third wave*/enactivist framework by saying that novel affordances are distributed in an ecology of artefacts and individuals.

Organizational implications: reconceptualizing practicality

A fundamental assumption in much of the current innovation research is that that the creation of knowledge and its applications belong to two distinct domains that are sequentially related: knowledge is created and transferred from its source (e.g. research centres) to industry and business, where it is applied. Although this representation fits the common-sense view of innovation, it is not always true. Taleb (2012) provocatively juxtaposes academicians and practitioners by emphasizing the retrospective tendency of the former to secure the paternity of discoveries and inventions actually made by the latter. Taleb calls this effect 'lecturing birds to fly', which is related to the commonsensical tendency of attributing to 'propositional' and formal knowledge a number of things that are actually discovered and/or learned through experience.

Knowledge has indeed also a 'pragmatic' dimension, and this pragmatic dimension (i.e. the 'useful knowledge' shared in a society) is a constitutive ingredient of economic growth (Kuznets, 1965). However, how this knowledge is actually exploited in terms of innovations is not a linear process based on a simple transposition 'from science to business'. Mokyr (2006) makes a distinction between 'propositional knowledge' (knowledge, typically of a scientific kind, about the regularities of nature) and 'prescriptive knowledge' (the knowledge, whether codified or tacit, that society can exploit by means of methods and techniques). Mokyr's distinction is, *mutatis mutandis*, consistent with Polanyi's distinction between 'right or wrong' knowledge and 'successful or unsuccessful' knowledge (Polanyi, 1962: p. 175; see also Ryle's (1949) distinction between *know-that* and *know-how*). According to Mokyr (2001), 'propositional knowledge...can exist and evolve on its own without being "expressed" in an underlying technique. Propositional knowledge is "expressed" by the techniques it generates, and its manifest entity is observable when the prescriptive knowledge is actually carried out' (p. 15). In Mokyr's view, the *practicality* instantiated in the specific technique is the unit of analysis of the evolutionary process (not simply the artefact, as in Basalla (1988), for instance). Indeed, he stated that 'a bicycle, for instance, requires quite different sets of instructions on how to build it and how to ride it. The unit of selection is the instruction set, not the bicycle itself' (Mokyr, 2000: p. 7). The idea of *practicality*, as a fundamental ingredient of innovation and change, will be discussed with reference to routines (as the unit of analysis of the evolutionary process, Nelson and Winter, 1982), by considering the different phases of development of the extended cognition hypotheses (see Section 2.1).

According to the *first wave* of the extended cognition hypothesis, practicality can be associated to organizational off-loading through the notion of routine introduced by Nelson and Winter (1982) and defined as the 'regular and behavioral patterns of firms' (p. 14). Routines rely on shared epistemic artefacts and, as such, can be considered the *memory* of organizations. Nelson and Winter (1982) stated the following: 'forms of external memory— files, message boards, manuals, computer memories, and magnetic tapes—... complement and support individual memories...maintained in a large part as a routine organizational function' (p. 105). In behavioural terms, organizational routines are stored as procedural memory (Cohen and Bacdayan, 1994). Insofar as these forms of external memory (cf. Section 2) reduce individuals' cognitive burden in organizations, Nelson and Winter's notion of routine can be somehow considered a precursor of the *first wave* of extended cognition.

With reference to the *second wave* of the extended cognition hypothesis, the 'complementarity' between internal and external resources can provide novel insight into the role of the tacit dimension of routines as a source of innovation. Routines are not only the memory organizations. As Nelson and Winter (1982) argued, they are the units of economic change as well. Furthermore, practicality (pertaining to the tacit dimension of routines) can be understood, from an extended perspective, as a way to explore exaptive potentials (new uses of organizational artefacts and resources). Indeed, the practical manipulation of artefacts and resources is not only goal-oriented and instrumental but also enables and even constitutes new reasoning processes. Therefore, we argue that practicality could be reconceptualized by looking at how the tacit manipulation of artefacts like routines enables (but also constrains) the cognitive processes involved in the recognition of new uses and functions (Yi et al., 2016). As discussed earlier, we should consider practicality both pragmatically (as the implementation of planned and goal-directed actions) and epistemically (as a way of enabling and constituting cognitive processes oriented to pursue novelty).

With reference to the *third wave*, individuals' engagement with their environment places a strong emphasis on interactive and distributed processes. Such interactive and distributed views are not new in management and innovation studies. Since the foundational contributions of Bourdieu (1977), Giddens (1984), and Latour (1990), a significant tradition has investigated the role of material factors in shaping organizational processes (e.g. Peschl and Fundneider, 2012; Orlikowski, 2007). In particular, emphasis has been placed on epistemic artefacts (discussed in Section 3.2) (see also Rheinberger, 1997) and their role in fostering organizational change (Miettinen and Virkkunen, 2005). With respect to this research tradition, the enactivist view places emphasis on organizational resources as genuinely cognitive ingredients of exaptive innovations. In frameworks such as that of 'participatory sense-making' (De Jaeger and Di Paolo, 2007), exaptive innovations could be, somehow, understood in terms of 'exaptation of routines'. The exaptation of routines would consist of reconfiguring procedural memories that are distributed in the organization to generate insight about the unconventional uses of resources.

Overall, the discussion above suggests considering extended cognition as a framework that, by putting emphasis on the pragmatic, epistemic, and transformative dimensions of actor-artefact interactions, could help us to reconceptualize organizational routines as extended-cognition devices leading to novelty via the generation of new uses and functions of artefacts and resources. Although the link between extended cognition and organizational routines is certainly still speculative and needs to be further developed, we see extended cognition as a 'launch pad' for a better understanding of the origins of novelty *within* the existing frameworks of evolutionary theory.

New insights from behavioural science and neuroscience

New exciting possibilities for understanding exaptive innovation processes through the lens of extended cognition are offered by new developments in behavioural science and neuroscience. These fields consist of different lines of research that investigate the cognitive dynamic of individuals' engagement with the real world of artefacts and resources. For instance, neuroscientific research on 'affordance landscapes' shows that action specification and action selection and execution occur simultaneously and not sequentially, as traditionally hypothesized (see Cisek, 2007; Pezzulo and Cisek, 2016). This supports a view of cognition as strictly linked to action execution. As such, this evidence challenges the general idea that the ideation of a plan of action and its implementation are two separate processes, at least in the context of plans of actions that require actions to be implemented. Clinical studies on 'apraxia', which is a disorder of skilled movement, could also provide significant insights on the cognitive phenomena involved in unusual (and potentially creative) uses of artefacts (Osiurak et al., 2009). Moreover, neuroscience also shows that 'neural reuse' is a principle of organization of the brain itself as brain circuits that evolved for specific functions are (in evolutionary timespans) *exapted* for other uses, while preserving the original ones (Anderson, 2010).

Other recent studies have explored the compatibility of extended cognition with the hypothesis of the *predictive brain* (called, more generally, *predictive processing*). This hypothesis looks at the brain as a device that constantly matches top-down predictions and expectations (typically made through a hierarchical, generative model) with bottom-up sensory inputs while aiming to minimize prediction error (Friston, 2010; Clark, 2013; Hohwy, 2013). The predictive brain is presented as a framework able to shed new light on embodied perception and, more generally, on embodied and enacted cognition (Kirchhoff, 2018; Kirchhoff and Kiverstein, 2019). The notion of *surprise* is central in the predictive brain framework. In brief, it is related to the idea that predictions and expectations based on top-down generative models are subjected to a 'free-energy' bound, according to which individuals try to minimize the surprise given by the difference between the model of the world and the actual experience of it (Friston, 2010) by revising or substantially altering the generative model. Therefore, surprise (or 'surprisal', in strict neural and computational terms) deserves special attention for its possible role in understanding innovation processes like those leading to new unconventional uses of artefacts and resources. A possibility is that new, unexpected cues experienced by the actor (like a candy bar melting in the pocket) as he/she interacts with an artefact (such as a radar containing a magnetron) act as surprises leading to a radical revision of the generative model and to thinking of new uses and functions of artefacts and resources (in our example, the magnetron is then seen as a cooking device, thus leading to the invention of the microwave).

Such surprises can be the product of active exploration because of the natural human propensity to seek variety, resulting in behaviour that increases the likelihood of experiencing novel, informative states (Schwartenbeck et al., 2013; see also Clark, 2018). Moreover, the way in which such surprises are the product of active exploration also involves degrees of 'attention', which is another central aspect of the predictive brain (Feldman and Friston, 2010), here understood as the faculty able to balance top-down and bottom-up processes. We argue that the hypothesis of the predictive brain could provide a number of insights into the idea of exaptation and 'happy accidents', thus shedding new light on the role of serendipity in innovation (Merton and Barber, 2004). In a way, the predictive brain suggests seeing exaptation and serendipity as the result of a mismatch between top-down cognitive processing (such as the predicted, common, uses of artefacts and resources, due to 'functional fixedness' or other biases:[2] see Felin et al., 2016; German and Barrett, 2005) and bottom-up processes (e.g., sensory evidence arising in ongoing manipulation of artefacts). As new, unexpected, and 'surprising' cues emerge via artefact manipulation, this can be the basis of new generative models through which the actor sees and makes sense of new uses of artefacts.

Conclusions

Unprestatability is a key feature of the history of business and technology. Taleb (2012) reports the following: Tiffany & Co., which is a luxury jewels chain, initially was a stationery store; Raytheon, which created the first driving system for missiles, initially produced refrigerators; Nokia, a mobile phone producer, started as a paper and rubber shoes factory; Oneida Silversmiths, which produces cutlery, was a religious community in the beginning. Such cases are nothing more than a small sample of otherwise extensive evidence. The nonlinear innovation dynamics has been theoretically framed usually in terms of emergent opportunities (Mintzberg and Waters, 1985) or in terms of contingent phenomena based on happy accidents (Dew, 2009). In this chapter, we have emphasized that the practical dimension of innovation is far from being just 'dirty work' (i.e. the mere implementation of preconceived plans) and can be reconceptualized by using the hypothesis of extended cognition in terms of the exploration of the exaptive potential of artefacts and resources. In particular, embodied factors are central and even required for the identification of novel affordances. On the basis of our discussion, practicality can be considered the ground on which 'contingency' happens and on which individuals are able to recognize and make sense of the happy accident. The history of science and technological innovation is,

---

[2] Like the 'omission bias' (Spranca et al., 1991), the 'status quo bias' and 'loss aversion' (Kahneman et al., 1991) lead to conservative behaviour.

actually, a history of undisciplined-but-alert manipulations of contingent resources instead of being a systematic, goal-directed application and implementation of existing propositional knowledge, as it is often represented (Gratzer, 2004).

The new and unconventional emphasis on the value of 'dirty work' is consistent with the evolutionary view according to which contingent resources (and constraints) enable the attainment of acceptable solutions instead of optimal ones (Gould and Lewontin, 1979). In his well-known contribution, François Jacob (1977) emphasizes that 'natural selection does not work as an engineer works. It works like a *tinkerer*—a tinkerer who does not know exactly what he is going to produce but uses whatever he finds around him whether it be pieces of string, fragments of wood, or old cardboards; in short it works like a tinkerer who uses everything at his disposal to produce some kind of workable object' (p. 1163, emphasis added). The evolutionary contrast between the systematic and finalized use of scientific propositional knowledge and the manipulation of contingent resources is a central argument in our discussion.

This emphasis on the practical manipulation of contingent resources can also shed new light on the so-called resource-based view (RBV) of competitive advantage. According to this view, sustainable competitive advantage relies on the presence of specific types of resources and capabilities (which must be valuable, rare, imperfectly imitable, and non-substitutable) (Wernerfelt, 1984; Barney, 1991; Peteraf, 1993) and is seen as the ability of an organization to mobilize and adapt such resources and capabilities (Teece et al., 1997; Makadok, 2001). A reconceptualization of practicality in extended terms could suggest new behavioural hypotheses for investigating the RBV. On one hand, as we discussed in Section 3, we know that many innovation processes are artefact-specific, to the extent that specific solutions are the product of extended reasoning processes enabled by specific resources. The specificity of contingent resources is a significant theoretical ingredient of both the extended cognition hypothesis and the RBV. On the other hand, a reconceptualization of practicality in extended terms could provide a fresh perspective on capabilities as integrated within current practices, routines, and resources (instead of considering them as a separate type of assets) insofar as the contextual exploitation of resources relies on dynamic capabilities, which are embodied and tacit, as they precede cognitive representation (Nayak et al., 2019).

We all know well that in a number of advanced economies practicality is somehow diminished as abstraction and propositional knowledge are seen as more important. However, this disposition towards abstraction could be a trap insofar as, as Baruch says, the 'skills of innovation and creativity developed with practical science are the bedrock of a knowledge economy' (Baruch, 2014: p. 114). The paradigmatic advancements of the last three decades in the cognitive, behavioural, and neuro-sciences are gradually unveiling the value of practicality. We suggest starting benefiting from them.

References

Adams, F. and Aizawa, K. 2010. *The bounds of cognition*. Blackwell Publishing.

Aizawa, K. 2010. The coupling-constitution fallacy revisited. *Cognitive Systems Research*, 11(4): 332–42.

Alvarez, S.A. and Barney, J.B. 2007. Discovery and creation: alternative theories of entrepreneurial action. *Strategic Entrepreneurship Journal*, 1(1–2): 11–26.

Anderson, M.L. 2010. Neural reuse: a fundamental organizational principle of the brain. *Behavioral and Brain Sciences*, 33(4): 245–66.

Andriani, P., Ali, A., and Mastrogiorgio, M. 2017. Measuring exaptation and its impact on innovation, search, and problem solving. *Organization Science*, 28(2): 320–38.

Andriani, P. and Cattani, G. 2016. Exaptation as source of creativity, innovation, and diversity: introduction to the special section. *Industrial and Corporate Change*, 25(1): 115–31.

Argote, L. and Ingram, P. 2000. Knowledge transfer: a basis for competitive advantage in firms. *Organizational Behavior and Human Decision Processes*, 82(1): 150–69.

Barney, J.B. 1991. Firm resources and sustained competitive advantage. *Journal of Management*, 17(1): 99–120.

Baruch, J. 2014. Practical science has a global reach and appeal. *Nature*, 507(7491): 141.

Basalla, G. 1988. *The evolution of technology*. Cambridge University Press.

Bourdieu, P. 1977. *Outline of a theory of practice*. Cambridge University Press.

Brooks, R.A. 1991. Intelligence without representation. *Artificial Intelligence*, 47(1–3): 139–59.

Cattani, G. 2006. Technological pre-adaptation, speciation, and emergence of new technologies: how Corning invented and developed fiber optics. *Industrial and Corporate Change*, 15(2): 285–318.

Cisek, P. 2007. Cortical mechanisms of action selection: the affordance competition hypothesis. *Philosophical Transactions of the Royal Society of London. Series B, Biological Sciences*, 362(1485): 1585–99.

Clark, A. 1997. Economic reason: the interplay of individual learning and external structure, In Drobak, J.N. and Nye, J.V.C. (eds.). *The frontiers of the new institutional economics*. Academic Press.

Clark, A. 2005. Intrinsic content, active memory and the extended mind. *Analysis*, 65(1): 1–11.

Clark, A. 2006. Language, embodiment, and the cognitive niche. *Trends in Cognitive Sciences*, 10(8): 370–4.

Clark, A. 2008a. *Supersizing the mind: embodiment, action, and cognitive extension.* Oxford University Press.

Clark, A. 2008b. Pressing the flesh: a tension in the study of the embodied, embedded mind? *Philosophy and Phenomenological Research*, 76(1): 37–59.

Clark, A. 2013. Whatever next? Predictive brains, situated agents, and the future of cognitive science. *Behavioral and Brain Sciences*, 36(3): 181–204.

Clark, A. 2018. A nice surprise? Predictive processing and the active pursuit of novelty. *Phenomenology and the Cognitive Sciences*, 17(3): 521–34.

Clark, A. and Chalmers, D. 1998. The extended mind. *Analysis*, 58(1): 7–19.

Cohen, M.D. and Bacdayan, P. 1994. Organizational routines are stored as procedural memory: evidence from a laboratory study. *Organization Science*, 5(4): 554–68.

Cohen, W.M. and Levinthal, D.A. 1990. Absorptive capacity: a new perspective on learning and innovation. *Administrative Science Quarterly*, 35(1): (39–67).

De Jaegher, H. and Di Paolo, E. 2007. Participatory sense-making. *Phenomenology and the Cognitive Sciences*, 6(4): 485–507.

Dew, N. 2009. Serendipity in entrepreneurship. *Organization Studies*, 30(7): 735–53.

Dew, N., Sarasvathy, S.D., and Venkataraman, S. 2004. The economic implications of exaptation. *Journal of Evolutionary Economics*, 14(1): 69–84.

Dewar, R.D. and Dutton, J.E. 1986. The adoption of radical and incremental innovations: an empirical analysis. *Management Science*, 32(11): 1422–33.

Eppinger, S. and Ulrich, K. 2015. *Product design and development (5th ed.)*. McGraw-Hill Higher Education.

Etzkowitz, H. and Leydesdorff, L. 2000. The dynamics of innovation: from national systems and 'Mode 2' to a triple helix of university–industry–government relations. *Research Policy*, 29(2): 109–23.

Faulkner, P. and Runde, J. 2009. On the identity of technological objects and user innovations in function. *Academy of Management Review*, 34(3): 442–62.

Feldman, H. and Friston, K. 2010. Attention, uncertainty, and free-energy. *Frontiers in Human Neuroscience*, 4(article 215).

Felin, T., Kauffman, S., Koppl, R., and Longo, G. 2014. Economic opportunity and evolution: beyond landscapes and bounded rationality. *Strategic Entrepreneurship Journal*, 8(4): 269–82.

Felin, T., Kauffman, S., Mastrogiorgio, A., and Mastrogiorgio, M. 2016. Factor markets, actors and affordances. *Industrial and Corporate Change*, 25(1): 133–47.

Friston, K. 2010. The free-energy principle: a unified brain theory? *Nature Reviews. Neuroscience*, 11(2): 127–38.

Gallagher, S. 2013. The socially extended mind. *Cognitive Systems Research*, 25–6: 4–12.

Gallagher, S. 2018. The extended mind: state of the question. *Southern Journal of Philosophy*, 56(4): 421–47.

Gallagher, S. and Allen, M. 2018. Active inference, enactivism and the hermeneutics of social cognition. *Synthese*, 195(6): 2627–48.

German, T.P. and Barrett, H.C. 2005. Functional fixedness in a technologically sparse culture. *Psychological Science*, 16(1): 1–5.

Gibson, J.J. 1977. The theory of affordances, In Shaw, R. and Bransford, J. (eds.). *Perceiving, acting, and knowing: toward an ecological psychology*. Lawrence Erlbaum.

Gibson, J.J. 1986. *The ecological approach to visual perception*. Erlbaum.

Giddens, A. 1984. *The constitution of society: outline of the theory of structuration*. Polity Press.

Gigerenzer, G. and Selten, R. 2002. *Bounded rationality: the adaptive toolbox*. MIT press.

Glăveanu, V.P. 2013. Rewriting the language of creativity: the Five A's framework. *Review of General Psychology*, 17(1): 69–81.

Gomila, T. and Calvo, P. 2008. Directions for an embodied cognitive science: toward an integrated approach, In Calvo, P. and Gomila, T. (eds.). *Handbook of cognitive science: an embodied approach*. Elsevier.

Gould, S.J. and Eldredge, N. 1977. Punctuated equilibria: the tempo and mode of evolution reconsidered. *Paleobiology*, 3(2): 115–51.

Gould, S.J. and Lewontin, R.C. 1979. The spandrels of San Marco and the Panglossian paradigm: a critique of the adaptationist programme. *Proceedings of the Royal Society of London. Series B, Biological Sciences*, 205(1161): 581–98.

Gould, S.J. and Vrba, E.S. 1982. Exaptation – a missing term in the science of form. *Paleobiology*, 8(1): 4–15.

Gratzer, W. 2004. *Eurekas and euphorias: the Oxford book of scientific anecdotes*. Oxford University Press.

Guilford, J.P. 1967. *The nature of human intelligence*. McGraw-Hill.

Hoffrage, U. and Pohl, R.F. 2003. Research on hindsight bias: a rich past, a productive present, and a challenging future. *Memory*, 11(4–5): 329–35.

Hohwy, J. 2013. *The predictive mind*. Oxford University Press.

Hurley, S.L. 1998. *Consciousness in action*. Harvard University Press.

Hutchins, E. 2008. The role of cultural practices in the emergence of modern human intelligence. *Philosophical Transactions of the Royal Society of London. Series B, Biological Sciences*, 363(1499): 2011–2019.

Jacob, F. 1977. Evolution and tinkering. *Science*, 196(4295): 1161–6.

James, W. 1907. *Pragmatism: a new name for some old philosophy, old ways of thinking: popular lectures on philosophy*. Longmans, Green, and Co.

Kadosh, R.C. and Walsh, V. 2009. Numerical representation in the parietal lobes: abstract or not abstract? *Behavioral and Brain Sciences*, 32(3–4): 313–28.

Kahneman, D., Knetsch, J.L., and Thaler, R.H. 1991. Anomalies: the endowment effect, loss aversion, and status quo bias. *Journal of Economic Perspectives*, 5(1): 193–206.

Kauffman, S. 2000. *Investigations*. Oxford University Press.

Kirchhoff, M. 2018. Predictive brains and embodied, enactive cognition: an introduction to the special issue. *Synthese*, 195(6): 2355–66.

Kirchhoff, M.D. and Kiverstein, J. 2019. *Extended consciousness and predictive processing: a third wave view*. Routledge.

Kirsh, D. 1995. The intelligent use of space. *Artificial Intelligence*, 73(1–2): 31–68.

Kirsh, D. 2010. Thinking with external representations. *AI and SOCIETY*, 25(4): 441–54.

Kirsh, D. and Maglio, P. 1994. On distinguishing epistemic from pragmatic action. *Cognitive Science*, 18(4): 513–49.

Koppl, R., Kauffman, S., Felin, T., and Longo, G. 2015. Economics for a creative world. *Journal of Institutional Economics*, 11(1): 1–31.

Kuznets, S. 1965. *Economic growth and structure*. W.W. Norton.

Lakoff, G. and Núñez, R. 2000. *Where mathematics comes from*. Basic Books.

Latour, B. 1990. Technology is society made durable. *The Sociological Review*, 38(issue S1): 103–31.

Longo, G., Montévil, M., and Kauffman, S. 2012. *No entailing laws, but enablement in the evolution of the biosphere*. Proceedings of the 14th annual conference on genetic and evolutionary computation.

Lundvall, B.Å. and Borrás, S. 2005. Science, technology, and innovation policy. In *Oxford handbook of innovation*. Oxford University Press.

Lyre, H. 2018. Socially extended cognition and shared intentionality. *Frontiers in Psychology*, 9: 831.

Magnani, L. 2004. Reasoning through doing. Epistemic Mediators in scientific discovery. *Journal of Applied Logic*, 2(4): 439–50.

Magnani, L. 2009. *Abductive cognition: the epistemological and eco-cognitive dimensions of hypothetical reasoning*. Springer.

Makadok, R. 2001. Toward a synthesis of the resource-based view and dynamic-capability views of rent creation. *Strategic Management Journal*, 22(5): 387–401.

Malafouris, L. 2013. *How things shape the mind*. MIT Press.

Menary, R. 2007. *Cognitive integration: mind and cognition unbounded*. Springer.

Menary, R. 2010a. Dimensions of mind. *Phenomenology and the Cognitive Sciences*, 9(4): 561–78.

Menary, R. 2010b. Cognitive integration and the extended mind, In Menary, R. (ed.). *The extended mind*. The MIT Press.

Merleau-Ponty, M.J.J. 1945. *Phénoménologie de la perception.* Gallimard.

Merton, R.K. and Barber, E. 2004. *The travels and adventures of serendipity: a study in sociological semantics and the sociology of science.* Princeton University Press.

Miettinen, R. and Virkkunen, J. 2005. Epistemic objects, artefacts and organizational change. *Organization*, 12(3): 437–56.

Mintzberg, H. and Waters, J.A. 1985. Of strategies, deliberate and emergent. *Strategic Management Journal*, 6(3): 257–72.

Mokyr, J. 2000. *Natural history and economic history: is technological change an evolutionary process?* Northwestern University, draft lecture, http://faculty.wcas. northwestern.edu/~jmokyr/papers. html.

Mokyr, J. 2001. Useful knowledge as an evolving system: the view from economic history. Paper presented at the conference on 'The Economy as an Evolving System'. Santa Fe, Nov. 16–18.

Mokyr, J. 2006. Useful knowledge as an evolving system: the view from economic history. In Blume, L.E. and Durlauf, S.N. (eds.). *The economy as an evolving complex system, III.* Oxford University Press.

Mokyr, J. 2010. The contribution of economic history to the study of innovation and technical change. In Hall, B.H. and Rosenberg, N. (eds.). *Handbook of the economics of innovation, 1.* North-Holland.

Nayak, A., Chia, R., and Canales, J.I. 2020. Non-cognitive microfoundations: understanding dynamic capabilities as idiosyncratically refined sensitivities and predispositions. *Academy of Management Review*, 45(2): 280–303.

Nelson, R. and Winter, S. 1982. *An evolutionary theory of economic change.* The Belknap Press.

Newell, A. and Simon, H.A. 1972. *Human problem solving.* Prentice-Hall.

Newen, A., De Bruin, L., and Gallagher, S. 2018. *The Oxford handbook of 4E cognition.* Oxford University Press.

Norman, D. 1988. *The design of everyday things.* Basic Books.

Norman, D. 1993. *Things that make us smart.* Perseus Books.

Orlikowski, W.J. 2007. Socio-material practices: exploring technology at work. *Organization studies*, 28(9): 1435–48.

Osiurak, F., Jarry, C., Allain, P., Aubin, G., Etcharry-Bouyx, F., Richard, I., Bernard, I., and Le Gall, D. 2009. Unusual use of objects after unilateral brain damage. The technical reasoning model. *Cortex. A Journal Devoted to the Study of the Nervous System and Behavior*, 45(6): 769–83.

Peschl, M.F. and Fundneider, T. 2012. Spaces enabling game-changing and sustaining innovations: why space matters for knowledge creation and innovation. *Journal of Organisational Transformation and Social Change*, 9(1): 41–61.

Peteraf, M.A. 1993. The cornerstones of competitive advantage: a resource-based view. *Strategic Management Journal*, 14(3): 179–91.

Petracca, E. 2017. A cognition paradigm clash: Simon, situated cognition and the interpretation of bounded rationality. *Journal of Economic Methodology*, 24(1): 20–40.

Pezzulo, G. and Cisek, P. 2016. Navigating the affordance landscape: feedback control as a process model of behavior and cognition. *Trends in Cognitive Sciences*, 20(6): 414–24.

Polanyi, M. 1962. *Personal knowledge: towards a post-critical philosophy*. Chicago University Press.

Radjou, N., Prabhu, J., and Ahuja, S. 2012. *Jugaad innovation: think frugal, be flexible, generate breakthrough growth*. John Wiley & Sons.

Rheinberger, H.J. 1997. *Toward a history of epistemic things: synthesizing proteins in the test tube*. Stanford University Press.

Risko, E.F. and Gilbert, S.J. 2016. Cognitive offloading. *Trends in Cognitive Sciences*, 20(9): 676–88.

Roese, N.J. and Vohs, K.D. 2012. Hindsight bias. *Perspectives on Psychological Science,* 7(5): 411–26.

Rosch, E. 1975. Cognitive representations of semantic categories. *Journal of Experimental Psychology: General*, 104(3): 192–233.

Ryle, G. 1949. *The concept of mind*. University of Chicago Press.

Sarasvathy, S.D. 2001. Causation and effectuation: toward a theoretical shift from economic inevitability to entrepreneurial contingency. *Academy of Management Review*, 26(2): 243–63.

Schwartenbeck, P., FitzGerald, T., Dolan, R.J., and Friston, K. 2013. Exploration, novelty, surprise, and free energy minimization. *Frontiers in Psychology*, 4: 710.

Schwarz, N. and Lee, S.W.S. 2018. Embodied cognition and the construction of attitudes. In Albarracín, D. and Johnson, B.T. (eds.). *The handbook of attitudes*. Routledge.

Smith, D.K. and Alexander, R.C. 1999. *Fumbling the future: how Xerox invented, then ignored, the first personal computer*. iUniverse.

Soler, E.A. and Santacana, A.B. 2013. Innovative scaffolding: understanding innovation as the disclosure of hidden affordances. *Revista Iberoamericana de Argumentación*, 7: 1–11.

Spranca, M., Minsk, E., and Baron, J. 1991. Omission and commission in judgment and choice. *Journal of Experimental Social Psychology*, 27(1): 76–105.

Sterelny, K. 2004. Externalism, epistemic artefacts and the extended mind, In Schantz, R. (ed.). *The externalist challenge. New studies on cognition and intentionality*. De Gruyter.

Sternberg, R.J. and Lubart, T.I. 1999. The concept of creativity: prospects and paradigms. *Handbook of Creativity*, 1: 3–15.

Suchman, L.A. 1987. *Plans and situated actions: the problem of human-machine communication*. Cambridge University Press.

Sutton, J. 2010. Exograms and interdisciplinarity: history, the extended mind and the civilizing process. In Menary, R. (ed.). *The extended mind*. MIT Press.

Taleb, N. 2012. *Antifragile: things that gain from disorder*. Random House.

Teece, D.J., Pisano, G., and Shuen, A. 1997. Dynamic capabilities and strategic management. *Strategic Management Journal*, 18(7): 509–33.

Tripsas, M. and Gavetti, G. 2000. Capabilities, cognition, and inertia: evidence from digital imaging. *Strategic Management Journal*, 21(10–11): 1147–61.

Uexküll, J. von. 1957. A stroll through the worlds of animals and men. A picture book of invisible worlds, In Schiller, C.H. (ed.). *Instinctive behaviour: the development of modern concept*. International Universities Press.

Vallée-Tourangeau, F., Steffensen, S.V., Vallée-Tourangeau, G., and Sirota, M. 2016. Insight with hands and things. *Acta Psychologica*, 170: 195–205.

Wernerfelt, B. 1984. A resource-based view of the firm. *Strategic Management Journal*, 5(2): 171–80.

Wheeler, M. 2014. Revolution, reform, or business as usual? The future prospects for embodied cognition, In Shapiro, L. (ed.). *The Routledge handbook of embodied cognition*. Routledge.

Wilson, M. 2002. Six views of embodied cognition. *Psychonomic Bulletin and Review*, 9(4): 625–36.

Wittgenstein, L. 1953. *Philosophische Untersuchungen, von Ludwig Wittgenstein* [Philosophical investigations, by Ludwig Wittgenstein]. Transl. GEM Anscombe. B. Blackwell.

Yi, S., Knudsen, T., and Becker, M.C. 2016. Inertia in routines: a hidden source of organizational variation. *Organization Science*, 27(3): 782–800.

Zhang, J. 1997. The nature of external representations in problem solving. *Cognitive Science*, 21(2): 179–217.

Zhou, K.Z. and Li, C.B. 2012. How knowledge affects radical innovation: knowledge base, market knowledge acquisition, and internal knowledge sharing. *Strategic Management Journal*, 33(9): 1090–102.

9

Organizing for Unprestateability

An Option-Based Approach

Gino Cattani and Mariano Mastrogiorgio

Unprestateable innovation: the need of an option-based approach

The concept of unprestateability (Longo et al., 2012) refers to the myriad of functions, uses, and applications of technologies and products that 'cannot be pre-stated' *ex ante* (Felin et al., 2014: p. 9). The classic example is that of the screwdriver, which is typically used to screw in a screw and embeds multiple functionalities that are context-dependent and inherently unpredictable (Longo et al., 2012). The centrality of unprestateability raises the need to reframe how the innovation process is managed. Innovation often consists of a linear process targeted towards goals that are prespecified, similar to the case of a molecule designed against a prespecified disease. However, several examples, such as the failed war on cancer by the National Cancer Institutes (Leaf, 2013), also illustrate the inherent fallacies of goal-oriented approaches to drug development, as evidenced by the low productivity rates despite the billions of dollars spent every year (Scannell et al., 2012).

This raises the following question: is there an alternative to the goal-oriented approach? The serendipity path seems to be promising (Andriani et al., 2017), but the underlying economic mechanisms are poorly understood. Our goal in this chapter is to extend the notion of serendipity with an option-based approach by depicting serendipitous innovation as the result of an unstructured process—rather than a linear and goal-oriented processes—that generates unexpected advances in novel domains, which represent 'options' for the firm. We will establish a link between the new evolutionary paradigm and the literature on options, with an emphasis on 'real options' (Myers, 1977) and 'redeployability' (Sakhartov and Folta, 2014).

The idea of approaching unprestateability with an option-based approach is not new. For instance, Taleb (2012) introduced the concept of 'antifragility',

Gino Cattani and Mariano Mastrogiorgio, *Organizing for Unprestateability: An Option-Based Approach* In: *New Developments in Evolutionary Innovation: Novelty Creation in a Serendipitous Economy.* Edited by: Gino Cattani and Mariano Mastrogiorgio, Oxford University Press (2021). © Gino Cattani and Mariano Mastrogiorgio. DOI: 10.1093/oso/9780198837091.003.0009 which is similar to 'optionality' because it refers to the ability of a generic system to benefit—rather than suffer—from the unpredictable variability of the environment. Our point of departure is that we do not see options in a classical financial sense but instead as opportunities for strategic choice that very often are 'shadow', i.e. not yet recognized (Bowman and Hurry, 1993). It is then important to understand how these shadow options are generated, recognized and activated in an organizational context (Cattani, 2006; Garud and Nayyar, 1994; Garud et al., 2018). The following sections develop this line of arguments.

An option-based approach to functional expansion: basic principles

The option-based approach originates in finance and has been utilized in other fields including strategy, innovation, and R&D (Trigeorgis and Reuer, 2017). In finance, an option classically refers to the right—but not the obligation—to buy (or sell) a given asset, such as a stock, for a given price at a prespecified future date. For instance, a 'call option' gives the right to buy a unit of a stock x at a 'strike price' p_s at a future date t. The investor who owns the option will exercise the right when the option is 'in the money' and brings a profit, that is, at time t the 'market price' of the stock p_m is higher than the strike price p_s. In fields other than finance, the underlying asset is a real asset rather than a financial security. As such, options are defined as 'real options', namely, 'opportunities to purchase real assets on possibly favorable terms' (Myers, 1977: p. 163). Owing to the variety of real assets, there are different types of real options, such as the 'growth option' that consists of entering a new market, the options to abandon or delay entry, and so on (Trigeorgis and Reuer, 2017). In the context of innovation and R&D, a real option can refer to the right to exploit a patent that will be exercised by investing in the development of a new product when market sales allow for the recovery of the initial investment (and possibly make a profit). Therefore, in the innovation case, the patent is the correspondent of stock x, further investments correspond to the strike price p_s, and future sales correspond to the market price p_m.

Another application of the real option logic is that of functional expansion in novel domains via exaptation. The idea is that a technological artefact reveals new functions in novel domains via contextual interaction. These newly discovered functions can be seen as options to 'grow' in novel domains and to be exercised via additional investments that aim to exploit those functions. An example is a drug launched in the market to treat a specific disease, which then reveals off-label treatments that open up growth options in new therapeutic categories.[1] To realize such options, pharmaceutical firms have to make additional investments in new clinical trials to obtain FDA approval for new treatments (Andriani et al., 2019). A specific connection point of the option-based approach with functional expansion is the concept of 'redeployability' of resources and capabilities (Cattani, 2006; Klepper and Simons, 2000; Levinthal, 1998), which, in the recent diversification literature, has been approached using the formalism of option theory (Sakhartov and Folta, 2014). Most studies on diversification have focused on the existence of an inverted U-shaped relationship between the level of diversification and firm performance, thus implying that more relatedness leads to higher per-formance, whereas diversification into unrelated domains eventually has a negative impact on performance (Palich et al., 2000). The general explan-ation for the positive linear effect of the relationship is the existence of scope economies, that is, the synergies from the contemporaneous use of resources and capabilities across related domains. A complementary explanation is the possibility of redeploying resources and capabilities by transferring them from one domain to another (Sakhartov and Folta, 2014). Redeploying resources and capabilities across domains is a function of the costs involved, which tend to be lower when the domains are related, as well as of the vola-tility of the original and target domain (Sakhartov and Folta, 2014).

The evolutionary roots of redeployability can be traced to Penrose (1959), who argued that resources can 'be used in different ways and for different purposes' (p. 76). Despite the increasing emphasis on redeployability in cur-rent research looking at the dynamic of technological speciation (Adner and Levinthal, 2002; Cattani, 2006; Garnsey et al., 2008; Levinthal, 1998), the issue of how it relates to functional expansion has been overlooked, with a few exceptions (Andriani et al., 2019). A key underlying assumption of the current approach to redeployability is the idea that the cost of redeploying resources and capabilities increases with the level of unrelatedness between the original domain and the new domain into which the firm diversifies. However, in the context of functional expansion via exaptation, this is not always the case. For instance, drug repurposing in new therapeutic categor-ies shows that functional shifts are often technologically conservative, that is, changes in technology (and in production processes) are not always required. Therefore, functional shifts must be seen as growth options in novel domains

---

[1] The drug's uses are identifiable via medical databases that detail what diseases and conditions the drugs can be used for. It is important to note that the list of uses cover both approved and unapproved uses. The latter are known as 'off-label uses' (DeMonaco et al., 2006).

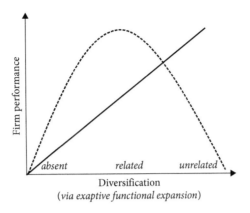

Figure 9.1 Exaptive functional expansion, diversification, and firm performance

to be exercised via a redeployment process that is not necessarily costly or, at least, not as costly as assumed in current research. Exaptive functional expansion can thus be seen as an important driver of diversification in related *and* unrelated domains that results from exercising redeployability options that are embedded in technologies, resources, and capabilities. This could imply a positively increasing—rather than an inverted U-shaped—relationship between diversification and performance (Figure 9.1).

As Ahuja and Novelli (2017) indicated, the assumed inverted U-shaped is highly unstable in empirical data, owing to a number of contingencies at the industry, firm, and technology level. The previous arguments suggest that exaptive functional expansion identifies another possible contingency that could affect diversification. This requires a better understanding of how to evaluate the optionality embedded in functional expansion via exaptation, as well as the organizational processes that facilitate the generation, recognition, and activation of options.

A stylized option-valuation setting

The option-valuation setting reported here comes from redeployability (Sakhartov and Folta, 2014; Sakhartov, 2018) and is enriched with insights from the literature on imperfect strategic factors markets (Barney, 1986; Denrell et al., 2003). The basic option-valuation formula is expressed as follows:

$$V^R = \max{}_M E \int_{t=0}^{t=T} e^{-rt} F_t dt,$$

where V^R is the value of redeployability of a firm's resources and capabilities, including technologies, given by the maximum of the expected value E of discounted cash flows F_t over the remaining lifetime of the firm, with respect to a vector M of resource redeployment weights (Sakhartov, 2018).

As in Sakhartov (2018), cash flows F_t can be expressed as follows:

$$F_t = I\left\{\left[m_{it}C_{it} + \left(1 - m_{it}\right)C_{jt}\right] - S\left[\max\left(0,\ m_{it} - m_{i,t-\delta}\right)C_{it} + \max\left(0, m_{i,t-\delta} - m_{it}\right)C_{jt}\right]\right\},$$

where cash flows F_t are split into cash flows C_{it} and C_{jt} obtained from redeploying resources at time t in domain i, in domain j or in both depending on the configuration of the redeployment weights m_{it} and $\left(1 - m_{it}\right)$. Specifically, I is an initial investment, m_{it} is the weight expressing the percentage of resources redeployed to domain i, and $\left(1 - m_{it}\right)$ refers to the percentage redeployed to domain j. For the sake of simplicity, only two domains are assumed, although the model can be extended to a multi-domain case. C_{it} and C_{jt} are the cash flows obtained in domains i and j, respectively, and are assumed to behave as time-varying stochastic processes. Finally, S measures the unit cost of redeploying resources, multiplied to how much is redeployed (in percentage terms) with respect to the previous period $t-\delta$ in both i and j. Therefore, the part of the formula on the right of the minus represents the overall cost of redeploying, which has to be subtracted from the cash flows.

As mentioned above, the expected value is maximized with respect to a vector M of resource redeployment weights, which is expressed as follows:

$$M = \left[m_{i0},\ m_{i,0+\delta},\ m_{it}\ ...\right],$$

The vector captures a firm's redeployment efforts over time in domain i and, by implication, in domain j, on the basis of the abovementioned relationship $m_{jt} = \left(1 - m_{it}\right)$. For more details, see Sakhartov and Folta (2014) and Sakhartov (2018).

The option-valuation formula expresses the 'true' value of redeployability. In a hypothetical situation of market efficiency, the formula could be used to estimate market-based indicators such as the stock value of the firm. However, the idea of market efficiency does not hold when the unprestateability of functional expansion via exaptation is taken into account, as discussed in the previous chapters. As Denrell et al. (2003) indicated, markets are inefficient in reflecting fundamental information, and the very idea of fundamental information, as well as the true value of redeployability, is problematic. Going back to the formula, M is a vector that contains the percentages/weights of resources redeployed in domain i over time (see above), where each redeployment is assumed to activate a specific product-ive path, according to which resource i is combined with other resources, and then with other resources, and so on, in combinations that are progres-sively more complex. For instance, as illustrated in Figure 9.2, a percentage $m_{i0} = 1$ in vector M means that, at time 0, all available resources are redeployed into domain i. As we can see, this redeployment activates the path indicated by the thick arrow, which identifies a combination that consists of combin-ing the redeployed resource (r_i) with another resource (r_a) into a new resource (r_b), which is in turn combined with resource r_c into a certain final product P.

We can express the fundamental value of P as a function of the cash flows generated by the product as $V_P = f(C)$. Thereafter, the fundamental value of r_b can be expressed as the cash flows function minus the cost of combining r_b into P, i.e. $V_b = f(C) - c_{r_b,P}$, and the fundamental value of r_i as the cash flows function minus the cost of combining r_b into P and r_i into r_b, i.e. $V_i = f(C) - c_{r_b,P} - c_{r_i,r_b}$.

It is important to emphasize that productive recombinations have a com-binatorial nature; therefore, the thick path is only one of the many possible paths. The fundamental value of a resource is the value of the best among all possible productive recombinations or, to put it differently, the value of the best use of a resource among all possible uses (Denrell et al., 2003). When markets are complete, the price signals observed in the market reflect the fundamental values (i.e. the value of the best possible use of a resource). However, resources are unique and complex assets, and markets for them do not exist in a classical sense—as aggregators of demand and supply produ-cing 'thick' price signals (Gans and Stern, 2010). Owing to market incom-pleteness, price signals cannot reflect the value of the best possible use of a resource unless economic agents have exhaustive knowledge of all possible uses (Denrell et al., 2003). This type of knowledge is not available because the uses and functions of resources and capabilities are unprestateable (Felin

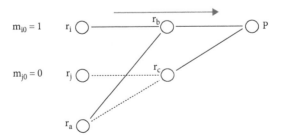

Figure 9.2 Resource redeployments and paths of use in productive recombinations

et al., 2016). Given the fundamental ambiguity of value imputations, the idea of fundamental value of a resource, or V^R—the true value of redeployability—is highly problematic. This is related to the broader debate on the complications of real options (Adner and Levinthal, 2004), and recent attempts to develop a 'realistic real option approach' (Leiblein et al., 2017) that takes these complications explicitly into account. An important complication is the idea of shadow optionality to which we now turn.

Shadow optionality

Applying real options to innovation and strategy faces several challenges such as the existence of different types of uncertainty, the difficulty to exercise and abandon options, and the interaction among the multiple options that firms possess (Trigeorgis and Reuer, 2017). Another important challenge is shadow optionality, which is intimately linked to the fundamental unprestateability that limits the ability of economic agents to see new uses and impute value to resources. The inability of seeing new uses and functions has well-known cognitive roots such as the existence of a 'functional fixedness' bias that limits the ability to discover new functions in a wide class of problems (McCaffrey, 2012). Going back to the previous figure, the presence of imperfections in strategic factor markets, combined with the unprestateability of new uses, implies that some paths of use in productive recombinations are shadowed (as represented by the cloud), that is V^R is inherently ambiguous (Figure 9.3).

The concept of *shadow options*, which was originally introduced by Bowman and Hurry (1993), refers to opportunities awaiting recognition (i.e. opportunities that 'firm resource endowments and capabilities might create in the future' (Trigeorgis and Reuer, 2017: p. 44)). This concept has been recently brought to the attention of evolutionary scholars by Andriani and

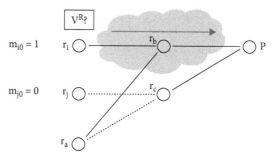

Figure 9.3 Shadow optionality in a redeployment setting

Cattani (2016), who indicated that shadow options often refer to new uses and functions embedded in existing technologies, resources, and capabilities and come to light 'when new information about possible applications for a firm's knowledge stock gradually emerges' (Andriani and Cattani, 2016: p. 12). Shadow options are relevant for three important reasons. First, the idea of shadow options refers to functional emergence out of a hidden state, meaning that unprestateability does not completely preclude foresight. This is consistent with the idea of Cattani (2006) of a 'watershed event' that separates a phase of knowledge accumulation that is not directed towards a new particular use from the phase in which this use is recognized and in which deliberate actions are taken to exploit it. This is when the shadow option becomes a real option that, in a classical sense, 'waits' to be exercised (Andriani and Cattani, 2016). Second, uncovering shadow options is a process that is inherently organizational because it depends on the ability of the firm to keep a memory of past knowledge and the ability to retrieve it when the time comes to seize new opportunities (Cattani, 2006; Garud and Nayyar, 1994). The key implication is that there is significant heterogeneity among companies as regards their ability to discover shadow options and attribute value to technologies, resources, and capabilities. This leads to a third point: heterogeneity in the ability to discover shadow options implies heterogeneity of opportunities in the markets for strategic factors, a critical condition for explaining the heterogeneity of performance at the firm level. As Trigeorgis and Reuer (2017) stated, 'firms that lack such early pre-investments, or do not appreciate the particular follow-on opportunities that stem from prior investments, may not be able to access the same future investment opportunity set, or do so on the same terms' (p. 44). Therefore, competitive advantage lies in the exploitation of arbitrage opportunities in strategic factor markets afforded by the ability to uncover shadow options (before others).

To illustrate this point, let us go back to the figure and consider the following simple example.

As Figure 9.4 shows, resource r_i is combined into resource r_b, which in turn is combined into a final product p generating cash flows (P = 10). As represented by the X sign, the market is incomplete for resource r_b, thus implying the absence of price signals regarding value. The market for r_i is thus inefficient, as reflected in a misalignment between the price signal ($P_i = 7$) and the fundamental value ($V_i = 8$), that is, the resource is undervalued. This situation presents an arbitrage opportunity. Let us also assume the existence of the costs of combining i into b and b into p, which are equal to $c_{i,b} = 1$ and $c_{b,p} = 1$, respectively. Finally, let us assume the existence of two firms: firm A, which is able to see through the cloud, and firm B, which is not (yet) aware of

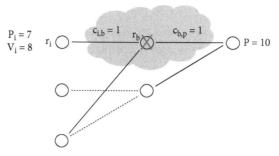

Figure 9.4 Shadow optionality, inefficiency, and arbitrage opportunities

the use path passing through r_b. Firm A can transform its knowledge advantage into a profit. For instance, firm A can borrow 9 dollars to buy r_i for 7 dollars and then combine it into r_b and p for a total cost of 2 dollars; the final product can be sold for 10 dollars, thus making a profit of 1 dollar after repaying the original loan. In a similar way, firm A can perform arbitrage leading to profit in a situation of overvaluation (e.g. via short-selling). The bottom line is the existence of a profit differential (a form of competitive advantage when sustained over time) thanks to the ability of firm A to *see through the cloud* of possible uses and functions, thus uncovering the shadow optionality that is latent in technologies, resources, and capabilities.

Inducing functional expansion through serendipity arrangements

As Trigeorgis and Reuer (2017) emphasized, there are different phases in the life of a real option. First, there is an 'identification' phase, which consists of the discovery of the shadow opportunities possessed by technologies, resources, and capabilities. Second, there is a 'management' phase, which consists of making sure that the option is preserved over time so that it can be exercised in the future. Third, there is the 'exercise' phase, which was defined previously. Although a significant emphasis has been placed on the last phases, less attention has been paid to the issue of discovery itself, that is, what are the organizational arrangements for discovering new uses and functions, thus transforming a shadow option into a real one (Trigeorgis and Reuer, 2017). A basis of discussion can be found in the recent work on 'serendipity arrangements' for inducing exaptation (Garud et al., 2018) and narrative approaches to exaptation (Garud et al., 2016). This work is part of the broader debate on the 'transformative capacity' of firms (Garud and

Nayyar, 1994), which refers to the ability to 'maintain internally developed technology over time' (p. 365), and redeploy it for new uses and functions.

The standard perspective views innovation as the result of science-push or demand-pull mechanisms directed towards prespecified uses and functions (of a technology, resource or capability). An alternative mechanism is exaptation, which refers to the context-driven co-option (for new uses and functions) of features that were originally adapted for a different use or had no use at all (Andriani and Cattani, 2016). It is important to stress the difficulty of inducing exaptation in organizational contexts, in terms of the discovery of new uses and functions, but also from the point of view of the management and exercise of the options embedded in them. An illustrative example is the drug Viagra, which was originally conceived against hypertension and then exapted against erectile dysfunctions. The discovery of the new functionality happened serendipitously during clinical trials that revealed a 'happy accident', that is, an increase in the blood flow to the genital area (Meyers, 2007). This raises the question of the organizational arrangements that make exaptation more likely. Furthermore, after the discovery, it took time to dissolve the scepticism, create a functioning market for the blue pills and align the organization towards its exploitation. A new market category of 'erectile dysfunctions' emerged but only slowly and gained legitimacy thanks to a progressive association of Viagra to natural disease conditions that could be sanitized rather than being associated to psychological taboos of 'impotence' (Loe et al., 2004).

The specific outcomes of exaptation cannot be predicted (Garud et al., 2018). However, following Cattani (2008), it is possible to investigate 'how firms can deliberately organize or prepare for serendipitous discoveries' (p. 590). In other words, it is possible to design 'serendipity arrangements' that make exaptation more likely (i.e. organizational conditions such as routines, practices, structures, and processes) (Garud et al., 2018). This links to the key distinction between prediction and control: the fact that we cannot foresee something does not imply that we cannot control it (Wiltbank et al., 2006). However, what are the serendipity arrangements that induce exaptation and, in general, functional expansion into new domains? By building on the idea that organizational 'narratives' can elicit innovation, Garud et al. (2018) have recently proposed a set of distributed serendipity arrangements: exaptive pools, exaptive events, and exaptive forums, which are respectively needed for maintaining, activating, and contextualizing innovative discoveries. Scientific discoveries and innovations can remain dormant on the shelves of a firm but then end up being reactivated after many years for different uses and functions, as illustrated by the case of the videocassette recorder (Irvine and Martin, 1984). Exaptive pools are arrangements designed to preserve these discoveries and inventions over time, like a sort of organizational memory, waiting for their latent optionality to emerge out of the shadow state. It is easier to preserve past discoveries and inventions for future possibilities when they are still in use. It is when they are inactive (i.e. they have no current use and function) or when they are tacit that more specific arrangements are needed for their preservation (Garud et al., 2018). Within the so-called 'exaptive pools', the different elements are loosely coupled and disconnected in space and time, thereby awaiting activation. It is their coupling that activates new uses and functions for a firm's resources and capabilities. This explains the importance of exaptive events, which consist of arrangements that are designed to foster these activations via intense organizational interactions. One example is Google's technology fairs, the objective of which is to foster interactions among engineers in a space- and time-compressed manner so that idea brainstorming leads to new inventions (Garud et al., 2018). The third type of arrangement are the so-called 'exaptive forums', which have a more stable basis and are intended to foster intra-actions (rather than interactions) among organizational members, to translate ideas into prototypes as part of a process that progressively moves from option identification and management to option exercise. An example of exaptive forums are physical spaces hosting incubators and technological accelerators.

The previous arguments point to the importance of certain types of organizational structures, cultures, and human resource (HR) policies in facilitating functional expansion and innovation via exaptation. In a study on the exaptive nature of drugs, Andriani et al. (2017) noted that the multiplication of contexts interacting with existing artefacts (i.e. what leads to new uses and functions) can be obtained with arrangements such as bottom-up innovation, access to distributed networks, and recombinant modularity. Similarly, Cuhna et al. (2010) discussed how to organize for serendipity by referring to other types of arrangements such as abandonment of hierarchy, exploration of the periphery via boundary spanning, teamwork, removal of tight deadlines, and so forth.

Examples of innovative arrangements abound among start-ups or tech companies, such as Google. As argued by Eric Schmidth, Google's former CEO, the best way to foster creativity and innovation in a firm is to create a *primordial ooze* in which smart creatives can play (Schmidt and Rosenberg, 2014). The secrets of Google's innovative success indeed lie in several design principles, such as a relatively flat organizational structure, small teams, and power assigned to who has an impact instead of simply having a formal role inside the hierarchy. Beyond structure, the organizational culture is important too. All this is combined with innovative HR policies for selecting, training, and retaining employees. A well-known example is the 70/20/10 rule, according to which employees can dedicate 70 per cent of their working time to the core business, whereas 20 per cent and 10 per cent can be freely allocated to emerging and radical new projects, respectively. This policy has been the source of several breakthroughs, many of them unexpected, such as Sky Map, Street View, or Gmail (Schmidt and Rosenberg, 2014). Therefore, a key message of this discussion is that structure, culture, and HR are all fundamental design variables for inducing functional expansion and leading to firm's growth in new domains via the latent optionality of resources and capabilities. In this regard, the flow of communication, discourse, and narration inside the organization is an important mediator. It seems well accepted that organizational discourse is less structured and more creative, thus leading to innovation, when the firm is structured in a flat or networked way rather than complying with the requisites of a Weberian type of hierarchical bureaucracy. In reality, beyond structure and HR systems, the culture itself is also important. As Bartel and Garud (2009) noted, prior research has explored systematically the issue of how innovation can be sustained through arrangements in structure and other types of systems. However, innovation can also be sustained by 'creating a *cultural infrastructure*', the key mechanisms of which are organizational narratives (Bartel and Garud, 2009: p. 109, emphasis added). Indeed, 'like the air we breathe, narratives are part of the fabric of organizing' (Garud et al., 2018: p. 130). In particular, drawing from a narrative approach, Garud et al. (2016) argued that the discovery of new functions is not purely driven by chance. Indeed, narratives can constitute relationships between resources and the contexts in which they are used. By elaborating narratives, individuals give meaning and functionality to what they encounter or experience, forge new feature-context connections, and unveil new uses or functions for existing resources.

Shadow optionality, serendipity, and competitive advantage

The previous discussion highlights the following critical points:

- Technological unprestateability implies that the goal-oriented approach to innovation is inherently limited: this approach is premised on the idea that innovation is a process targeted towards prespecified goals. Owing to its flexibility, the options approach better characterizes the essence of the innovation process.

- The options approach views a firm's resources and capabilities as embodying growth options in the form of new uses and functions. These growth options represent opportunities for corporate diversification; however, owing to the imperfections of strategic factor markets, combined with the cognitive limitations of economic agents, options cannot be conceptualized in a classical financial sense but can be conceptualized more realistically as shadow options.
- Shadow options are options awaiting recognitions, that is, at any particular point in time, some new uses and functions remain hidden to the firm or hidden to the firm but not to others.
- Firms differ in their ability to uncover shadow options, and this implies heterogeneity in value inferences in strategic factor markets; in turn, this entails performance differences, which are the basis of firm-level performance heterogeneity.
- This heterogeneity is deeply organizational because it is rooted in the presence (or absence) of serendipity arrangements for the preservation, identification, and exercise of the options embedded in a firm's existing resources and capabilities.

In light of all this, we argue that evolutionary research should carefully consider optionality as an organizing approach for unprestateability. To this end, it is useful to see options as 'realistic real options' (Leiblein et al., 2017), that is, complex tools for resource allocation where management and organizational realities play an important role. This is certainly consistent with the recent trends in real options' research. Indeed, a promising research direction consists of disentangling 'the roles of management and organizational considerations in ROT [real options theory]' (Trigeorgis and Reuer, 2017: p. 57). An example of this new direction is the recent work by Leiblein et al. (2017), who argued that the common view on competitive advantage still falls short of properly explaining where heterogeneity among firms comes from. Although some scholars point to behavioural origins (Gavetti, 2012), we point to interfirm differences coming from the ability to execute real options. As we argued before, this heterogeneity lies in the capacity of firms to maintain, reactivate, and synthetize their organizational knowledge, and learn about new uses and functions of technologies, resources, and capabilities.

References

Adner, R. and Levinthal, D.A. 2002. The emergence of emerging technologies. *California Management Review*, 45(1): 50–66.

Adner, R. and Levinthal, D.A. 2004. What is not a real option: considering boundaries for the application of real options to business strategy. *Academy of Management Review*, 29(1): 74–85.

Ahuja, G. and Novelli, E. 2017. Redirecting research efforts on the diversification-performance linkage: the search for synergy. *The Academy of Management Annals*, 11(1): 342–90.

Andriani, P. and Cattani, G. 2016. Exaptation as a source of creativity, innovation, and diversity in evolutionary sciences: introduction to the special section. *Industrial and Corporate Change*, 25(1): 115–31.

Andriani, P., Ali, A., and Mastrogiorgio, M. 2017. Measuring exaptation and its impact on innovation, search and problem-solving. *Organization Science*, 28(2): 320–38.

Andriani, P., Cattani, G., Givry, P. 2019. Unused services of a firm's resources: a Penrosian view of shadow options. *Academy of Management Proceedings*, 2019(1).

Barney, J.B. 1986. Strategic factor markets: expectations, luck, and business strategy. *Management Science*, 32(10): 1231–41.

Bartel, C.A. and Garud, R. 2009. The role of narratives in sustaining organizational innovation. *Organization Science*, 20(1): 107–17.

Bowman, E.H. and Hurry, D. 1993. Strategy through the option lens: an integrated view of resource investments and the incremental-choice process. *Academy of Management Review*, 18(4): 760–82.

Cattani, G. 2006. Technological preadaptation, speciation and emergence of new technologies: how Corning invented and developed fiber optics. *Industrial and Corporate Change*, 15(2): 285–318.

Cattani, G. 2008. Reply to Dew's 2007. commentary: 'Pre-adaptation, exaptation and technological speciation: a comment on Cattani (2006)'. *Industrial and Corporate Change*, 17(3): 585–96.

Cunha, M.P., Clegg, S.R., and Mendonca, S. 2010. On serendipity and organizing. *European Management Journal*, 28(5): 319–30.

DeMonaco, H.J., Ali, A., and Von Hippel, E. 2006. The major role of clinicians in the discovery of off-label drug therapies. *Pharmacotherapy*, 26(3): 323–32.

Denrell, J., Fang, C., and Winter, S.G. 2003. The economics of strategic opportunity. *Strategic Management Journal*, 24(10): 977–90.

Felin, T., Kauffman, S., Koppl, R., and Longo, G. 2014. Economic opportunity and evolution: beyond landscapes and bounded rationality. *Strategic Entrepreneurship Journal*, 8(4): 269–82.

Felin, T., Kauffman, S., Mastrogiorgio, A., and Mastrogiorgio, M. 2016. Factor markets, actors and affordances. *Industrial and Corporate Change*, 25(1): 133–47.

Gans, J.S. and Stern, S. 2010. Is there a market for ideas? *Industrial and Corporate Change*, 19(3): 805–37.

Garnsey, E.W., Lorenzoni, G., and Ferriani, S. 2008. Technology speciation through entrepreneurial spin-off: the Acorn-ARM story. *Research Policy*, 37(2): 210–24.

Garud, R. and Nayyar, P.R. 1994. Transformative capacity: continual structuring by intertemporal technology transfer. *Strategic Management Journal*, 15(5): 365–85.

Garud, R., Gehman, J., and Giuliani, A.P. 2016. Technological exaptation: a narrative approach. *Industrial and Corporate Change*, 25(1): 115–31.

Garud, R., Gehman, J., and Giuliani, A.P. 2018. Serendipity arrangements for exapting science-based innovations. *Academy of Management Perspectives*, 32(1): 125–40.

Gavetti, G. 2012. Toward a behavioral theory of strategy. *Organization Science*, 23(1): 267–85.

Irvine, J. and Martin, B.R. 1984. *Foresight in science: picking the winners*. Pinter Publications.

Klepper, S. and Simons, K.L. 2000. Dominance by birthright: entry of prior radio producers and competitive ramifications in the US television receiver industry. *Strategic Management Journal*, 21(10–11): 997–1016.

Leaf, C. 2013. *The truth in small doses: why we're losing the war on cancer-and how to win it*. Simon & Schuster Paperbacks.

Leiblein, M.J., Chen, J.S., and Posen, H.E. 2017. Resource allocation in strategic factor markets: a realistic real options approach to generating competitive advantage. *Journal of Management*, 43(8): 2588–608.

Levinthal, D.A. 1998. The slow pace of rapid technological change: gradualism and punctuation in technological change. *Industrial and Corporate Change*, 7(2): 217–47.

Loe, M. 2004. *The rise of Viagra: how the little blue pill changed sex in America*. New York University Press.

Longo, G., Montevil, M., and Kauffman, S. 2012. No entailing laws, but enablement in the evolution of the biosphere. In *Proceedings of the Genetic and Evolutionary Computation Conference*.

McCaffrey, T. 2012. Innovation relies on the obscure: a key to overcome the classic problem of functional fixedness. *Psychological Science*, 23(3): 215–18.

Meyers, M.A. 2007. *Happy accidents: serendipity in major medical breakthroughs in the twentieth century*. Arcade Publishing.

Myers, S.C. 1977. Determinants of corporate borrowing. *Journal of Financial Economics*, 5(2): 147–76.

Palich, L.E., Cardinal, L.B., and Miller, C.C. 2000. Curvilinearity in the diversification-performance linkage: an examination of over three decades of research. *Strategic Management Journal*, 21(2): 155–74.

Penrose, E. 1959. *Limits to the size and growth of firms*. Oxford University Press.

Sakhartov, A.V. 2018. Stock market undervaluation of resource redeployability. *Strategic Management Journal*, 39(4): 1059–82.

Sakhartov, A.V. and Folta, T.B. 2014. Resource relatedness, redeployability, and firm value. *Strategic Management Journal*, 35(12): 1781–97.

Scannell, J.W., Blanckley, A., Boldon, H., and Warrington, B. 2012. Diagnosing the decline in pharmaceutical R&D efficiency. *Nature Reviews*, 11: 191–200.

Schmidt, E. and Rosenberg, J. 2014. *How Google works*. Grand Central Publishing.

Taleb, N.N. 2012. *Antifragile: things that gain from disorder*. Penguin Books.

Trigeorgis, L. and Reuer, J.J. 2017. Real options theory in strategic management. *Strategic Management Journal*, 38(1): 42–63.

Wiltbank, R., Dew, N., Read, S., and Sarasvathy, S.D. 2006. What to do next? The case for non-predictive strategy. *Strategic Management Journal*, 27(10): 981–98.

10

The Cultural Evolution of Creative Ideas and Social Innovations

A Complex Systems Approach

Mike Unrau and Liane Gabora

Introduction

The role of technological innovation in driving cultural and economic change is widely appreciated. Less appreciated but equally important is the role of social innovation. We define *social innovation* as a new and broadly effective solution to a problem that is social in nature (e.g. gang violence or unemployment due to economic collapse) for which the value created accrues primarily to society as a whole as opposed to individuals. By incorporating insights from complex systems science and, more specifically, the complex-systems-inspired theory of creativity, which is referred to as 'honing theory' (HT) (Gabora, 2017), we demonstrate how social innovation can be fruitfully viewed as a creative process. Therefore, the wealth of theoretical and experimental research into creativity sheds new light on the nature of social problems, how they are represented in the minds of individuals and groups, and how these representations can shift to yield new approaches and solutions. Our approach to creativity and social innovation incorporates concepts from complex systems science—for example, the transition from confusion to insight (in the case of creativity) or social unrest to a strengthened civil society (in the case of social innovation), where both are described as processes of self-organization yielding a lower-entropy state. This chapter also discusses the cultural and economic impacts of social innovation and its role in cultural evolution.

We begin by addressing the sense in which elements of culture, including but not limited to technology (i.e. also including languages, mannerisms, activities, stories, and so forth) can be said to evolve. Thereafter, we outline

Mike Unrau and Liane Gabora, *The Cultural Evolution of Creative Ideas and Social Innovations: A Complex Systems Approach*
In: *New Developments in Evolutionary Innovation: Novelty Creation in a Serendipitous Economy.* Edited by:
Gino Cattani and Mariano Mastrogiorgio, Oxford University Press (2021). © Mike Unrau and Liane Gabora.
DOI: 10.1093/oso/9780198837091.003.0010

our view of how the creative process *fuels* cultural innovation. We then discuss how creative processes in a social innovation context fuel cultural evolution and economic change. We offer a speculative account of how concepts from complex systems theory may shed light on the dynamics of how social innovations affect cultural and economic change.

In what sense does technology evolve?

The significance of Darwin's theory of evolution by natural selection was that it integrated scattered biological knowledge into a united framework, thus enabling us to see how species fit together in a unified 'tree of life'. Given that languages, technology, and so forth change over time in a manner reminiscent of biological evolution, it seems reasonable to view culture as a second evolutionary process. By *culture* we mean extrasomatic adaptations, including behaviour and artefacts, that are socially rather than sexually transmitted. The elements of culture diversify and become more complex over time and exhibit phenomena observed in biological evolution, including niches, drift, epistasis, and punctuated equilibrium (Bentley et al., 2004; Durham, 1991; Gabora, 1995, 2001). Furthermore, cultural evolution has mechanisms for introducing variation and preserving fit variants, similar to biological evolution.

Given the similarities between these two evolutionary processes, it should be determined if the framework developed by population geneticists to formally describe and explain evolution by natural selection (Fisher, 1930; Wright, 1931; Haldane, 1932) can also apply to culture. Indeed, there is a history of attempts to frame culture as a Darwinian or *selectionist* process (Boyd and Richerson, 1985; Cavalli-Sforza and Feldman, 1981). The approach remains widespread; the formal frameworks of population genetics and phylogenetics is being adapted for application in anthropology (Brewer et al., 2017; Creanza et al., 2017; Mesoudi, 2017), archaeology (O'Brien and Lyman, 2000), economics (Hodgson, 2002; Essletzbichler, 2011; Nelson and Winter, 2002), neuroscience (Edelman, 1987, 2014), and creativity (Campbell, 1960; Simonton, 1999a,b, 2011), and is being applied to the evolution of languages (Pagel, 2017; Fitch, 2005).

However, culture cannot be accommodated by a Darwinian framework (Gabora, 2004, 2008, 2011, 2013, 2019). First, *cultural variation is not randomly generated*. To the extent that this is the case, the distribution of variants reflects *whatever is biasing the generation away from random in the first place*, rather than Darwinian selection, i.e. differential selection on the distribution of randomly generated heritable variation in a population over generations. Cultural Darwinians sometimes concede this point (e.g. Heyes, 2018) but fail to recognize its implications for the assumed validity of a Darwinian framework.

Second, there are two kinds of traits in biological evolution: (1) *inherited traits* (e.g. eye colour), which are transmitted *vertically* from parent to off-spring by way of genes, and (2) *acquired traits* (e.g. a tattoo), which are obtained during an organism's lifetime and are transmitted *horizontally* to others. Vetsigian et al. (2006) showed that crossing what they refer to as the *Darwinian threshold* from a non-Darwinian to a Darwinian evolutionary process required the emergence of a *self-assembly code* (such as the genetic code), i.e. a set of instructions for how to reproduce. The low-level information-bearing components of the code must be organized in an orderly manner so that they can be parsed into meaningful units; otherwise, the precisely orchestrated process by which it is expressed to generate off-spring is disrupted. *A Darwinian explanation works in biology to the extent that acquired change is negligible relative to inherited change;* otherwise, the first, which can operate instantaneously, overwhelms the second, which takes generations. There is no evidence that cultural evolution has crossed this threshold. Indeed, cultural evolution does not possess the signature characteristic of having crossed this threshold: a lack of transmission of acquired traits. *In cultural evolution, there are no vertically transmitted inherited traits, and all change is more acquired.* Therefore, cultural evolution is not due to the mechanism Darwin proposed (i.e. differential replication of heritable variation in response to selection). Indeed, considering that (as Darwin himself noted) his theory concerns the consequences of competition among *existing* organisms, it does not address how they come into existence in the first place.

This precludes a *selectionist* but not an *evolutionary* framework for culture. There is increasing recognition of the impact of non-Darwinian processes on evolution (e.g. Arnheim and Taylor, 1969; Kauffman, 1993; Killeen, 2019; King and Jukes, 1969; Koonin, 2009; Ling et al., 2015; Woese, 2002). The improbability that a structure as complex as RNA could arise spontaneously led to the now predominant view that the earliest life forms evolved without a self-assembly code via the self-organization of autocatalytic molecular net-works and the horizontal (lateral) exchange of catalytic molecules between them, with natural selection emerging later from this more haphazard ances-tral evolutionary process (Baum, 2018; Cornish-Bowden and Cárdenas, 2017; Gabora, 2006; Hordijk et al., 2018; Hordijk et al., 2010; Kauffman, 1993; Steel, 2000; Vetsigian et al., 2006). Kauffman (1993) showed that when catalytic molecules interact, they generate new molecules such that their diversity increases; therefore, there is a probability that some subset of them reaches a critical point where there is a catalytic pathway to every member, a state he referred to as *autocatalytic closure*.[1] Autocatalytic sets emerge for a range of hypothetical chemistries (i.e. different collections of catalytic molecules). It has been suggested that autocatalytic networks can also explain *conceptual closure (CC)*, which is the origin of the kind of cognitive structure that makes *cultural* evolution possible (Gabora, 1998, 2000, 2013; Gabora and Steel, 2017). Just as interactions between catalytic molecules generate new molecules, forging associations among concepts generates new concepts, which in turn enables new associations. CC is attained when some subset of them reaches a critical point where there is an associative pathway to every member.

In short, *self-other reorganization* (SOR) posits that culture evolves through the interplay of communal exchange *between* minds and self-organizing processes *within* minds (Gabora, 2019). SOR bridges the cultural evolution literature with the literature on creative thinking and psychological growth. Since, unlike the Darwinian approach, SOR *is* compatible with the transmission of non-random acquired change, support has come from demonstrations of this phenomenon in studies of creative people (Ranjan et al., 2013; Scotney et al., 2018; Weissmeyer et al., 2019).

Creativity: the process that drives cultural evolution

Creativity research has emphasized the generation of multiple ideas over what is sometimes called *honing*—reflecting on a question or idea by viewing it from different perspectives, with the output of each such reflection providing the input to the next, recursively (Gabora, 2017). Therefore, the creator comes to a deeper and more nuanced understanding of it. The honing of an idea is shepherded by an overarching conceptual framework, the structure of which reflects the individuals' *worldview:* their self-organizing web of understandings about their world and their place in that world (in other words, the creator's mind as experienced 'from the inside'). As in other self-organizing systems, a worldview interacts with and adapts to its environment to minimize internal *entropy*, which is a measure of uncertainty and internal disorder. The concept of entropy, which comes from information theory and thermodynamics, refers to the amount of uncertainty and disorder in a system. Open

---

[1] Although 'closure' has different mathematical meanings and sometimes refers to a condition that bounds a set, Kauffman (1993) (following Erdos and Rényi) used it to state that the set surpasses a threshold density of connectedness by way of catalysis events.

systems (e.g. living organisms) obtain energy (or information) from the environment, use it to maintain semi-stable, far-from-equilibrium states, and displace entropy into the environment, thereby keeping their own entropy low. Hirsh et al. (2012) used the term *psychological entropy* to refer to anxiety-provoking uncertainty and claimed that humans continually try to keep it at a manageable level. Elsewhere, the term has been used to refer to *arousal*-provoking uncertainty, which can be experienced negatively as anxiety or positively as a wellspring for creativity or both (Gabora, 2017). Redefining psychological entropy in terms of arousal as opposed to anxiety is consistent with the finding that creative people exhibit higher tolerance of ambiguity and greater openness to experience (Feist, 1998), which may predispose them to states of cognitive uncertainty. Creative people also exhibit higher variability in arousal (Martindale and Armstrong, 1974), which may reflect a predilection to enter situations that increase psychological entropy, relish them, and resolve them.

According to the 'honing theory' (HT) of creativity (Gabora, 2017), the creative process makes use of psychological entropy, a macro-level variable acting at the level of the worldview, to drive intuitions and emotions that help the individual track and monitor creative progress. Honing continues until psychological entropy decreases to an acceptable level. To use Piaget's terminology, during honing, each new 'take' on the idea is assimilated, and the worldview changes in response to accommodate this new understanding. In honing theory, insight is explained in terms of self-organized criticality (SOC) (Gabora, 1998, 2017; Schilling, 2005). SOC is a phenomenon wherein, through simple local interactions, complex systems tend to find a critical state poised at the cusp of a transition between order and chaos, from which a single small perturbation occasionally exerts a disproportionately large effect (Bak et al., 1988). While most thoughts have little effect on one's worldview, an *insightful* idea is one for which one thought triggers another, which triggers another, and so forth in an avalanche of conceptual change.

While it is tempting to assume that creative thought entails the generation of multiple, distinct ideas, there may be just one underlying mental representation that affords some degree of ambiguity in its interpretation. Even though the different designs for a possible work of art or prototypes of an invention take different forms when expressed in the physical world, this does not mean they derive from different underlying ideas in the mind. The designs or prototypes may be different external realizations of the same underlying idea at different stages of a creative honing process. As the idea loses potentiality and gains concreteness, psychological entropy dissipates.

How creativity drives innovation in a social system

As discussed in Chapter 4, when an open system acquires energy, resources, and/or information from its environment, entropy may be displaced, thus creating a semi-stable state. By way of this kind of change of state, the system may evolve (Schrödinger, 1944). In cultural evolution, what is evolving is human worldviews, and psychological entropy provides an arousal-provoking signal that a more evolved state is possible. As we saw above, psychological entropy may be generated by a problem, need, inconsistency, gap in knowledge, missing element, or disruption, and through self-other reorganization it *transitions*[2] from an entropic or disordered state towards a more ordered or stable state. In an individual worldview, this happens via *creativity*. In a collective worldview,[3] we propose that the old structures that are transformed into new ones undergo a transition between these two states via a *social system innovation*.

A social system innovation is an innovation that takes place in a social system, such as a new way in which an economy, organization, group, or sociotechnical system functions. In contemporary usage, the term 'innovation' often refers to creative processes or outcomes (Pavitt, 2006; Badiru, 2020). When an innovation pertains to the creation of a process or outcome in a social system for a broader societal value in addressing a social challenge, it is called a *social innovation* (Ward, 1909; Phills et al., 2008; Andrew and Klein, 2010). While any innovation may address a social problem or need, a social innovation directs its value towards novel solutions for the benefit of the societal whole.[4] All innovations have similar processes, including the generation of novelty, the transitioning of novelty into artefacts, and the filling of unmet needs or functions in society (Pavitt, 2006; Badiru, 2020; Gabora, 2018).

Here is an example that we will return to throughout the chapter: a small oil 'boomtown' experiences a 'bust' and a person loses her job but develops

---

[2] We will use the term 'transition' to describe the transformation or even replacement of the deep structure (or regime) of a system through the constant iterative changes that reinforce each other towards the emergence of a new structure (Grin et al., 2010: p. 326).

[3] This term is used as a collective of the individual worldviews of a group or society and their coherently connected web of interrelations, as opposed to a whole entity operating independently. Therefore, the term encompasses how individuals in a social group collectively weave their narratives and understandings by interacting with the world. Here, the term 'collective' is not meant as in collectivism, or as a political structure; rather, it is a multitude that includes the plurality of all variations of individual worldviews within it (Aerts et al., 1994: p. 21).

[4] Although innovations can have positive and negative impacts upon a social system and be designed as such (think of the nuclear bomb as a radical innovation of the time), social innovations are geared towards positive impacts relative to what is paradigmatically and collectively decided as a 'benefit' in that particular society's milieu. For example, the 'intelligence test' was geared to solve a social problem at the turn of the nineteenth century, but a hundred years later is considered to have been collectively damaging (see McGowan, 2017).

an idea to start a wind power business. The individual's worldview experiences a disruption and triggers personal stress, which stimulates a creative solution. Let us look at the same scenario from a collective perspective. After the resource town experiences the economic collapse, a town meeting instigates a shared vision that inspires a few individuals to work on a local wind power project. The meeting results in a new policy that encourages a burgeoning renewable power sector that stimulates a new energy source, strong social networks, *and* the local economy. The collective worldview undergoes a disruption that triggers economic stress, which stimulates the advance of a social innovation. In either case, in the *transition* from an entropic or disordered state to a stable or ordered state, ideas are honed to dissipate entropy by organizing, replicating, and exchanging different perspectives.

Let us consider the process as *active* in social systems when people are seeking solutions via creative ideas and as *passive* when people are not seeking solutions but ideas arise out of necessity owing to external pressures or shocks.[5] When it is passive, the innovation process could be likened to what happens in the punctuated equilibrium theory of evolutionary biology, in which rapid evolutionary events interrupt speciation stasis for short periods of time (Eldredge and Gould, 1972). Likewise, a sudden or short-term event in a social system in which the innovation process is passive may stimulate increased idea generation. Entropic disruptions happen in societal systems (such as the economy) with unpredictability: steady growth may be interrupted by runaway entropy production, and social structures can be threatened (Bailey, 1996). Perhaps jobs are lost and an increase in poverty ensues. However, the proposal here is that innovations introduce energy, resources, and information that fight against entropy (in a type of 'negative entropy' or *negentropy*) by allowing the system to change or evolve and/or stimulating self-organization in interrelated systems or subsystems.[6]

The role of creative destruction

A social system innovation, we propose, is like individual creativity in that it can emerge in response to an entropic, disordered, or even destructed state. An entropic worldview can innovate to originate novel output. Worldviews

---

[5] Here, we associate active and passive innovation with *transport phenomena* in biology (Rosenberg and Johanson, 1948). Plawsky (2014) summarizes the concept by saying it is the process of going from nonequilibrium to equilibrium states or vice versa.

[6] In terms of the 'puzzle' example from Chapter 4, the friend in the trunk of the car may not put the puzzle back together in its original arrangement but instead glues different pieces together creatively to make a sculpture. This action helps the friend acquire an unmet need: getting out of the trunk of a car.

move towards stability when they *self-organize* new components out of older or destructed ones, *self-replicate* or reconstitute a successful component such as by iterating itself in a new context and *exchange* components for novel restructuring (Gabora, 2018: p. 4). The result might include enough of a worldview modification to evolve not only knowledge creation but also technological advancement and the development of a new economic paradigm. In social systems, this can be described as *creative destruction* because old elements are destroyed in the creation of new ones (Schumpeter, 1942). The economy is a collective network of social agreements (positive or negative) that is part of our culture (Freeman, 1990; Rawls, 1993) and is thus subject to collective worldview change. Old elements of an entropic collective world-view are 'destroyed' to create new ordered ones through novel restructuring. A *de*structed state transitions through creative means to a '*re*structed' one.

Schumpeter applies the term creative destruction to the economic structures of capitalism by claiming that capitalism has creative destruction built within it and must evolve or die (Schumpeter, 1942). Any economic system that utilizes its resources to its advantage continuously in an immediate timeframe may fail compared with a system that utilizes its resources continuously over the long term. In this case, innovation is the active or passive process that moves from any inherent limiting elements in an economic system that are destructive (e.g. the continuously immediate utilization of resources to the cost of the long term) to the dynamic elements that respond to the limiting ones but are resilient enough to find balance in the unpredictability of the long term. In this situation, innovation can be seen as *holonic*, that is, fully considering the part (the need to utilize resources in the immediate timeframe advantageously) and fully considering the whole (the need to utilize resources over the long term). Koestler (1967) used the term *holon*, which was based on his observations of biological and social systems, to refer to a whole that is also a part of another whole (see also Botti and Giret, 2008).

If a destructive agent in an economic system is gradualistic and causes little obvious morphological change, then the innovation process in the system may be less noticeable. An economic system may 'hum along', recursively altering the system continuously in a short-term timeframe with minimal increments. However, if the destruction is abrupt (such as in a punctuated equilibrium model and in an unforeseen crisis of resources in an exogenous shock), the resulting process out of crisis into opportunity essentially creates possibilities or demands for innovation. The economic system's utilization of resources, continuously at incremental adjustments, builds up tension in the system when long-term considerations are unforeseen and therefore suddenly 'explode' into chaos. Such destructive crises are often seen as negative.

However, if they are viewed from this Schumpeterian point of view, such crises have built-in possibility for innovation. The types of resulting innovations are not necessarily system-linear or domain-specific but can be across domains and even exapted.[7]

The driver of a social system such as an economy (whether it be gradualistic or punctuated) is the innovative process by which old elements of an entropic collective worldview are 'destroyed' to create new ordered ones. A transition process such as this one is instigated through different possible forces, such as perturbations (shock), incremental change (gradualistic), and the recombination of, or shift between, systems, scopes, and temporal or geospatial scales (Geels and Schot, 2010; Turchin, 1977; Goldstein et al., 2010). The heuristic *adaptive cycle* (Gunderson and Holling, 2002) describes the nonlinear path that many social systems take (and others, such as environmental systems) and shows how a perturbation or shock initiates creative destruction to *release* the tightly bound or rigid limitations of the system, thus instigating a phase of innovation or *reorganization* and is followed by a system's slower *exploitation* and *conservation* (for another interpretation, see Fath et al., 2015). Once a system reaches its critical point, it shifts to redirect its resources to adaptive change via self-organization and low recurrence, fighting against entropy towards negentropy via innovation and reorganization. Innovation drives the social system's transformation toward new growth, similar to creativity in psychological systems and emergence in complex natural systems. It also highlights honing theory's proposal that cultural evolution occurs through the honing of creative ideas in individual or collective worldviews (Gabora, 2017). We propose that Schumpeter's term 'creative destruction' can also be used to describe metaphorically the processes within social systems that represent the transition towards entropic states of instability ("destruction"), *and* the transition toward negentropic states of stability ("creation"). A social system's transition from a disordered state to a novel stable state occurs through innovation.

An economic example and a social innovation response

Let us examine how economic systems evolve by using the example of the utilization of resources. Oil has been claimed to be 'the lifeblood of the modern economy' (Bentley, 2016: p. 1) because it comprises the largest portion of

---

[7] *Exaptation* refers to the cooption of a characteristic that originally evolved for one purpose and was then used for a different purpose. For example, although feathers evolved to provide insulation, they were later co-opted for flight (see Gould and Vrba, 1982).

the world's traded supply of energy. When oil is in short supply, social disturbance can occur, as exemplified by the oil crisis of 1973, the European fuel protests of 2000, and the 2018 Brazilian state of emergency. *Peak oil*, or the notion that oil supply will peak and then reduce in supply (Hubbert, 1956), suggests that further social disruptions may yet occur (Bentley, 2016). As resource availability depletes or becomes more challenging to access, and as we shift from conventional oil supply to nonconventional oil supplies such as oil sands and shale, supply decreases, and prices tend to increase. When this happens, energy descent occurs, and disruption to economic and social systems develops, thus creating a gap in the supply-to-demand (Bentley, 2016).

In current oil-based economies (e.g. Alberta, Canada), the energy demand is being met with technological innovations, such as new extraction methods like fracking, 3D seismic imaging, and MWD (Measurement While Drilling) technology and new methods are emerging all the time. However, other innovations to increase energy supply have also arisen outside of the demand for oil, namely, novel uses of renewable resources such as algae, alcohol waste, lake-bed sediment, and even human body heat (Kim et al., 2018). Whether or not these become useful large-scale solutions with broad impact as unique and new alternatives to meet the energy demand, they indicate the movement from a disrupted economy's gradualist growth to innovatively adapt, exapt, or create new avenues for supply. As an example of a type of evolutionary exaptation of older technology, windmills were originally developed to pump water or grind grains but more recently have been modernized and used for electricity generation. As a result, windmill electricity generation has become one of the fastest growing methods of electrical power creation in the world (Natural Resources Canada, 2016). The shifting away of importance from total profitability to human and environmental sustainability in a 'triple bottom line' or social enterprise structure has brought to economic systems a social innovation paradigm shift from the Friedman doctrine of the 1970s (Cordes, 2014). Perhaps, as Schumpeter implies, the short-term continuous utilization of non-renewable oil-derived energy will lead to failure as supply decreases or as climate change impacts increase, compared with more resilient innovations that utilize renewable resources over the long term. These are examples of innovation arising in the transition from an entropic state to a steady-state that honing theory holds as creativity in worldviews. Although such innovations may have happened passively or with little intention or intervention originally, as demands for energy increase, they are now occurring more actively in creating positive interventions for faster and longer-term results. A large-scale renewable energy source is highly sought after; it seems that the green economy is not an obscure tangent but is an increasing percentage of the global economy that is based on natural cycles rather than a linear economic design (Danaher et al., 2016). Volvo's commitment to producing 'all electric' vehicles in 2019 similarly indicates an economic evolution towards a renewable energy source (Ewing, 2017); innovations will increase in demand if other companies and industries take a similar stance.

Innovations in social systems have also resulted from the peak oil dilemma. The *transition movement* or 'Transition', as it is called, is a direct response to oil dependency and climate change (Hopkins, 2010). In an example of a shift in focus from global economic drivers to communal self-sufficiency across domains (social enterprise, community development, community currency, and local politics), this movement has hundreds of 'transition towns' that have committed to such an emphasis. The movement has shown signs of having its own culture and could be considered a fusion between a social and an environmental movement that 'transitions' away from oil dependency towards a 'permanent culture' (Mollison and Holmgren, 1978). *Permaculture*, which is a social design principle that responds to the need for agricultural sustainability, was conceived at a time when Carson's now classic book *Silent Spring* (1962) aroused a global consciousness of environmental issues. These social design principles have expanded across multiple domains and were exapted beyond agricultural-based permaculture to social perma-culture, financial permaculture, and a permaculture-based local-regional economy (Henfrey and Penha-Lopes, 2015). Cultural evolution here is not linear or one-dimensional, and the resulting innovations (both technological and social) cannot be attributed only to the disruptions triggered by low peak oil or environmental and economic degradation; still, the innovation process is non-arbitrary in that some innovative outputs can be attributed to the cause, as in the transition case (Hopkins, 2010). Innovations in a com-plex system accumulate change in the sense that, once an element such as permaculture has been introduced into the collective worldview, it can be drawn upon for future iterations or adaptations (or even simply as a refer-ence point) regardless of its immediate success, reach, or broad adoption.

Transition is an example of a *social innovation*, which is further defined as a 'complex process of introducing new products, processes, or programs that profoundly change the basic routines, resource and authority flows, or beliefs of the social system in which the innovation occurs. Such successful social innovations have durability and broad impact' (Westley and Antadze, 2010: p. 2). Whether transitioning from an oil-based economic state towards a renewable sustainable state or from a global economic oil-dependent culture towards a sustainable economic or social permaculture, such systems are moving from a state of entropic disorder to a steady-state system of order via *creativity* in individual worldviews and via *innovation* in the collective worldviews of a social system. Although speculative, this is important because shifts in social systems that have the negentropic driver of innovation may lead researchers to search for transitional indicators of system (re)configuration, co-evolutionary processes, and multi-actor interactions such as social movements through entropic instability, variance, and competition (Prigogine and Stengers, 1984; Kondepudi and Prigogine, 1998, 2015; Kubicek and Marek, 1983). Once these indicators of entropy are observed in the context of the systemic negentropic change, social innovation interventions can be designed to actively or passively leverage the system toward behaviours or resource flows that increase value to the broader society.

A complex systems approach to social innovation and its relationship to worldviews

Social innovation can be seen as filling the gap of an unmet social need, a perceived unresolved social challenge to overcome, or a complex social problem to solve. Unmet needs that manifest as large-scale social challenges, such as persistent poverty, war, lack of education, or the economic collapse of a resource town, are inherently difficult to address successfully. The unmanageability of complex systems leads to challenges that are sometimes called *wicked problems* (Rittel and Webber, 1973) and to the unpre-stateability of any clear governing behaviour that would allow for a direct resolution (Kauffman, 1993). Similar to a psychological entropic state, these social complex problems (disorder) trigger an active or passive process towards innovative solutions (order) and, when approached with social innovation interventions and implementation, can create greater resilience and show promise of long-term stability (Westley, 2013). Social innovation is about change at the social systemic level and as such transcends sectors across domains and scales (Westley and Antadze, 2010; compare to creativity in Ranjan et al., 2013). The underlying mechanisms of change in social innovation evolves as culture evolves; therefore, the methods of social innovation tend to go beyond the strategies and theories that define them (Phills et al., 2008). When social innovations arise out of creative destruction and/or instigate it, they can become a type of *disruptive innovation* (Christensen et al., 2006). They disrupt the dominant social system and institutions as they restructure them to create new ones, thereby challenging relationships of power and resources and disturbing the basic habitualizations and belief systems of those who blindly work to uphold them (Murray et al., 2008; Westley and Antadze, 2010). For example, in Seoul, South Korea, after decades of authoritarian governments that favoured a corporate in-group domination of civil society, a new mayor created an innovative participatory process claiming that 'citizens are mayors', and gave unprecedented political access to the 'everyday lives of citizens' (Kim et al., 2015: p. 171). With politically backed efforts, such as participatory city budgeting, citizen-created municipal news content, citizen-led policy creation and adoption, and real-time political meeting feedback platforms, these social innovations in municipal communications challenged established monopolies and crossed multiple domains.

Social innovations can be seen as having six key elements: 1) *novelty* (or the uniqueness of an idea, product, process or initiative) within the context of the field, domain, or system that it is being applied to; 2) *implementation*, or how the novel idea is implemented into the field, domain, or system and how well it can be done; 3) *need*, which describes the system's need to be met; 4) *effectiveness*, which describes whether the innovation is more effective than the previous normalized or standard solutions; 5) *enhancement*, the ability for the innovation to alter society's capacity to act; and 6) *resilience*, or the innovation's ability to adapt to stress and change while retaining its basic function and structure (as described by *The Young Foundation*; Caulier-Grice et al., 2012). The recent development in social innovation that has heightened the focus on social entrepreneurism and social enterprise has spurred growth in the *social economy*, which is the 'third sector' of the economy other than the government and private sector, placing people and place (environment) before profit (or in conjunction with it; CIRIEC International, 2016). This third sector is a burgeoning competitor in the global economic system, with, for example, 22 per cent of the EU population as members of associated businesses (European Commission, 2018). The social economy can be seen as a *holonic system*, which describes a system that is both a whole and a part, in that the social economy is part of the global economy, but its components (such as social enterprises, cooperative corporate structures, and B-Corp networks) are robust smaller systems on their own.

Let us look at the scaling up of individual creative ideas to social innovations as per a negentropic process. Creative ideas start in the mind of an individual or group of individuals, from the detection of a psychologically entropic state concerning a social condition that provokes uncertainty and is arousal-inducing. Social innovations start similarly, but they occur passively or are conceived of actively in the context of a collective worldview entropic state transitioning to a social condition that is better than the current/

previous condition (Caulier-Grice et al., 2012). If individual ideas are adopted or co-authored by supportive groups or communities, they can be implemented into the disrupted system that requires change and may evolve to include other strategies from the community to support the process or products required to facilitate such change. Finally, such collective ideas are integrated to address the complex dynamics of the social system, including blockages and resistances that created the disruption in the first place (McGowan et al., 2017). This describes a considerable leap from the individual (micro holon) to the social system (macro holon) in which new ideas innovate over time to articulate or 'bake' in the individual or group and percolate within the community and are then implemented, occurring in rapid succession owing to a sudden perturbation or shock to the system in a short period of time. The scaling up of an idea from the micro level to the macro level happens at different temporal frames for a multitude of reasons, including the ability of the idea to meet or overcome the limitations of the domain(s) in which the scaling happens within or across. Other reasons include social factors, such as the honing of ideas from the field of professionals that influences what should be implemented.

Therefore, social innovations can initiate system change that involves cross-scale and cross-domain dynamics, reacting to and meeting needs in a way that can leave the system more durable, effective, and resilient in the long term (Westley and Antadze, 2010). For example, in the late nineteenth and early twentieth centuries, a few individuals challenged the notion of a new national park system as only 'islands of civilization in a sea of wilderness' (Dearden and Rollins, 2008: p. 112). Instead, they wanted to protect these areas in a cross-scale innovation that gathered thousands more to challenge industries, agricultures, and governments from regional to federal levels so that parks would become resilient biophysical and natural ecosystems with a focus on ecological integrity (Antadze, 2017). Now, a national park is seen more as an 'island of wilderness within a sea of civilization' (Dearden and Rollins, 2008: p. 290). Social movements that challenge the societal norm, such as the parks example or the Transition movement mentioned earlier, are 'early warning systems' that signal a dysfunction within a social system or a disruptive or entropic state (Henderson, 1993). Lateral information flows and citizen-led networks of social movements instigate self-organization through artefact-sharing and meaning-making, where the individual and collective worldviews respond to the gaps or interstices in destabilized social structures by challenging authority flows and beliefs towards novel, durable, and broad-scale solutions (Westley and Antadze, 2017; Henderson, 1993). Social movements often initiate social innovations;

therefore, such movements are indicative of entropic processes within social systems as birthing places for novelty and the generation of innovation.

New innovations tend to adapt or exapt current components or previous components upon which they were built. As worldviews evolve, so do innovations; however, the 'trajectory' of this evolution may be nonlinear. If a system has an innovation trajectory that is seemingly irregular but then 'narrows' towards a specific 'direction', whatever the point of the direction that the trajectory is headed can be called an *attractor* (Lorenz, 1995; Klüver, 2000). As worldviews and innovations iterate, reinforce, and amplify each other, their trajectories could feed back into disorderly chaos; however, if they create a stable pattern of interaction held by attractors strong enough, even if disrupted endogenously or exogenously, they will return to that stable pattern (McGowan et al., 2017: p. 7). Like several rivers flowing back into the same sea (Kauffman, 1995), the 'area' where this pattern returns to is called a *basin of attraction*. For example, as collective worldviews respond to disruptions in an oil-based economy by fluctuating to variant possible solutions that include a sustainable perspective, a novel renewable-oriented innovation that has resilient features may appear and become an attractor. To return to our earlier example of a resource town that has gone 'bust', consider the disruptive innovator who has an idea to start a wind power business, and others take interest. Instead of the other innovative ideas 'leaving' the system, they return to support the novelty of the original attractor idea. If the attractor becomes a stable basin, meaning that the idea of the disruptive innovator keeps attracting the other ideas to support the direction of the attractor, the collective worldview may become more dominant and resilient. However, for reasons such as demographic stochasticity, random variation in population size (people coming and going or liking and disliking the ideas), temporal phases within the transition and perturbations (or shocks) to the basin (Stevens, 2009), not all attractors create a basin of attraction. Still, new ideas will adapt or exapt old ideas upon which they were based.

In our example of a resource boomtown, a simple attractor would be the trajectory of all the insufficient but dominant routines, resource flows, authority flows, and social networks within the town's community, organizations, and governments (Goldstein et al., 2010; Klüver, 2000) that aid its continuing use of dominant economic resources (oil). The town makes changes to its economic or social structure only to keep it *stable* so that the system variables do not affect the attractor or amplify the system to chaotic or disorderly levels. In other words, the boomtown continues 'business as usual' and, thus, is oil dependent. However, complex systems are sensitive to initial conditions, so much so that even small initial disruptions can cause drastic outcomes (as in the *butterfly effect*[8]). Furthermore, even though outcomes cannot be predicted in complex systems directly, the parameters that outcomes fall into can be predicted; such processes are '*not random but look random*' (Lorenz, 1995: p. 4; italics in original). Even though patterns of iteration occur in chaotic or random ways, complex systems self-organize and can evolve into surprisingly stable patterns. This may happen via a *strange attractor* (Ruelle and Takens, 1971; Kauffman, 1993; McCarthy, 2017), which occurs because of its sensitivity to initial conditions and due to the nearby trajectories converging upon it. It is '"strange" because it is orderly when it is expected to be random' (Rogers et al., 2005: p. 5) and can catalyse a chaotic system towards a patterned and stable structure (Dyer, 2012). Snowflakes are created in the chaos of a storm but display unique fractal patterns of self-replication and creativity that comes out of seeming disorder. Patterns of system behaviour that transition from instability toward stabilized structures can be applied to individual psychology and social systems as well (McCarthy, 2017). As described earlier, insight, through the lens of self-organized criticality, arises when a critical but semi-stable state is reached between order and chaos (punctuated equilibrium is an example of self-organized criticality) (Bak and Boettcher, 1997). If our example simple attractor is 'business as usual', a strange attractor would be the trajectory or goal that, through a catalyser or shift to the system that creates a social innovation, arises out of chaos but emerges as a unique pattern of social net-works, interactions, and structures (Goldstein et al., 2010). For instance, the town may experience a flood that destroys much of the resource industry's infrastructure. However, upon the social connectivity and 'help your neigh-bour' attitude that organizes and restabilizes the town, a 'shared vision' emerges that decides that the flooding may have been induced by climate change; as such, the town should seek innovation towards a novel renewable resource to create a sustainable opportunity (Gilstrap, 2005). If a strange attractor's basin of attraction becomes large, it will be 'highly resistant to disturbances' (Klüver, 2000: p. 114). A social innovation can be generally resilient even when there are disruptions.

While complex systems can fluctuate between stable and chaotic states, strange attractors show us that something balanced can result when a system moves towards disorder. Self-organization limits complexity just within the 'edge of chaos' in what some researchers call the *goldilocks principle* (Boulding, 1981), which refers to conditions that are 'just right' (Klüver, 2000; McCarthy, 2017). The notion that a system can be chaotic and stable may

---

[8] A famous analogy is that a butterfly flapping its wings in Brazil causes a hurricane in Texas (Lorenz, 1972).

seem paradoxical; however, when there is simultaneously order and chaos patterning that does not lead to the extensive domination of chaos *or* order (yet existing in between both), the system can be called *chaordic* (Hock, 1999; van Eijnatten, 2004).[9] For example, in a system that includes a storm (chaos) and wind turbine (stability), if neither dominate but instead complement each other, electricity can result. The storm needs to be strong enough to produce wind but not so strong that it renders the turbine useless. The tension between destruction and creation, entropy (disorder) and negentropy (order), and instability and stability may fluctuate owing to endogenous or exogenous reasons at different rates and scales. However, from a chaordic place, self-organizing, self-replicating, and exchanging elements within a social system become emergent in the sense that chaordic conditions allow for emergent structures to arise, thus leading to other emerging structures. In an iterative and evolving process, innovations create conditions that lead to other innovations (McCarthy, 2017). This implies that order *and* disorder (negentropy and entropy) are an integral part of innovation. Psychological entropy is an integral part of creativity and idea concretization. Similarly, we propose that creative destruction is an integral part of social innovation and implementation. This is not to emphasize the entropic or destructive process but rather to accentuate the role of creativity/innovation in the negentropic resiliency and evolution of a social system. This evolving systems dynamic can be seen as the result of the creative transition from entropy toward stability in not only individual worldviews but also the innovative transition from social disruptions toward stability in a collective worldview system.

In our earlier example of an oil boomtown, when its economy collapses owing to a flood that leaves the economic situation and social network disrupted, a newly unemployed individual who is desperate to find a solid job has an idea. Psychological entropy arouses creative ideation. The individual collaborates with others and they hone their ideas in communal exchange. They see an unmet need within the community for an energy source; therefore, they begin a community wind power project that turns into a social enterprise that creates not only individual but communal economic stability. Perhaps modern technology is exapted from traditional resources, a social innovation project is sparked, and a social economy develops not only economic stability but also social network bonds. The initiative spurs the community to fund the project by encouraging its citizens to be investors, thus resulting in a complex social network that is resilient and supports community

---

[9] Although chaos theory implies both chaos and order, van Eijnatten (2004) uses the term 'chaordic' to describe a chaotically ordered complex, and thus distinguishes it from the common use of the word 'chaos' as disorder or mayhem.

commitment, participation, and contribution. Although not all actors in the system are benefactors, the collective begins to see that the destructive nature of the oil-based economic collapse was essential to their greater success. They find chaordic dynamism, such that the strange attractor of the shared vision of social innovation was neither dominating the system to become too large a project for the situation nor was dominated by the wicked problems of unemployment and social disruption, thus leading to a resilient outcome. The shared community effort helps to set up a system of replication of their model for exchange with others, scaling up their innovation. The government takes on the initiative, crossing fields and domains out of community effort and into political policy. For the town, the ideas of economic collapse become part of their new social innovation theory, thus evolving the collective worldviews of the townspeople towards long-term utilization of resource sustainably (see the 'Sunshine Project' of Japan as a general example; Maruyama et al., 2007). The entropic disorder of their collective worldview, triggered by economic collapse, initiated social and other innovations in a transition towards a self-mended sustainable and resilient communal perspective.

When a social system is in dynamic tension between order and chaos, the tension allows such systems to 'continue to self-organize and remain resilient in the face of broader system change' (McCarthy, 2017: p. 135). Social innovations may lead to other social innovations, much as concepts may generate new concepts in a self-organizing network of understanding. The overall structure of the worldview in which this occurs evolves via restructuring (fuelled by the drive to reduce psychological entropy) and the communal exchange of ideas among individuals. This is the basis for cultural evolution. We refer to the process by which this happens in an individual worldview as creativity, and suggest that social innovation is one process by which this happens in a collective worldview. That is, through the iterative self-organizing of groups, communities, or societies, disruption may shift to solutions that are effective and resilient. Both psychological and group novelty generation processes involve a dynamic movement between entropy and stability. Complex systems theory, negentropy, creative destruction, as well as collective worldviews and the concept of self-other reorganization, can shed light on both creativity and social innovation, thus aiding us in our understanding of how innovation thrives and how resilient societies evolve.

Conclusion

When a system such as a mind or a social group is poised in the regime between order and chaos, innovations may emerge through the modifications or exaptations of previous innovations. Such innovations may 'hop' domains or scales in their drive to meet unmet needs. Creative individuals and groups exemplify the adage that creativity and destruction are intrinsically linked. In social systems, innovations can result from the disruption of unresolved complex challenges, such as the wicked problems of resource boomtowns undergoing economic collapse. We argue that as much as individual psychological entropy instigates creativity, creative destruction instigates social innovation. This in turn elicits social change towards resiliency, as in the Transition movement example. We suggest that both individual creativity and social innovation involve a psychological transition between entropy and stability that can manifest as change in the external world. Communities can significantly reinvent themselves within even extreme economic challenges through the communal exchange of ideas in a network of worldviews. As such, evolutionary thinking will need to include a serious consideration of how worldviews transform and evolve through the honing of creative ideas, and how this elicits the transition between entropy and stability or chaos and order, as a key feature of how social innovations occur. Destruction is not only a link to creativity but indeed is a part of it. This positions a destruction-creativity dynamic as a fundamental link through which the network of worldviews evolves culture, society, and, ultimately, our individual and collective human experience.

References

Aerts, D., Apostel, L., De Moor, B., Hellemans, S., Maex, E., Van Belle, H., and Van der Veken, J. 1994. *World views: from fragmentation to integration*. VUB Press.

Andrew, C. and Klein, J.L. 2010. *Social innovation: what it is and why is it important to understand it better*. Centre de recherche sur les innovations sociales. Collection Études théoriques, no ET1003.

Antadze, N. 2017. National parks in the United States. In Westley, F., McGowan, K. and Tjörnbo, O. (eds.). *The evolution of social innovation*. Edward Elgar Publishing.

Arnheim, N. and Taylor, C.E. 1969. Non-Darwinian evolution: consequences for neutral allelic variation. *Nature*, 223(5209): 900–3.

Badiru, A.B. 2020. *Innovation: a systems approach*. Taylor & Francis Group.

Bailey, K. 1996. Advances in social entropy theory. *Sociologia-Slovak Sociological Review*, Fall: 89–98.

Bak, P. and Boettcher, S. 1997. Self-organized criticality and punctuated equilibria. *Physica D: Nonlinear Phenomena*, 107(2–4): 143–50.

Bak, P., Tang, C., and Wiesenfeld, K. 1988. Self-organized criticality. *Physical Review A*, 38(1): 364–74.

Baum, D.A. 2018. The origin and early evolution of life in chemical composition space. *Journal of Theoretical Biology*, 456: 295–304.

Bentley, R.A., Hahn, M.W., and Shennan, S.J. 2004. Random drift and cultural change. *Proceedings of the Royal Society of London. Series B*, 271: 1143–50.

Bentley, R.W. 2016. *Introduction to peak oil*. Springer International Publishing.

Botti, V. and Giret, A. 2008. *ANEMONA: a multi-agent methodology for holonic manufacturing systems*. Springer.

Boulding, K.E. 1981. *Evolutionary economics*. Sage Publications.

Boyd, R. and Richerson, P. 1985. *Culture and the evolutionary process*. University of Chicago Press.

Brewer, J., Gelfand, M., Jackson, J.C., MacDonald, I.F., Peregrine, P.N., Richerson, P.J., Turchin, P., Whitehouse, H., and Wilson, D.S. 2017. Grand challenges for the study of cultural evolution. *Nature Ecology and Evolution*, 1(3): 1–3.

Campbell, D.T. 1960. Blind variation and selective retention in creative thought as in other knowledge processes. *Psychological Review*, 67(6): 380–400.

Carson, R. 1962. *Silent spring*. Houghton Mifflin.

Caulier-Grice, J., Davies, A., Patrick, R., and Norman, W. 2012. Defining social innovation. Social innovation overview: a deliverable of the project 'The theoretical, empirical and policy foundations for building social innovation in Europe' (TEPSIE). European Commission–7th Framework Programme, Brussels: European Commission, DG Research.

Cavalli-Sforza, L.L. and Feldman, M.W. 1981. *Cultural transmission and evolution: a quantitative approach*. Princeton University Press.

Christensen, C.M., Baumann, H., Ruggles, R., and Sadtler, T.M. 2006. Disruptive innovation for social change. *Harvard Business Review*, (December issue).

CIRIEC International. 2016. *Recent evolutions of the social economy in the European Union*. European Economic and Social Committee (Publication No. CES/CSS/12/2016/23406).

Cordes, C. 2014. The rise of triple-bottom-line businesses. In Worldwatch Institute (ed.). *State of the world 2014: governing for sustainability*. Island Press.

Cornish-Bowden, A. and Cárdenas, M.L. 2017. Life before LUCA. *Journal of Theoretical Biology*, 434: 68–74.

Creanza, N., Kolodny, O., and Feldman, M.W. 2017. Cultural evolutionary theory: how culture evolves and why it matters. *Proceedings of the National Academy of Sciences of the United States of America*, 114(30): 7782–9.

Danaher, K., Biggs, S., and Mark, J. 2016. *Building the green economy: success stories from the grassroots*. Taylor and Francis.

Dearden, P. and Rollins, R. 2008. *Parks and protected areas in Canada: planning and management*. Oxford University Press.

Durham, W. 1991. *Coevolution: genes, culture, and human diversity*. Stanford University Press.

Dyer, W. 2012. Mapping pathways. In Williams, M. and Vogt, W.P. (eds.). *The SAGE handbook of innovation in social research methods*. SAGE Publications.

Edelman, G. 2014. Neural Darwinism. *New Perspectives Quarterly*, 31(1): 25–7.

Edelman, G.M., 1987. *Neural Darwinism: the theory of neuronal group selection*. Basic Books.

Eldredge, N. and Gould, S.J. 1972. Punctuated equilibria: an alternative to phyletic gradualism. In Schopf, Freeman TJM (ed.). *Models in paleobiology*. Cooper and Company.

Essletzbichler, J. 2011. Darwin's conjecture: the search for general principles of social and economic evolution. *Regional Studies*, 45(7): 1015–16.

EU European Commission on Growth: Internal Market, Industry, Entrepreneurship and SMEs. (2018, November 22). Social economy in the EU.

Ewing, J. 2017. *Volvo, betting on electric, moves to phase out conventional engines*. The New York Times (July 5).

Fath, B.D., Dean, C.A., and Katzmair, H. 2015. Navigating the adaptive cycle: an approach to managing the resilience of social systems. *Ecology and Society*, 20(2).

Feist, G.J. 1998. A meta-analysis of personality in scientific and artistic creativity. *Personality and Social Psychology Review*, 2(4): 290–309.

Fisher, R.A. 1930. *The genetical theory of natural selection*. Clarendon Press.

Fitch, W.T. 2005. The evolution of language: a comparative review. *Biology and Philosophy*, 20(2–3): 193–203.

Freeman, S. 1990. Reason and agreement in social contract views. *Philosophy and Public Affairs*, 19(2): 122–57.

Gabora, L. 1995. Meme and variations: a computational model of cultural evolution. In Nadel, L. and Stein, D. (eds.). *Lectures in complex systems*. Addison-Wesley.

Gabora, L. 1998. Autocatalytic closure in a cognitive system: a tentative scenario for the origin of culture. *Psycholoquy*, 9(67).

Gabora, L. 2001. *Cognitive mechanisms underlying the origin and evolution of culture* [Doctoral Dissertation]. Center Leo Apostel For Interdisciplinary Studies, Vrije Universiteit Brussel, Brussels, Belgium.

Gabora, L. 2004. Ideas are not replicators but minds are. *Biology and Philosophy*, 19(1): 127–43.

Gabora, L. 2006. Self-other organization: why early life did not evolve through natural selection. *Journal of Theoretical Biology*, 241(3): 443–50.

Gabora, L. 2008. The cultural evolution of socially situated cognition. *Cognitive Systems Research*, 9(1–2): 104–14.

Gabora, L. 2011. Five clarifications about cultural evolution. *Journal of Cognition and Culture*, 11(1–2): 61–83.

Gabora, L. 2013. An evolutionary framework for culture: selectionism versus communal exchange. *Physics of Life Reviews*, 10(2): 117–45.

Gabora, L. 2017. Honing theory: a complex systems framework for creativity. *Nonlinear Dynamics, Psychology, and Life Sciences*, 21(1): 35–88.

Gabora, L. 2018a. The creative process of cultural evolution. In Leung, A., Kwan, L., and Liou, S. (eds.). *Handbook of culture and creativity: basic processes and applied innovations*. Oxford University Press.

Gabora, L. 2018b. Why a population genetics framework is inappropriate for cultural evolution. https://www.researchgate.net/publication/329057836_Why_a_Population_Genetics_Framework_is_Inappropriate_for_Cultural_Evolution.

Gabora, L. 2019. Creativity: linchpin in the quest for a viable theory of cultural evolution. *Current Opinion in Behavioral Sciences*, 27: 77–83.

Gabora, L. and Steel, M. 2017. Autocatalytic networks in cognition and the origin of culture. *Journal of Theoretical Biology*, 431: 87–95.

Gabora, L. 2000. Conceptual closure. How memories are woven into an interconnected worldview. *Annals of the New York Academy of Sciences*, 901: 42–53.

Geels, F.W. and Schot, J. 2010. The dynamics of transitions: a socio-technical perspective. In Grin, J. Rotmans, J., and Schot, J. (eds.). *Transitions to sustainable development: new directions in the study of long term transformative change*. Routledge.

Gilstrap, D.L. 2005. Strange attractors and human interaction: leading complex organizations through the use of metaphors. *Complicity: An International Journal of Complexity and Education*, 2(1): 55–69.

Goldstein, J., Hazy, J.K., and Silberstang, J. 2010. A complexity science model of social innovation in social enterprise. *Journal of Social Entrepreneurship*, 1(1): 101–25.

Gould, S.J. and Vrba, E.S. 1982. Exaptation—a missing term in the science of form. *Paleobiology*, 8(1): 4–15.

Grin, J., Rotmans, J., and Schot, J. 2010. Conclusion: how to understand transitions? How to influence them? Synthesis and lessons for further research. In Grin, J., Rotmans, J., and Schot, J. (eds.). *Transitions to sustainable development: new directions in the study of long term transformative change*. Routledge.

Gunderson, L.H. and Holling, C.S. 2002. *Panarchy: understanding transformations in human and natural systems*. Island Press.

Haldane, J.B.S. 1932. *The causes of evolution*. Princeton University Press.

Henderson, H. 1993. Social innovation and citizen movements. *Futures*, 25(3): 322–38.

Henfrey, T. and Penha-Lopes, G. 2015. *Permaculture and climate change adaptation: inspiring ecological, social, economic and cultural responses for resilience and transformation*. Permanent Publications.

Heyes, C. 2018. Enquire within: cultural evolution and cognitive science. *Philosophical Transactions of the Royal Society Series B*, 373.

Hirsh, J.B., Mar, R.A., and Peterson, J.B. 2012. Psychological entropy: a framework for understanding uncertainty-related anxiety. *Psychological Review*, 119(2): 304–20.

Hock, D. 1999. *Birth of the chaordic age*. Berrett-Koehler Publishers.

Hodgson, G.M. 2002. Darwinism in economics: from analogy to ontology. *Journal of Evolutionary Economics*, 12(3): 259–81.

Hopkins, R. 2010. *Localisation and resilience at the local level: the case of Transition Town Totnes* (Doctoral dissertation). Retrieved from ProQuest Dissertations Publishing (U560577).

Hordijk, W., Hein, J., and Steel, M. 2010. Autocatalytic sets and the origin of life. *Entropy*, 12(7): 1733–42.

Hordijk, W., Steel, M., and Dittrich, P. 2018. Autocatalytic sets and chemical organizations: modelling self-sustaining reaction networks at the origin of life. *New Journal of Physics*, 20(1).

Hubbert, M.K. 1956. Nuclear energy and fossil fuels. In The American Petroleum Institute (ed.). *Drilling and production practice*. Shell, Houston, TX Development Company (7–25).

Kauffman, S.A. 1993. *The origins of order*. Oxford University Press.

Kauffman, S.A. 1995. *At home in the universe*. Oxford University Press.

Killeen, P.R. 2019. The non-Darwinian evolution of behavers and behaviors. *Behavioural Processes*, 161: 45–53.

Kim, C.S., Lee, G.S., Choi, H., Kim, Y.J., Yang, H.M., Lim, S.H., Lee, S., and Cho, B.J. 2018. Structural design of a flexible thermoelectric power generator for wearable applications. *Applied Energy*, 214(C): 131–8.

Kim, J., Rim, S., Han, S., and Park, A. 2015. Seoul city's social innovation strategy: new models of communication to strengthen citizen engagement. In Nicholls, A., Simon, J., and Gabriel, M. (eds.). *New frontiers in social innovation research*. Palgrave Macmillan Publishers.

King, J.L. and Jukes, T.H. 1969. Non-Darwinian evolution. *Science*, 164(3881): 788–98.

Klüver, J. 2000. *The dynamics and evolution of social systems: new foundations of a mathematical sociology*. Springer.

Koestler, A. 1967. *The ghost in the machine*. Hutchinson.

Kondepudi, D. and Prigogine, I. 1998/2015. *Modern thermodynamics: from heat engines to dissipative structures* (2nd ed.). John Wiley.

Koonin, E.V. 2009. Darwinian evolution in the light of genomics. *Nucleic Acids Research*, 37(4): 1011–34.

Kubicek, M. and Marek, M. 1983. *Computational methods in bifurcation theory and dissipative structures*. Springer-Verlag.

Ling, S., Hu, Z., Yang, Z., Yang, F., Li, Y., Lin, P., Chen, K., Dong, L., Cao, L., Tao, Y., Hao, L., Chen, Q., Gong, Q., Wu, D., Li, W., Zhao, W., Tian, X., Hao, C., Hungate, E.A., Catenacci, D.V., Hudson, R.R., Li, W.H., Lu, X., and Wu, C.I. 2015. Extremely high genetic diversity in a single tumor points to prevalence of non-Darwinian cell evolution. *Proceedings of the National Academy of Sciences of the United States of America*, 112(47): E6496–E6505.

Lorenz, E.N. 1972. *Predictability: does the flap of a butterfly's wings in Brazil set off a tornado in Texas?* Presented before the American Association for the Advancement of Sciences.

Lorenz, E.N. 1995. *The essence of chaos.* UCL Press Limited.

Martindale, C. and Armstrong, J. 1974. The relationship of creativity to cortical activation and its operant control. *Journal of Genetic Psychology*, 124(2nd half): 311–20.

Maruyama, Y., Nishikido, M., and Iida, T. 2007. The rise of community wind power in Japan: enhanced acceptance through social innovation. *Energy Policy*, 35(5): 2761–9.

McCarthy, D. 2017. Synthesis: self-organization, strange attractors and social innovation. In Westley, F., McGowan, F., and Tjörnbo, O. (eds.). *The evolution of social innovation.* Edward Elgar Publishing.

McGowan, K. 2017. The intelligence test. In Westley, F., McGowan, F., and Tjörnbo, O. (eds.). *The evolution of social innovation.* Edward Elgar Publishing.

McGowan, K., Westley, F., and Tjörnbo, O. 2017. The history of social innovation. In Westley, F. McGowan, K., and Tjörnbo, O. (eds.). *The evolution of social innovation.* Edward Elgar Publishing.

Mesoudi, A. 2017. Pursuing Darwin's curious parallel: prospects for a science of cultural evolution. *Proceedings of the National Academy of Sciences of the United States of America*, 114(30): 7853–60.

Mollison, B. and Holmgren, D. 1978. *Permaculture one: a perennial agriculture for human settlements.* Transworld Publishers.

Murray, R., Mulgan, G., and Caulier-Grice, J. 2008. How to innovate: the tools for social innovation. Retrieved from http://youngfoundation.org/wp-content/uploads/2012/10/How-to-innovate-the-tools-for-social-innovation.pdf.

Natural Resources Canada (Government of Canada). 2016. Wind energy. Retrieved from https://www.nrcan.gc.ca/energy/energy-sources-distribution/renewables/wind-energy/7299.

Nelson, R.R. and Winter, S.G. 2002. Evolutionary theorizing in economics. *The Journal of Economic Perspectives*, 16(2): 23–46.

O'Brien, M.J. and Lyman, R.L. 2000. Applying evolutionary archaeology: a systematic approach. Kluwer Academic/Plenum Publishers.

Pagel, M. 2017. Darwinian perspectives on the evolution of human languages. *Psychonomic Bulletin and Review*, 24(1): 151–7.

Pavitt, K. 2006. Innovation processes. In Fagerberg, J. and Mowery, D.C. (eds.). *The Oxford handbook of innovation*. Oxford University Press.

Phills, J.A., Deiglmeier, K., and Miller, D.T. 2008. Rediscovering social innovation. *Stanford Social Innovation Review*, 6(4): 34–43.

Plawsky, J.L. 2014. *Transport phenomena fundamentals* (3rd ed.). CRC Press, Taylor & Francis Group.

Prigogine, I. and Stengers, I. 1984. *Order out of chaos: man's new dialogue with nature*. Bantam Press Books.

Ranjan, A., Gabora, L., and O'Connor, B. 2013a. The cross-domain re-interpretation of artistic ideas. In Knauff, M., Pauen, M., Sebanz, N., and Wachsmuth, I. (eds.). *Proceedings of the 35th annual meeting of the Cognitive Science Society*. Cognitive Science Society, Austin TX (3251–3256).

Ranjan, A., Gabora, L., and O'Connor, B. 2013b. *Evidence that cross-domain re-interpretations of creative ideas are recognizable*. Proceedings of the Association for the Advancement of Artificial Intelligence (AAAI) spring Symposium. (Creativity and Cognitive Development: A perspective from Artificial Creativity, Developmental Artificial Intelligence, and Robotics). AAAI Press, Menlo Park, CA.

Rawls, J. 1993. *Political liberalism*. Columbia University Press.

Rittel, H.W.J. and Webber, M.M. 1973. Dilemmas in a general theory of planning. *Policy Sciences*, 4(2): 155–69.

Rogers, E.M., Medina, U.E., Rivera, M.A., and Wiley, C.J. 2005. Complex adaptive systems and the diffusion of innovations. *The Innovation Journal: The Public Sector Innovation Journal*, 10(3): 1–26.

Rosenberg, T. and Johanson, M. 1948. On accumulation and active transport in biological systems. I. Thermodynamic considerations. *Acta Chemica Scandinavica*, 2: 14–33.

Ruelle, D. and Takens, F. 1971. On the nature of turbulence. *Communications in Mathematical Physics*, 20(3): 167–92.

Schilling, C. 2005. *The body in culture, technology and society*. Sage.

Schrödinger, E. 1944. *What is life? The physical aspect of the living cell*. Cambridge University Press.

Schumpeter, J. 1942. *Capitalism, socialism and democracy*. Harper.

Scotney, V., Weissmeyer, S., and Gabora, L. 2018. Cross-domain influences on creative processes and products. In Kalish, C., Rau, M., Zhu, J., and Rogers, T. (eds.). *Proceedings of the 40th annual meeting of the Cognitive Science Society*. Cognitive Science Society, Austin, TX (2452–7).

Scotney, V.S., Weissmeyer, S., Carbert, N., and Gabora, L. 2019. The ubiquity of cross-domain thinking in the early phase of the creative process. *Frontiers in Psychology*, 10: 1426. doi: 10.3389/fpsyg.2019.01426

Simonton, D.K. 1999a. Creativity as blind variation and selective retention: is the creative process Darwinian? *Psychological Inquiry*, 10(4): 309–28.

Simonton, D.K. 1999b. *Origins of genius: Darwinian perspectives on creativity*. Oxford University Press, Oxford, UK.

Simonton, D.K. 2011. Creativity and discovery as blind variation: Campbell's (1960) BVSR model after the half-century mark. *Review of General Psychology*, 15(2): 158–74.

Steel, M. 2000. The emergence of a self-catalysing structure in abstract origin-of-life models. *Applied Mathematics Letters*, 13(3): 91–5.

Stevens, M.H.H. 2009. Multiple basins of attraction. In Stevens, M.H.H. (ed.). *A primer of ecology with R*. Springer.

Turchin, V.F. 1977. *The phenomenon of science: a cybernetic approach to human evolution*. Columbia University Press.

van Eijnatten, F.M. 2004. Chaordic systems thinking: some suggestions for a complexity framework to inform a learning organization. *Learning Organization*, 11(6): 430–49.

Vetsigian, K., Woese, C., and Goldenfeld, N. 2006. Collective evolution and the genetic code. *Proceedings of the National Academy of Sciences in the United States of America*, 103(28): 10696–701.

Ward, L.F. 1909. *Pure sociology: a treatise on the origin and spontaneous development of society*. The Macmillan Company.

Westley, F. 2013. Social innovation and resilience: how one enhances the other. *Stanford Social Innovation Review*, Summer: 6–8.

Westley, F. and Antadze, N. 2010. Making a difference: strategies for scaling social innovation for greater impact. *The Innovation Journal: The Public Sector Innovation Journal*, 15(2): 2–19.

Woese, C.R. 2002. On the evolution of cells. *Proceedings of the National Academy of Sciences in the United States of America*, 99(13): 8742–7.

Wright, S. 1931. Evolution in Mendelian populations. *Genetics*, 16(2): 97–159.

Conclusions

Gino Cattani and Mariano Mastrogiorgio

We began this book by highlighting that, since the 1970s, several important developments have profoundly changed the field of evolutionary biology. Of particular interest here are the concepts of punctuated equilibrium, speciation, and exaptation and their centrality for understanding the emergence of novelty. Despite their influence in evolutionary biology, these advancements have received only limited attention in evolutionary approaches to economics, innovation, and strategy. By reviewing and contextualizing these advancements within the current evolutionary debate in economics, innovation, and strategy, our goal was to show how they can shed new light on some of the key assumptions of evolutionary theory, such as the idea that economic systems are in a continual state of disequilibrium. In much of the existing literature, for instance, innovation is treated as an activity that aims to respond to a direct type of question: given a problem, what is the solution? This implies that a new technology is usually 'a working architecture of parts and modules that performs a specific function that permits the satisfaction of a predefined need' (Andriani and Cattani, 2016: p. 116). However, innovation is often the result of a process that starts from the assumption that existing forms (e.g. technologies) have an inherent (and unpredictable) creative potential. This creative potential consists of 'the appearance of novel functions for which the forms were not originally designed or selected for' (Andriani and Cattani, 2016: p. 117). Accordingly, a central theme throughout the book was the recognition that many new technologies originate from an inherently exaptive process—often via horizontal transfer of functional modules—in which technologies previously designed for a particular function or with no function at all are later on co-opted for a new function.

The recent finding in biology that certain proteins are *multifunctional* (Chapple and Brun, 2015; Chapple et al., 2015) further elucidates the origins of novelty via exaptation. As Andriani et al. (2020) emphasized, 'the multiple

Gino Cattani and Mariano Mastrogiorgio, *Conclusion* In: *New Developments in Evolutionary Innovation: Novelty Creation in a Serendipitous Economy.* Edited by: Gino Cattani and Mariano Mastrogiorgio, Oxford University Press (2021). © Gino Cattani and Mariano Mastrogiorgio. DOI: 10.1093/oso/9780198837091.003.0011 functions of a biological entity either can be performed simultaneously or can switch or be revealed when triggered by cellular localization or environment changes' (p. 77). Multifunctionality in biology sheds light on the role of exaptation in the evolution of complex organismal systems.[1] This is closely related to our previous discussion of an option-based approach. Indeed, the investment in a resource should be evaluated on the basis of not only its real option value but also—and perhaps even more importantly—its shadow option value. The fact that most resources embody a variety of different services explains why a firm's productive opportunity space is greater than one can infer simply by looking at the current uses of those resources. The heterogeneity among the services that are embodied in a firm's material resources, therefore, 'permits the same resources to be used in different ways and for different purposes if the people who work with them get different ideas about how they can be used' (Penrose, 1959: p. 76).

A key insight of conceptualizing resources as bundles of services is that the range of unused services of a resource bundle affords a set of innovation opportunities that a firm may decide to pursue. This raises the question of whether it is possible, at least in principle, to anticipate shadow option returns, which are often inherently exaptive (Andriani and Cattani, 2016), from a real option investment. In the pharmaceutical industry, for instance, we know that investment in drug development is likely to generate additional uses for the same drug at zero or low cost (DeMonaco et al., 2006), some of which may become blockbusters (e.g. Viagra); this is consistent with the increasingly important strategy among pharma companies of 'taking drugs developed for one disorder and "repositioning" them to tackle another' (Nosengo, 2016: p. 314). More generally, firms can try to organize or prepare for serendipitous discoveries (Garud et al., 1997; Cattani, 2006). However, this does not imply that new technologies and their applications can be foreseen. Rather, it means that firms' ability to capitalize on technological opportunities that arise from their past R&D can be improved significantly via organizational design and ad hoc routines and practices. Understanding the type of strategies that firms deploy to enhance innovation via exaptation is a

---

[1] A particular type of multifunctional proteins are known as 'moonlighting' proteins (Jeffery, 1999), which are able to perform multiple *unrelated* functions with no change in polypeptide sequence. These are also known as 'multitask' (Franco-Serrano et al., 2018) or 'extreme multifunctional' proteins (Chapple and Brun, 2015; Chapple et al., 2015; Zanzoni et al., 2019). As moonlighting functions are 'often revealed and triggered by a modification in subcellular localization or an environmental change (e.g. healthy versus pathological states), it therefore appears that the moonlighting/exapted function contributes to the homeostasis of the systems by responding to the new conditions, rather than indicating an evolution towards a specialization' (Andriani et al., 2020: p. 78).

very important topic that future innovation research might find worthy of further examination.

This book proposes several approaches for the computational and empirical analysis of the evolutionary phenomena of interest (punctuated equilibrium, speciation, and exaptation). To date, only a few studies have attempted to quantify the occurrence of exaptive events. By using data on the pharma industry, for instance, Andriani et al. (2017) estimated that approximately 42 per cent of new functions derived from existing drugs have an exaptive nature during the study period. They also found that most radical innovations in their sample were exaptive and that all radical innovations occurred in market areas that were distant from the drug's original market. Given that each drug is approved for a specific market and for a set of specific conditions, Andriani and Cattani (2020) documented the temporal order of emergence of further uses to establish whether general patterns of shadow options emergence can be identified. Accordingly, they have developed quantitative measures to estimate the likelihood with which shadow options unfold. They also examined the organizational conditions that foster the emergence of shadow options by tracing Corning's glass-based innovations and applications over a century (1880–1980) of the company's history. Similarly, Ferreira et al. (2020) explored the notion that exaptation arises from the usage of scientific ideas in other domains than the area to which they were originally applied. In particular, they adopted normalized entropy and an inverse participation ratio as observables that reveal and quantify the concept of exaptation in the context of scientific evolution. These are but a few important steps towards quantifying exaptation. Future research may continue to proceed along similar paths to achieve a deeper understanding of the mechanisms through which exaptation occurs, as well as its relevance in explaining innovation relative to alternative mechanisms already discussed extensively in the innovation literature.

We would like to conclude by emphasizing how a systematic investigation of these mechanisms can also help reconcile some of the differences between biological and cultural evolution, thereby recasting the old debate about the usefulness of building biological analogies. The analogy between biological and cultural evolution has long been a matter of heated discussion. Critical differences have haunted biological analogies. For instance, Penrose's (1952) classic critique of the tendency to impose sweeping biological models upon economic phenomena was premised on the assumption that the structures and processes underlying organic and cultural evolution are substantively different. According to Darwin (1859), for instance, biological evolution follows a bifurcating evolutionary process whose branches are the result of descent with modification—through vertical gene transmission or inheritance—from a common root or ancestor, as represented by the so-called 'Tree of Life'. However, the evolution of many cultural phenomena, including technology, does not neatly fit this pattern and exhibits instead a reticular structure (Carignani et al., 2019; Ziman, 2000).

The developments in evolutionary biology discussed in this book suggest greater *substantive* similarity underneath the *surface* similarity between biological and cultural—including technological—evolution. It is today recognized, for instance, that descent with modification is but one of the possible transmission mechanisms, and a tree-like evolutionary pattern is an incomplete representation of biological evolution, which itself exhibits a reticular structure (Bapteste et al., 2004). Focusing on the evolutionary phenomena of interest in this volume—namely, punctuated equilibrium, speciation, and exaptation, and the mechanisms responsible for their occurrence—may contribute to bringing to an end what has long been considered an intractable disanalogy between biological and technological evolution.

References

Andriani, P. and Cattani, G. 2016. Exaptation as source of creativity, innovation, and diversity: introduction to special section. *Industrial and Corporate Change*, 25(1): 115–31.

Andriani, P., Ali, A., and Mastrogiorgio, M. 2017. Measuring exaptation and its impact on innovation, search, and problem solving. *Organization Science*, 28(2): 339–54.

Andriani, P. and Cattani, G. 2020. *Unused services of a firm's resources: a Penrosian view of shadow options*. Working paper.

Andriani, P., Brun, C., Carignani, G., and Cattani, G. 2020. Exaptation and beyond: multilevel function evolution in biology and technology. In La Porta, C., Zapperi, S., and Pilotti, L. (eds.). *Understanding innovation through exaptation*, pp. 69–84. Springer Nature: The Frontiers Collection.

Bapteste, E., Boucher, Y., Leigh, J., and Doolittle, W.F. 2004. Phylogenetic reconstruction and lateral gene transfer. *Trends in Microbiology*, 12(9): 406–11.

Carignani, G., Cattani, G., and Zaina, G. 2019. Evolutionary chimeras: a Woesian perspective of radical Innovation. *Industrial and Corporate Change*, 28(3): 511–28.

Cattani, G. 2006. Technological preadaptation, speciation and emergence of new technologies: how Corning invented and developed fiber optics. *Industrial and Corporate Change*, 15(2): 285–318.

Chapple, C.E. and Brun, C. 2015. Redefining protein moonlighting. *Oncotarget* 6(19): 16812–13.

Chapple, C.E., Robisson, B., Spinelli, L., Guien, C., Becker, E., and Brun, C. 2015. Extreme multifunctional proteins identified from a human protein interaction network. *Nature Communications*, 6: 7412.

Darwin, C. 1859. *On the origin of species.* John Murray Eds.

DeMonaco, H.J., Ali, A., and Von Hippel, E. 2006. The major role of clinicians in the discovery of off-label drug therapies. *Pharmacotherapy*, 26(3): 323–32.

Ferreira, M.R., Reisz, N., Schueller, W., Servedio, V.D.P., Thurner, S., and Loreto, V. 2020. Quantifying exaptation in scientific evolution. In La Porta, C., Zapperi, S., and Pilotti, L. (eds.). *Understanding innovation through exaptation.* Springer Nature: The Frontiers Collection.

Franco-Serrano, L., Hernández, S., Calvo, A., Severi, M.A., Ferragut, G., Pérez-Pons, J., Piñol, J., Pich, Ò., Mozo-Villarias, Á., Amela, I., et al. 2018. MultitaskProtDB-II: an update of a database of multitasking/moonlighting proteins. *Nucleic Acids Research*, 46: D645–8.

Garud, R., Nayyar, P.R., and Shapira, Z.B. 1997. Technological innovation: oversights and foresights. In Garud, R., Nayyar, P.R., and Shapira, Z.B. (eds.). *Technological innovation: oversights and foresights.* Cambridge University Press.

Jeffery, C.J. 1999. Moonlighting proteins. *Trends in Biochemical Sciences*, 24(1): 8–11.

Nosengo, N. 2016. Can you teach old drugs new tricks? *Nature*, 534(7607): 314–16.

Penrose, E.T. 1952. Biological analogies in the theory of the firm. *American Economic Review*, 42(5): 804–19.

Penrose, E. 1959. *Limits to the size and growth of firms.* Oxford University Press.

Zanzoni, A., Ribeiro, D.M., and Brun, C. 2019. Understanding protein multifunctionality: from short linear motifs to cellular functions. *Cellular and Molecular Life Sciences*, 76(22): 4407–12.

Ziman, J. 2000. *Technological innovation as an evolutionary process.* Cambridge University Press.

Index of Authors

For the benefit of digital users, indexed terms that span two pages (e.g., 52–53) may, on occasion, appear on only one of those pages.

Index

For the benefit of digital users, indexed terms that span two pages (e.g., 52–53) may, on occasion, appear on only one of those pages.